# The World's Best Poetry

THE GRANGER ANTHOLOGY

SERIES I  VOLUME IX

## TRAGEDY AND HUMOR

**Edited by Bliss Carman**

GRANGER BOOK CO., INC.
GREAT NECK, NEW YORK

LC 81-83524 ISBN 0-89609-210-0

Printed and Bound in the United States of America

# TABLE OF CONTENTS.

# PREFACE TO THE NEW EDITION.

THE GRANGER ANTHOLOGY, published in several multivolume servies, is a comprehensive conspectus of international poetry in English designed to form the core of a library's poetry collection. *The World's Best Poetry*, in ten volumes, constitutes Series I. It covers the entire range of poetic literature and encompasses all topics and national literatures (in the best English translations) necessary to constitute a basic and inclusive poetry collection for the small to medium-sized library. Each volume contains a complete author-title index; the final volume concludes with author-title and title-first line indexes for the complete series.

*The World's Best Poetry* is a comprehensive and well-balanced anthology of 2,400 poems written prior to 1904 by 1,100 poets from all parts of the world; it is a superb representation of the best poetic literature of all nationalities and is an appropriate introductory series to THE GRANGER ANTHOLOGY. The scope of this series is so broad in theme and time that it might serve as a book of reference or as a comprehensive exhibit of the history and growth of poetry.

The arrangement is neither chronological, alphabetical, nor by nationality or sex of authors, but it is arranged by special subjects according to the ideas of the poets. Each volume is devoted to major topics; each volume is indexed so as to form a complete and independent work for the subject theme. The tenth and final volume of this series contains an additional 2,700 quotations from poems grouped under more than 300 headings for general topics, in addition to the general indexes for all volumes. Brief biographical notes for each poet are included.

The complete work is contained in ten volumes:

Volume I    Home and Friendship
       II   Love
       III  Sorrow and Consolation
       IV   The High Life (religious poetry)
       V    Nature
       VI   Fancy and Sentiment
       VII  Descriptive and Narrative
       VIII National Spirit
       IX   Tragedy and Humor
       X    Poetical Quotations; General Indexes

The plan of the work is simple and yet it is unique. It is distinctive in its totality, arrangement, inclusiveness, and quality of material presented.

# The World's Best Poetry

THE GRANGER ANTHOLOGY
SERIES I VOLUME IX

## TRAGEDY AND HUMOR

# POEMS OF TRAGEDY.

## IPHIGENEIA AND AGAMEMNON.

IPHIGENEIA, when she heard her doom
At Aulis, and when all beside the king
Had gone away, took his right hand, and said:
" O father! I am young and very happy.
I do not think the pious Calchas heard
Distinctly what the goddess spake; old age
Obscures the senses. If my nurse, who knew
My voice so well, sometimes misunderstood,
While I was resting on her knee both arms,
And hitting it to make her mind my words,
And looking in her face, and she in mine,
Might not he, also, hear one word amiss,
Spoken from so far off, even from Olympus? "
The father placed his cheek upon her head,
And tears dropt down it; but the king of men
Replied not. Then the maiden spake once more:
" O father! sayest thou nothing? Hearest thou
        not
Me, whom thou ever hast, until this hour,
Listened to fondly, and awakened me
To hear my voice amid the voice of birds,
When it was inarticulate as theirs,
And the down deadened it within the nest? "
He moved her gently from him, silent still;

3

And this, and this alone, brought tears from her,
Although she saw fate nearer.  Then with sighs:
" I thought to have laid down my hair before
Benignant Artemis, and not dimmed
Her polished altar with my virgin blood;
I thought to have selected the white flowers
To please the nymphs, and to have asked of each
By name, and with no sorrowful regret,
Whether, since both my parents willed the change,
I might at Hymen's feet bend my clipt brow;
And (after these who mind us girls the most)
Adore our own Athene, that she would
Regard me mildly with her azure eyes,—
But, father, to see you no more, and see
Your love, O father! go ere I am gone!"
Gently he moved her off, and drew her back,
Bending his lofty head far over hers;
And the dark depths of nature heaved and burst.
He turned away,—not far, but silent still.
She now first shuddered; for in him, so nigh,
So long a silence seemed the approach of death,
And like it.   Once again she raised her voice:
" O father! if the ships are now detained,
And all your vows move not the gods above,
When the knife strikes me there will be one prayer
The less to them; and purer can there be
Any, or more fervent, than the daughter's prayer
For her dear father's safety and success?"
A groan that shook him shook not his resolve.
An aged man now entered, and without
One word stepped slowly on, and took the wrist
Of the pale maiden.   She looked up, and saw
The fillet of the priest and calm, cold eyes.

Then turned she where her parent stood, and cried :
" O father! grieve no more; the ships can sail."

WALTER SAVAGE LANDOR.

---

## THE SACRIFICE OF POLYXENA.

### FROM " HECUBA."

[It had been determined by the victorious Greeks to
sacrifice Polyxena, the daughter of Priam, King of Ilium,
and his wife Hecuba, on the tomb of the slain Achilleus.
Odysseus. sent by the Greeks to fetch the maiden, turned
a deaf ear to the entreaties of the mother, and Polyxena
herself addresses the Greek :]

" I SEE thee, how beneath thy robe, O King,
Thy hand is hidden, thy face turned from mine,
Lest I should touch thee by the beard and pray :
Fear not : thou hast escaped the god of prayers
For my part. I will rise and follow thee,
Driven by strong need; yea, and not loth to die.
Lo! if I should not seek death, I were found
A cowardly, life-loving, selfish soul!
For why should I live? Was my sire not King
Of all broad Phrygia? Thus my life began;
Then I was nurtured on fair bloom of hope
To be the bride of kings; no small the suit,
I ween, of lovers seeking me : thus I
Was once—ah, woe is me! of Idan dames
Mistress and queen, 'mid maidens like a star
Conspicuous, peer of gods, except for death;
And now I am a slave : this name alone
Makes me in love with death—so strange it is."

[Later in the drama follows the account of the heroic
death of Polyxena, described to the unhappy Hecuba by
the herald Talthybius.]

" THE whole vast concourse of the Achaian host
Stood round the tomb to see your daughter die.
Achilleus' son, taking her by the hand,
Placed her upon the mound, and I stayed near;
And youths, the flower of Greece, a chosen few,
With hands to check thy heifer, should she bound,
Attended.  From a cup of carven gold,
Raised full of wine, Archilleus' son poured forth
Libation to his sire, and bade me sound
Silence throughout the whole Achaian host.
I, standing there, cried in the midst these words:—
' Silence, Achaians! let the host be still!
Hush, hold your voices!'  Breathless stayed the
        crowd;
But he:—' O son of Peleus, father mine,
Take these libations pleasant to thy soul,
Draughts that allure the dead: come, drink the
        black
Pure maiden's blood wherewith the host and I
Sue thee: be kindly to us; loose our prows,
And let our barks go free; give safe return
Homeward from Troy to all, and happy voyage.'
Such words he spake, and the crowd prayed assent.
Then from the scabbard, by its golden hilt,
He drew the sword, and to the chosen youths
Signalled that they should bring the maid; but she,
Knowing her hour was come, spake thus, and said:
' O men of Argos, who have sacked my town,
Lo, of free will I die! Let no man touch
My body: boldly will I stretch my throat.

Nay, but I pray you set me free, then slay;
That free I thus may perish : 'mong the dead,
Being a queen, I blush to be called slave.'
The people shouted, and King Agamemnon
Bade the youths loose the maid, and set her free;
She, when she heard the order of the chiefs,
Seizing her mantle, from the shoulder down
To the soft centre of her snowy waist
Tore it, and showed her breasts and bosom fair
As in a statue. Bending then with knee
On earth, she spake a speech most piteous :—
'See you this breast, O youth? If breast you will,
Strike it; take heart : or if beneath my neck,
Lo! here my throat is ready for your sword!'
He, willing not, yet willing,—pity-stirred
In sorrow for the maiden,—with his blade
Severed the channels of her breath : blood flowed;
And she, though dying, still had thought to fall
In seemly wise, hiding what eyes should see not.
But when she breathed her life out from the blow,
Then was the Argive host in divers way
Of service parted; for some, bringing leaves,
Strewed them upon the corpse; some piled a pyre,
Dragging pine trunks and boughs; and he who
        bore none,
Heard from the bearers many a bitter word :—
'Standest thou, villain? hast thou then no robe,
No funeral honors for the maid to bring?
Wilt thou not go and get for her who died
Most nobly, bravest-souled, some gift?' Thus they
Spake of thy child in death :—O thou most blessed
Of women in thy daughter, most undone!"

                From the Greek of EURIPIDES.
        Translation of JOHN ADDINGTON SYMONDS.

## PARRHASIUS.

THERE stood an unsold captive in the mart,
A gray-haired and majestical old man,
Chained to a pillar.  It was almost night,
And the last seller from the place had gone,
And not a sound was heard but of a dog
Crunching beneath the stall a refuse bone,
Or the dull echo from the pavement rung,
As the faint captive changed his weary feet.
He had stood there since morning, and had borne
From every eye in Athens the cold gaze
Of curious scorn.  The Jew had taunted him
For an Olynthian slave.  The buyer came
And roughly struck his palm upon his breast,
And touched his unhealed wounds, and with a
       sneer
Passed on; and when, with weariness o'erspent,
He bowed his head in a forgetful sleep,
The inhuman soldier smote him, and, with threats
Of torture to his children, summoned back
The ebbing blood into his pallid face.

'T was evening, and the half-descended sun
Tipped with a golden fire the many domes
Of Athens, and a yellow atmosphere
Lay rich and dusky in the shaded street
Through which the captive gazed.  He had borne
       up
With a stout heart that long and weary day,
Haughtily patient of his many wrongs,
But now he was alone, and from his nerves

The needless strength departed, and he leaned
Prone on his massy chain, and let his thoughts
Throng on him as they would.  Unmarked of him
Parrhasius at the nearest pillar stood,
Gazing upon his grief.  The Athenian's cheek
Flushed as he measured with a painter's eye
The moving picture.  The abandoned limbs,
Stained with the oozing blood, were laced with
      veins
Swollen to purple fulness; the gray hair,
Thin and disordered, hung about his eyes;
And as a thought of wilder bitterness
Rose in his memory, his lips grew white,
And the fast workings of his bloodless face
Told what a tooth of fire was at his heart.

The golden light into the painter's room
Streamed richly, and the hidden colors stole
From the dark pictures radiantly forth,
And in the soft and dewy atmosphere
Like forms and landscapes magical they lay.
The walls were hung with armor, and about
In the dim corners stood the sculptured forms
Of Cytheris, and Dian, and stern Jove,
And from the casement soberly away
Fell the grotesque long shadows, full and true,
And like a veil of filmy mellowness,
The lint-specks floated in the twilight air.
Parrhasius stood, gazing forgetfully
Upon his canvas.  There Prometheus lay,
Chained to the cold rocks of Mount Caucasus—
The vulture at his vitals, and the links
Of the lame Lemnian festering in his flesh;

And, as the painter's mind felt through the dim,
Rapt mystery, and plucked the shadows forth
With its far reaching fancy, and with form
And color clad them, his fine, earnest eye
Flashed with a passionate fire, and the quick curl
Of his thin nostril, and his quivering lip
Were like the winged god's breathing from his
    flight.

    " Bring me the captive now!
My hand feels skilful, and the shadows lift
From my waked spirit airily and swift,
        And I could paint the bow
Upon the bended heavens—around me play
Colors of such divinity to-day.

    " Ha! bind him on his back!
Look—as Prometheus in my picture here!
Quick—or he faints!—stand with the cordial near!
        Now—bend him to the rack!
Press down the poisoned links into his flesh!
And tear agape that healing wound afresh!

    " So—let him writhe! How long
Will he live thus? Quick, my good pencil, now!
What a fine agony works upon his brow!
        Ha! gray-haired, and so strong!
How fearfully he stifles that short moan!
Gods! if I could but paint a dying groan!

    " ' Pity ' thee! So I do!
I pity the dumb victim at the altar—
But does the robed priest for his pity falter?
        I 'd rack thee though I knew

A thousand lives were perishing in thine—
What were ten thousand to a fame like mine?

"'Hereafter!' Ay—hereafter!
A whip to keep a coward to his track!
What gave Death ever from his kingdom back
    To check the sceptic's laughter?
Come from the grave to-morrow with that story,
And I may take some softer path to glory.

"No, no, old man! we die
Even as the flowers, and we shall breathe away
Our life upon the chance wind, even as they!
    Strain well thy fainting eye—
For when that bloodshot quivering is o'er,
The light of heaven will never reach thee more.

"Yet there's a deathless name!
A spirit that the smothering vault shall spurn,
And like a steadfast planet mount and burn;
    And though its crown of flame
Consumed my brain to ashes as it shone,
By all the fiery stars! I'd bind it on!—

"Ay—though it bid me rifle
My heart's last fount for its insatiate thirst—
Though every life-strung nerve be maddened
    first—
    Though it should bid me stifle
The yearning in my throat for my sweet child,
And taunt its mother till my brain went wild—

"All—I would do it all—
Sooner than die, like a dull worm, to rot,

Thrust foully into earth to be forgot!
　　Oh heaven!—but I appall
Your heart, old man! forgive—ha! on your lives
Let him not faint!—rack him till he revives!

　　" Vain—vain—give o'er! His eye
Glazes apace.　He does not feel you now—
Stand back!　I 'll paint the death-dew on his
　　　　brow!
　　Gods! if he do not die
But for one moment—one—till I eclipse
Conception with the scorn of those calm lips!

　　" Shivering! Hark! he mutters
Brokenly now—that was a difficult breath—
Another?　Wilt thou never come, oh Death!
　　Look! how his temple flutters!
Is his heart still?　Aha! lift up his head!
He shudders—gasps—Jove help him!—so—he 's
　　　　dead."

How like a mounting devil in the heart
Rules the unreigned ambition!　Let it once
But play the monarch, and its haughty brow
Glows with a beauty that bewilders thought
And unthrones peace forever.　Putting on
The very pomp of Lucifer, it turns
The heart to ashes, and with not a spring
Left in the bosom for the spirit's lip,
We look upon our splendor and forget
The thirst of which we perish!　Yet hath life
Many a false idol.　There are hopes
Promising well; and love-touched dreams for
　　　　some;

And passions, many a wild one; and fair schemes
For gold and pleasure—yet will only this
Balk not the soul—Ambition, only, gives,
Even of bitterness, a beaker full!
Friendship is but a slow-awaking dream,
Troubled at best; Love is a lamp unseen,
Burning to waste, or, if its light is found,
Nursed for an idle hour, then idly broken;
Gain is a grovelling care, and Folly tires,
And Quiet is a hunger never fed;
And from Love's very bosom, and from Gain,
Or Folly, or a Friend, or from Repose—
From all but keen Ambition—will the soul
Snatch the first moment of forgetfulness
To wander like a restless child away.
Oh, if there were not better hopes than these—
Were there no palm beyond a feverish fame—
If the proud wealth flung back upon the heart
Must canker in its coffers—if the links
Falsehood hath broken will unite no more—
If the deep yearning love, that hath not found
Its like in the cold world, must waste in tears—
If truth and fervor and devotedness,
Finding no worthy altar, must return
And die of their own fulness—if beyond
The grave there is no heaven in whose wide air
The spirit may find room, and in the love
Of whose bright habitants the lavish heart
May spend itself—what thrice-mocked fools are
    we!

NATHANIEL PARKER WILLIS.

## LUCIUS JUNIUS BRUTUS OVER THE BODY OF LUCRETIA.

### FROM "BRUTUS."

WOULD you know why I summoned you together?
Ask ye what brings me here?  Behold this dagger,
Clotted with gore!  Behold that frozen corse!
See where the lost Lucretia sleeps in death!
She was the mark and model of the time,
The mould in which each female face was formed,
The very shrine and sacristy of virtue!
Fairer than ever was a form created
By youthful fancy when the blood strays wild,
And never-resting thought is all on fire!
The worthiest of the worthy!  Not the nymph
Who met old Numa in his hallowed walks,
And whispered in his ear her strains divine,
Can I conceive beyond her;—the young choir
Of vestal virgins bent to her.  'T is wonderful
Amid the darnel, hemlock, and base weeds,
Which now spring rife from the luxurious com-
        post
Spread o'er the realm, how this sweet lily rose,—
How from the shade of those ill-neighboring plants
Her father sheltered her, that not a leaf
Was blighted, but, arrayed in purest grace,
She bloomed unsullied beauty.  Such perfections
Might have called back the torpid breast of age
To long-forgotten rapture; such a mind
Might have abashed the boldest libertine

And turned desire to reverential love
And holiest affection! O my countrymen!
You all can witness when that she went forth
It was a holiday in Rome; old age
Forgot its crutch, labor its task,—all ran,
And mothers, turning to their daughters, cried,
" There, there 's Lucretia!" Now look ye where
    she lies!
That beauteous flower, that innocent sweet rose,
Torn up by ruthless violence,—gone! gone! gone!
  Say, would you seek instruction? would ye ask
What ye should do? Ask ye yon conscious walls,
Which saw his poisoned brother,—
Ask yon deserted street, where Tullia drove
O'er her dead father's corse, 't will cry, Revenge!
Ask yonder senate-house, whose stones are purple
With human blood, and it will cry, Revenge!
Go to the tomb where lies his murdered wife,
And the poor queen, who loved him as her son,
Their unappeasèd ghosts will shriek, Revenge!
The temples of the gods, the all-viewing heavens,
The gods themselves, shall justify the cry,
And swell the general sound, Revenge! Revenge!
  And we will be revenged, my countrymen!
Brutus shall lead you on; Brutus, a name
Which will, when you 're revenged, be dearer to
    him
Than all the noblest titles earth can boast.
  Brutus your king!—No, fellow-citizens!
If mad ambition in this guilty frame
Had strung one kingly fibre, yea, but one,—
By all the gods, this dagger which I hold
Should rip it out, though it intwined my heart.

Now take the body up.   Bear it before us
To Tarquin's palace; there we 'll light our torches,
And in the blazing conflagration rear
A pile, for these chaste relics, that shall send
Her  soul  amongst  the  stars.   On!  Brutus  leads
      you!

                              JOHN HOWARD PAYNE.

---

## THE  ROMAN  FATHER.

FROM " VIRGINIA."

STRAIGHTWAY Virginius led the maid
    A little space aside,
To where the reeking shambles stood,
    Piled up with horn and hide;
Close to yon low dark archway,
    Where, in a crimson flood,
Leaps down to the great sewer
    The gurgling stream of blood.

Hard by, a flesher on a block
    Had laid his whittle down:
Virginius caught the whittle up,
    And hid it in his gown.
And then his eyes grew very dim,
    And his throat began to swell,
And in a hoarse, changed voice he spake,
    " Farewell, sweet child! Farewell!

" O, how I loved my darling!
    Though stern I sometimes be,
To thee, thou know'st, I was not so,—
    Who could be so to thee?

And how my darling loved me!
  How glad she was to hear
My footstep on the threshold
  When I came back last year!

" And how she danced with pleasure
  To see my civic crown,
And took my sword, and hung it up,
  And brought me forth my gown!
Now, all those things are over,—
  Yes, all thy pretty ways,
Thy needlework, thy prattle,
  Thy snatches of old lays;

" And none will grieve when I go forth,
  Or smile when I return,
Or watch beside the old man's bed,
  Or weep upon his urn.
The house that was the happiest
  Within the Roman walls,
The house that envied not the wealth
  Of Capua's marble halls,

" Now, for the brightness of thy smile,
  Must have eternal gloom,
And for the music of thy voice,
  The silence of the tomb.
The time is come!  See how he points
  His eager hand this way!
See how his eyes gloat on thy grief,
  Like a kite's upon the prey!

" With all his wit; he little deems
  That, spurned, betrayed, bereft,

2

Thy father hath, in his despair,
　One fearful refuge left.
He little deems that in this hand
　I clutch what still can save
Thy gentle youth from taunts and blows,
　The portion of the slave;

" Yea, and from nameless evil,
　That passes taunt and blow,—
Foul outrage which thou knowest not,
　Which thou shalt never know.
Then clasp me round the neck once more,
　And give me one more kiss;
And now, mine own dear little girl,
　There is no way but this."

With that he lifted high the steel,
　And smote her in the side,
And in her blood she sank to earth,
　And with one sob she died.
Then, for a little moment,
　All people held their breath;
And through the crowded forum
　Was stillness as of death;

And in another moment
　Brake forth, from one and all,
A cry as if the Volscians
　Were coming o'er the wall.
Some with averted faces
　Shrieking fled home amain;
Some ran to call a leech; and some
　Ran to lift up the slain.

Some felt her lips and little wrist,
    If life might there be found;
And some tore up their garments fast,
    And strove to stanch the wound.
In vain they ran, and felt, and stanched;
    For never truer blow
That good right arm had dealt in fight
    Against a Volscian foe.

When Appius Claudius saw that deed,
    He shuddered and sank down,
And hid his face some little space
    With the corner of his gown;
Till, with white lips and bloodshot eyes,
    Virginius tottered nigh,
And stood before the judgment-seat,
    And held the knife on high.

" O dwellers in the nether gloom,
    Avengers of the slain,
By this dear blood I cry to you
    Do right between us twain;
And even as Appius Claudius
    Hath dealt by me and mine,
Deal you by Appius Claudius,
    And all the Claudian line!"

So spake the slayer of his child,
    And turned and went his way;
But first he cast one haggard glance
    To where the body lay,
And writhed, and groaned a fearful groan,
    And then, with steadfast feet,

Strode right across the market-place
 Unto the Sacred Street.


Then up sprang Appius Claudius:
 "Stop him; alive or dead!
Ten thousand pounds of copper
 To the man who brings his head."
He looked upon his clients;
 But none would work his will.
He looked upon his lictors;
 But they trembled, and stood still.


And as Virginius through the press
 His way in silence cleft,
Ever the mighty multitude
 Fell back to right and left.
And he hath passed in safety
 Unto his woful home,
And there ta'en horse to tell the camp
 What deeds are done in Rome.
   THOMAS BABINGTON, LORD MACAULAY.


## MARK ANTONY, OVER THE BODY OF CÆSAR.

FROM "JULIUS CÆSAR," ACT III. SC. 2.


ANTONY.—O mighty Cæsar! dost thou lie so
 low?
Are all thy conquests, glories, triumphs, spoils,
Shrunk to this little measure?—Fare thee well.—

*(To the people.)*

Friends, Romans, countrymen, lend me your
    ears;
I come to bury Cæsar, not to praise him.
The evil that men do lives after them;
The good is oft interrèd with their bones;
So let it be with Cæsar. The noble Brutus
Hath told you Cæsar was ambitious:
If it were so, it was a grievous fault;
And grievously hath Cæsar answered it.
Here, under leave of Brutus and the rest,
(For Brutus is an honorable man;
So are they all, all honorable men,)
Come I to speak in Cæsar's funeral.
He was my friend, faithful and just to me:
But Brutus says he was ambitious;
And Brutus is an honorable man.
He hath brought many captives home to Rome,
Whose ransom did the general coffers fill:
Did this in Cæsar seem ambitious?
When that the poor have cried, Cæsar hath wept:
Ambition should be made of sterner stuff:
Yet Brutus says he was ambitious;
And Brutus is an honorable man.
You all did see that on the Lupercal
I thrice presented him a kingly crown,
Which he did thrice refuse: was this ambition?
Yet Brutus says he was ambitious;
And, sure, he is an honorable man.
I speak not to disprove what Brutus spoke,
But here I am to speak what I do know.
You all did love him once,—not without cause!
What cause withholds you, then, to mourn for
    him?

O judgment, thou art fled to brutish beasts,
And men have lost their reason!—Bear with me;
My heart is in the coffin there with Cæsar,
And I must pause till it come back to me.

.        .        .        .        .        .

But yesterday, the word of Cæsar might
Have stood against the world! now lies he there
And none so poor to do him reverence.
O masters! if I were disposed to stir
Your hearts and minds to mutiny and rage,
I should do Brutus wrong, and Cassius wrong,
Who, you all know, are honorable men:
I will not do them wrong; I rather choose
To wrong the dead, to wrong myself, and you,
Than I will wrong such honorable men.
But here 's a parchment, with the seal of Cæsar,—
I found it in his closet,—'t is his will.
Let but the commons hear this testament,
(Which, pardon me, I do not mean to read,)
And they would go and kiss dead Cæsar's wounds,
And dip their napkins in his sacred blood:
Yea, beg a hair of him for memory,
And, dying, mention it within their wills,
Bequeathing it, as a rich legacy,
Unto their issue.

  4 Citizen.—We 'll hear the will: read it, Mark
   Antony.

  Citizens.—The will, the will! we will hear Cæsar's will.

  Antony.—Have patience, gentle friends, I must
   not read it;

It is not meet you know how Cæsar loved you.
You are not wood, you are not stones, but men;

And, being men, hearing the will of Cæsar,
It will inflame you, it will make you mad:
'T is good you know not that you are his heirs,
For if you should, O, what would come of it!

    4 CITIZEN.—Read the will; we 'll hear it, An-
      tony;
You shall read us the will,—Cæsar's will.

    ANTONY.—Will you be patient? Will you stay
      awhile?
I have o'ershot myself to tell you of it.
I fear I wrong the honorable men
Whose daggers have stabbed Cæsar; I do fear it.

    4 CITIZEN.—They were traitors: honorable
      men!

    CITIZENS.—The will! the testament!

    2 CITIZEN.—They were villains, murderers: the
      will! read the will!

    ANTONY.—You will compel me, then, to read the
      will!
Then make a ring about the corse of Cæsar,
And let me show you him that made the will.
Shall I descend? and will you give me leave?

    CITIZENS.—Come down.

    ANTONY.—Nay, press not so upon me; stand
      far off.

    CITIZENS.—Stand back; room; bear back.

    ANTONY. If you have tears, prepare to shed
      them now.
You all do know this mantle: I remember
The first time ever Cæsar put it on;
'T was on a summer's evening, in his tent;
That day he overcame the Nervii:—
Look, in this place ran Cassius' dagger through:
See what a rent the envious Casca made:

Through this the well-belovèd Brutus stabbed;
And, as he plucked his cursèd steel away,
Mark how the blood of Cæsar followed it,
As rushing out of doors, to be resolved
If Brutus so unkindly knocked, or no;
For Brutus, as you know, was Cæsar's angel:
Judge, O you gods, how dearly Cæsar loved him!
This was the most unkindest cut of all;
For when the noble Cæsar saw him stab,
Ingratitude, more strong than traitors' arms,
Quite vanquished him: then burst his mighty
        heart;
And, in his mantle muffling up his face,
Even at the base of Pompey's statua,
Which all the while ran blood, great Cæsar fell.
O, what a fall was there, my countrymen!
Then I, and you, and all of us fell down,
Whilst bloody treason flourished over us.
O, now you weep; and I perceive you feel
The dint of pity: these are gracious drops.
Kind souls, what, weep you when you but behold
Our Cæsar's vesture wounded?   Look you here,
Here is himself, marred, as you see, with traitors.

.        .        .        .        .        .

    Good friends, sweet friends, let me not stir you
        up
To such a sudden flood of mutiny.
They that have done this deed are honorable;—
What private griefs they have, alas, I know not,
That made them do it;—they are wise and hon-
        orable,
And will, no doubt, with reasons answer you.
I come not, friends, to steal away your hearts;

I am no orator, as Brutus is;
But, as you know me all, a plain blunt man,
That love my friend; and that they know full well
That gave me public leave to speak of him:
For I have neither wit, nor words, nor worth,
Action, nor utterance, nor the power of speech,
To stir men's blood: I only speak right on;
I tell you that which you yourselves do know;
Show you sweet Cæsar's wounds, poor, poor dumb
    mouths,
And bid them speak for me: but were I Brutus,
And Brutus Antony, there were an Antony
Would ruffle up your spirits, and put a tongue
In every wound of Cæsar, that should move
The stones of Rome to rise and mutiny.

    ALL.—We 'll mutiny.

    1 CITIZEN.—We 'll burn the house of Brutus.

    3 CITIZEN.—Away, then! come, seek the conspir-
    ators.

    ANTONY.—Yet hear me, countrymen; yet hear
    me speak.

    ALL.—Peace, ho! Hear Antony, most noble An-
    tony.

    ANTONY.—Why, friends, you go to do you know
    not what.

Wherein hath Cæsar thus deserved your loves?
Alas, you know not!—I must tell you, then.
You have forgot the will I told you of.

    ALL.—Most true;—the will!—let 's stay and
    hear the will.

    ANTONY.—Here is the will, and under Cæsar's
    seal:—

To every Roman citizen he gives,

To every several man, seventy-five drachmas.

  2 CITIZEN.—Most noble Cæsar!—we 'll revenge
    his death.

  3 CITIZEN.—O royal Cæsar!

ANTONY.—Hear me with patience.

CITIZENS.—Peace, ho!

ANTONY.—Moreover, he hath left you all his
    walks,

His private arbors, and new-planted orchards
On this side Tiber; he hath left them you,
And to your heirs forever,—common pleasures,
To walk abroad, and recreate yourselves.
Here was a Cæsar! when comes such another?

  1 CITIZEN.—Never, never!—Come away, away!
We 'll burn his body in the holy place,
And with the brands fire the traitors' houses.
Take up the body. . . . . .

    [*Exeunt Citizens, with the body.*]

ANTONY.—Now let it work. Mischief, thou art
  afoot,

Take thou what course thou wilt.

                SHAKESPEARE.

---

## THE SACK OF THE CITY.

THY will, O King, is done! Lighting but to con-
    sume,
  The roar of the fierce flames drowned even the
    shouts and shrieks;
Reddening each roof, like some day-dawn of
    bloody doom,
  Seemed they in joyous flight to dance above
    their wrecks.

Slaughter his thousand giant arms hath tossed on
    high,
  Fell fathers, husbands, wives, beneath his
    streaming steel;
Prostrate the palaces huge tombs of fire lie,
  While gathering overhead the vultures scream
    and wheel.

Died the pale mothers;—and the virgins, from
    their arms,
  O Caliph, fiercely torn, bewailed their young
    years' blight;
With stabs and kisses fouled, all their yet quiver-
    ing charms
  At our fleet coursers' heels were dragged in
    mocking flight.

Lo, where the city lies mantled in pall of death!
  Lo, where thy mighty arm hath passed, all
    things must bend!
As the priests prayed, the sword stopped their
    accursèd breath,—
  Vainly their sacred book for shield did they
    extend.

Some infants yet survived, and the unsated steel
  Still drinks the life-blood of each whelp of
    Christian hound.
To kiss thy sandal's foot, O King, thy people
    kneel,
  With golden circlet to thy glorious ankle bound.
        From the French of VICTOR-MARIE HUGO.

## THE SLAYING OF SOHRAB.

### FROM " SOHRAB AND RUSTUM."

HE spake; and Rustum answered not, but
    hurled
His spear.  Down from the shoulder, down it
    came—
As on some partridge in the corn, a hawk,
That long has towered in the airy clouds,
Drops like a plummet.  Sohrab saw it come,
And sprang aside, quick as a flash.  The spear
Hissed, and went quivering down into the sand,
Which it sent flying wide.  Then Sohrab threw
In turn, and full struck Rustum's shield.  Sharp
    rang
The iron plates, rang sharp, but turned the spear.
And Rustum seized his club, which none but he
Could wield—an unlapped trunk it was, and huge,
Still rough; like those which men, in treeless
    plains,
To build them boats, fish from the flooded rivers,
Hyphasis or Hydaspes, when, high up
By their dark springs, the wind in winter-time
Has made in Himalayan forests wrack,
And strewn the channels with torn boughs—so
    huge
The club which Rustum lifted now, and struck
One stroke; but again Sohrab sprang aside,
Lithe as the glancing snake, and the club came
Thundering to earth, and leapt from Rustum's
    hand.
And Rustum followed his own blow, and fell

To his knees, and with his fingers clutched the
    sand.
And now might Sohrab have unsheathed his
    sword,
And pierced the mighty Rustum while he lay
Dizzy, and on his knees, and choked with sand;
But he looked on, and smiled, nor bared his
    sword;
But courteously drew back, and spoke, and
    said :—
  " Thou strik'st too hard; that club of thine will
    float
Upon the summer floods, and not my bones.
But rise, and be not wroth; not wroth am I.
No, when I see thee, wrath forsakes my soul.
Thou sayest thou art not Rustum; be it so.
Who art thou then, that canst so touch my soul?
Boy as I am, I have seen battles too;
Have waded foremost in their bloody waves,
And heard their hollow roar of dying men;
But never was my heart thus touched before.
Are they from heaven, these softenings of the
    heart?
O thou old warrior, let us yield to Heaven!
Come, plant we here in earth our angry spears,
And make a truce, and sit upon this sand,
And pledge each other in red wine, like friends;
And thou shalt talk to me of Rustum's deeds.
There are enough foes in the Persian host
Whom I may meet, and strike, and feel no pang;
Champions enough Afrasiab has, whom thou
May'st fight: fight them, when they confront thy
    spear.

But oh, let there be peace 'twixt thee and me!"
 He ceased. But while he spake Rustum had
  risen,
And stood erect, trembling with rage. His club
He left to lie, but had regained his spear,
Whose fiery point now in his mailed right hand
Blazed bright and baleful—like that autumn star,
The baleful sign of fevers. Dust had soiled
His stately crest, and dimmed his glittering arms.
His breast heaved; his lips foamed; and twice his
  voice
Was choked with rage. At last these words broke
  way :—
 "Girl! nimble with thy feet, not with thy
  hands!
Curled minion, dancer, coiner of sweet words!
Fight! Let me hear thy hateful voice no more!
Thou art not in Afrasiab's gardens now
With Tartar girls, with whom thou art wont to
  dance;
But on the Oxus sands, and in the dance
Of battle, and with me, who make no play
Of war. I fight it out, and hand to hand.
Speak not to me of truce, and pledge, and wine!
Remember all thy valor; try thy feints
And cunning; all the pity I had is gone;
Because thou hast shamed me before both the
  hosts,
With thy light skipping tricks, and thy girl's
  wiles."
 He spoke; and Sohrab kindled at his taunts,
And he too drew his sword. At once they rushed
Together; as two eagles on one prey

Come rushing down together from the clouds,
One from the east, one from the west. Their
    shields
Dashed with a clang together; and a din
Rose, such as that the sinewy woodcutters
Make often in the forest's heart at morn,
Of hewing axes, crashing trees; such blows
Rustum and Sohrab on each other hailed.
And you would say that sun and stars took part
In that unnatural conflict; for a cloud
Grew suddenly in heaven, and darkened the sun
Over the fighters' heads; and a wind rose
Under their feet, and moaning swept the plain,
And in a sandy whirlwind wrapped the pair.
In gloom they twain were wrapped, and they
    alone;
For both the on-looking hosts on either hand
Stood in broad daylight, and the sky was pure,
And the sun sparkled on the Oxus stream.
But in the gloom they fought, with bloodshot eyes
And laboring breath. First Rustum struck the
    shield
Which Sohrab held stiff out. The steel-spiked
    spear
Rent the tough plates, but failed to reach the
    skin:
And Rustum plucked it back with angry groan.
Then Sohrab with his sword smote Rustum's helm
Nor clove its steel quite through; but all the crest
He shore away; and that proud horse-hair plume,
Never till now defiled, sunk to the dust;
And Rustum bowed his head. But then the gloom
Grew blacker; thunder rumbled in the air,

And lightnings rent the cloud; and Ruksh, the
     horse,
Who stood at hand, uttered a dreadful cry.
No horse's cry was that, most like the roar
Of some pained desert lion, who all day
Has trailed the hunter's javelin in his side,
And comes at night to die upon the sand.
The two hosts heard the cry, and quaked for fear;
And Oxus curdled as it crossed his stream.
But Sohrab heard, and quailed not—but rushed
     on,
And struck again; and again Rustum bowed
His head. But this time all the blade, like glass,
Sprang in a thousand shivers on the helm,
And in his hand the hilt remained alone.
Then Rustum raised his head; his dreadful eyes
Glared, and he shook on high his menacing spear,
And shouted "Rustum!" Sohrab heard that
     shout,
And shrank amazed; back he recoiled one step,
And scanned with blinking eyes the advancing
     form;
And then he stood bewildered; and he dropped
His covering shield, and the spear pierced his
     side.
He reeled, and staggering back, sunk to the
     ground.
And then the gloom dispersed, and the wind fell,
And the bright sun broke forth, and melted all
The cloud; and the two armies saw the pair—
Saw Rustum standing, safe upon his feet,
And Sohrab wounded, on the bloody sand.
     Then with a bitter smile, Rustum began:—

" Sohrab, thou thoughtest in thy mind to kill
A Persian lord this day, and strip his corpse,
And bear thy trophies to Afrasiab's tent;
Or else that the great Rustum would come down
Himself to fight, and that thy wiles would move
His heart to take a gift, and let thee go.
And then all the Tartar host would praise
Thy courage or thy craft, and spread thy fame,
To glad thy father in his weak old age.
Fool! thou art slain, and by an unknown man!
Dearer to the red jackals shalt thou be,
Than to thy friends, and to thy father old."
    And with a fearless mien Sohrab replied:—
    " Unknown thou art; yet thy fierce vaunt is
        vain.
Thou dost not slay me, proud and boastful man!
No! Rustum slays me, and this filial heart.
For were I matched with ten such men as thou,
And I were he who till to-day I was,
They should be lying here, I standing there.
But that belovèd name unnerved my arm—
That name, and something, I confess, in thee,
Which troubles all my heart, and made my shield
Fall; and thy spear transfixed an unarmed foe.
And now thou boastest, and insult'st my fate.
But hear thou this, fierce man—tremble to hear!
The mighty Rustum shall avenge my death!
My father, whom I seek through all the world,
He shall avenge my death, and punish thee!"

.        .        .        .        .

So Rustum knew not his own loss; but stood
Over his dying son, and knew him not.
    But with a cold, incredulous voice, he said:—
3

"What prate is this of fathers and revenge?
The mighty Rustum never had a son."
    And, with a failing voice, Sohrab replied:—
"Ah yes, he had! and that lost son am I.
Surely the news will one day reach his ear—
Reach Rustum, where he sits, and tarries long,
Somewhere, I know not where, but far from here;
And pierce him like a stab, and make him leap
To arms, and cry for vengeance upon thee—
Fierce man, bethink thee—for an only son!
What will that grief, what will that vengeance be!
Oh, could I live till I that grief had seen!
Yet him I pity not so much, but her,
My mother, who in Ader-baijan dwells
With that old king, her father, who grows gray
With age, and rules over the valiant Koords.
Her most I pity, who no more will see
Sohrab returning from the Tartar camp,
With spoils and honor, when the war is done,
But a dark rumor will be bruited up,
From tribe to tribe, until it reach her ear;
And then will that defenceless woman learn
That Sohrab will rejoice her sight no more;
But that in battle with a nameless foe,
By the far-distant Oxus, he is slain."

.        .        .        .        .        .

And Rustum gazed on him with grief, and said:
    "O Sohrab, thou indeed art such a son
Whom Rustum, wert thou his, might well have
        loved!
Yet here thou errest, Sohrab, or else men
Have told thee false—thou art not Rustum's son.
For Rustum had no son.  One child he had—

But one—a girl; who with her mother now
Plies some light female task, nor dreams of us;
Of us she dreams not, nor of wounds, nor war."

But Sohrab answered him in wrath; for now
The anguish of the deep-fixed spear grew fierce,
And he desired to draw forth the steel,
And let the blood flow free, and so to die.
But first he would convince his stubborn foe;
And, rising sternly on one arm, he said:

" Man, who art thou, who dost deny my words?
Truth sits upon the lips of dying men;
And falsehood, while I lived, was far from mine.
I tell thee, pricked upon this arm I bear
That seal which Rustum to my mother gave,
That she might prick it on the babe she bore."

He spoke: and all the blood left Rustum's
     cheeks;
And his knees tottered; and he smote his hand
Against his breast, his heavy mailèd hand,
That the hard iron corselet clanked aloud;
And to his heart he pressed the other hand,
And in a hollow voice he spake, and said:

" Sohrab, that were a proof which could not lie.
If thou show this, then art thou Rustum's son."

Then, with weak, hasty fingers, Sohrab loosed
His belt, and near the shoulder bared his arm,
And showed a sign in faint vermilion points
Pricked. As a cunning workman, in Pekin,
Pricks with vermilion some clear porcelain vase,
An emperor's gift; at early morn he paints,
And all day long; and, when night comes, the
     lamp
Lights up his studious forehead and thin hands:

So delicately pricked the sign appeared
On Sohrab's arm—the sign of Rustum's seal.
It was that griffin, which of old reared Zal,
Rustum's great father, whom they left to die,
A helpless babe, among the mountain rocks,
Him that kind creature found and reared and
    loved.
Then Rustum took it for his glorious sign.
And Sohrab bared that figure on his arm,
And himself scanned it long with mournful eyes,
And then he touched it with his hand and said:
   "How sayest thou? Is that sign the proper sign
Of Rustum's son, or of some other man's?"
   He spoke: but Rustum gazed, and gazed, and
    stood
Speechless; and then he uttered one sharp cry—
"O, boy—thy father!"—and his voice choked
    there,
And then a dark cloud passed before his eyes,
And his head swam, and he sank down to earth.
But Sohrab crawled to where he lay, and cast
His arms about his neck, and kissed his lips.
And with fond, faltering fingers stroked his
    cheeks,
Trying to call him back to life. And life
Came back to Rustum, and he oped his eyes,
And they stood wide with horror; and he seized
In both his hands the dust which lay around,
And threw it on his head, and smirched his hair—
His hair, and face, and beard, and glittering
    arms;
And strong, convulsive groanings shook his breast,
And his sobs choked him; and he clutched his
    sword

To draw it, and for ever let life out.
But Sohrab saw his thought, and held his hands;
And with a soothing voice he spoke, and said:
  "Father, forbear! for I but meet to-day
The doom that at my birth was written down
In heaven, and thou art heaven's unconscious
      hand.
Surely my heart cried out that it was thou,
When first I saw thee; and thy heart spoke too,
I know it. But fate trod those promptings down
Under its iron heel; fate, fate engaged
The strife, and hurled me on my father's spear.
But let us speak no more of this—I find
My father; let me feel that I have found.
Come, sit beside me on this sand, and take
My head betwixt thy hands, and kiss my cheeks,
And wash them with thy tears, and say, ' My
      son!'
Quick! quick! for numbered are my sands of life,
And swift; for like the lightning to this field
I came, and like the wind I go away—
Sudden, and swift, and like a passing wind.
But it was writ in heaven that this should be."
  So said he: and his voice released the heart
Of Rustum, and his tears broke forth; he cast
His arms round his son's neck, and wept aloud,
And kissed him. And awe fell on both the hosts
When they saw Rustum's grief; and Ruksh, the
      horse,
With his head bowing to the ground, and mane
Sweeping the dust, came near, and in mute woe,
First to the one, then to the other moved
His head, as if inquiring what their grief

Might mean; and from his dark, compassionate
    eyes,
The big, warm tears rolled down, and caked the
    sand.
But Rustum chid him with stern voice, and said:
  " Ruksh, now thou grievest; but, O Ruksh, thy
     feet
Should then have rotted on thy nimble joints,
When first they bore thy master to this field."
    But Sohrab looked upon the horse, and said:
  " Is this then Ruksh?  How often, in past days,
My mother told me of thee, thou brave steed—
My terrible father's terrible horse! and said
That I should one day find thy lord and thee.
Come, let me lay my hand upon thy mane.
O Ruksh, thou art more fortunate than I;
For thou hast gone where I shall never go,
And snuffed the breezes of my father's home,
And thou hast trod the sands of Seïstan,
And seen the river of Helmund, and the lake
Of Zirrah; and the aged Zal himself
Has often stroked thy neck, and given thee food—
Corn in a golden platter soaked with wine—
And said—' O Ruksh! bear Rustum well!'  But I
Have never known my grandsire's furrowed face,
Nor seen his lofty house in Seïstan,
Nor slaked my thirst at the clear Helmund
    stream;
But lodged among my father's foes, and seen
Afrasiab's cities only, Samarcand,
Bokhara, and lone Khiva in the waste,
And the black Toorkmun tents; and only drunk
The desert rivers, Moorghab and Tejend,

Kohik, and where the Kalmuks feed their sheep,
The northern Sir; and this great Oxus stream—
The yellow Oxus, by whose brink I die."
    And, with a heavy groan, Rustum replied:
" Oh that its waves were flowing over me!
Oh that I saw its grains of yellow silt
Roll tumbling in the current o'er my head!"
    And, with a grave, mild voice, Sohrab replied:
" Desire not that, my father! Thou must live;
For some are born to do great deeds, and live;
As some are born to be obscured, and die.
Do thou the deeds I die too young to do,
And reap a second glory in thine age;
Thou art my father, and thy gain is mine.
But come! thou seest this great host of men
Which follow me; I pray thee, slay not these!
Let me entreat for them—what have they done?
They followed me, my hope, my fame, my star.
Let them all cross the Oxus back in peace.
But me thou must bear hence, not send with them,
But carry me with thee to Seïstan,
And place me on a bed, and mourn for me—
Thou, and the snow-haired Zal, and all thy
        friends.
And thou must lay me in that lovely earth,
And heap a stately mound above my bones,
And plant a far-seen pillar over all;
That so the passing horseman on the waste
May see my tomb a great way off, and say:
*Sohrab, the mighty Rustum's son, lies there,*
*Whom his great father did in ignorance kill—*
And I be not forgotten in my grave."
    And, with a mournful voice, Rustum replied:

" Fear not! as thou hast said, Sohrab, my son,
So shall it be; for I will burn my tents,
And quit the host, and bear thee hence with me,
And carry thee away to Seïstan,
And place thee on a bed, and mourn for thee,
With the snow-headed Zal, and all my friends.
And I will lay thee in that lovely earth,
And heap a stately mound above thy bones,
And plant a far-seen pillar over all;
And men shall not forget thee in thy grave;
And I will spare thy host—yea, let them go—
Let them all cross the Oxus back in peace.
What should I do with slaying any more?
For would that all whom I have ever slain
Might be once more alive—my bitterest foes,
And they who were called champions in their
        time,
And through whose death I won that fame I
        have—
And I were nothing but a common man,
A poor, mean soldier, and without renown;
So thou mightest live too, my son, my son!
Or rather, would that I, even I myself,
Might now be lying on this bloody sand,
Near death, and by an ignorant stroke of thine.
Not thou of mine; and I might die, not thou;
And I, not thou, be borne to Seïstan;
And Zal might weep above my grave, not thine;
And say—*O son, I weep thee not too sore,*
*For willingly, I know, thou met'st thine end!*—
But now in blood and battles was my youth,
And full of blood and battles is my age;
And I shall never end this life of blood."

Then at the point of death, Sohrab replied:—
" A life of blood indeed, thou dreadful man!
But thou shalt yet have peace; only not now,
Not yet. But thou shalt have it on that day
When thou shalt sail in a high-masted ship,
Thou and the other peers of Kai-Khosroo,
Returning home over the salt, blue sea,
From laying thy dear master in his grave."
    And Rustum gazed on Sohrab's face, and
        said:—
" Soon be that day, my son, and deep that sea!
Till then, if fate so wills, let me endure."
    He spoke: and Sohrab smiled on him, and took
The spear, and drew it from his side, and eased
His wound's imperious anguish. But the blood
Came welling from the open gash, and life
Flowed with the stream; all down his cold white
        side
The crimson torrent ran, dim now, and soiled—
Like the soiled tissue of white violets
Left, freshly gathered, on their native bank
By romping children, whom their nurses call
From the hot fields at noon. His head drooped
        low;
His limbs grew slack; motionless, white, he lay—
White, with eyes closed; only when heavy gasps,
Deep, heavy gasps, quivering through all his
        frame,
Convulsed him back to life, he opened them,
And fixed them feebly on his father's face.
Till now all strength was ebbed, and from his
        limbs
Unwillingly the spirit fled away,

Regretting the warm mansion which it left,
And youth and bloom, and this delightful world.
   So, on the bloody sand, Sohrab lay dead.
And the great Rustum drew his horseman's cloak
Down o'er his face, and sate by his dead son.
As those black granite pillars, once high-reared
By Jemshid in Persepolis, to bear
His house, now, mid their broken flights of steps,
Lie prone, enormous, down the mountain-side—
So in the sand lay Rustum by his son.
   And night came down over the solemn waste,
And the two gazing hosts, and that sole pair,
And darkened all; and a cold fog, with night,
Crept from the Oxus.

                          MATTHEW ARNOLD.

------

## KHAMSIN.

Oh, the wind from the desert blew in!—
                          Khamsin,
The wind from the desert blew in!
It blew from the heart of the fiery south,
From the fervid sand and the hills of drouth,
And it kissed the land with its scorching mouth;
The wind from the desert blew in!

It blasted the buds on the almond bough,
And shrivelled the fruit on the orange-tree;
The wizened dervish breathed no vow,
So weary and parched was he.
The lean muezzin could not cry;
The dogs ran mad, and bayed the sky;

The hot sun shone like a copper disk,
And prone in the shade of an obelisk
The water-carrier sank with a sigh,
For limp and dry was his water-skin;
And the wind from the desert blew in.

The camel crouched by the crumbling wall,
And oh the pitiful moan it made!
The minarets, taper and slim and tall,
Reeled and swam in the brazen light;
And prayers went up by day and night,
But thin and drawn were the lips that prayed.
The river writhed in its slimy bed,
Shrunk to a tortuous, turbid thread;
The burnt earth cracked like a cloven rind;
And still the wind, the ruthless wind,
                    Khamsin,
The wind from the desert blew in.

Into the cool of the mosque it crept,
Where the poor sought rest at the Prophet's
        shrine;
Its breath was fire to the jasmine vine;
It fevered the brow of the maid who slept,
And men grew haggard with revel of wine.
The tiny fledglings died in the nest;
The sick babe gasped at the mother's breast.
Then a rumor rose and swelled and spread
From a tremulous whisper, faint and vague,
Till it burst in a terrible cry of dread,
*The plague! the plague! the plague!*—
                Oh the wind, Khamsin,
The scourge from the desert, blew in!
                    CLINTON SCOLLARD.

## THE DIVER.

"OH, where is the knight or the squire so bold,
    As to dive to the howling charybdis below?—
I cast into the whirlpool a goblet of gold,
    And o'er it already the dark waters flow :
Whoever to me may the goblet bring,
Shall have for his guerdon that gift of his king."

He spoke, and the cup from the terrible steep,
    That rugged and hoary, hung over the verge
Of the endless and measureless world of the deep,
    Swirled into the maelstrom that maddened the
        surge.
" And where is the diver so stout to go—
I ask ye again—to the deep below? "

And the knights and the squires that gathered
        around,
    Stood silent—and fixed on the ocean their eyes ;
They looked on the dismal and savage profound,
    And the peril chilled back every thought of the
        prize.
And thrice spoke the monarch—" The cup to win,
Is there never a wight who will venture in? "

And all as before heard in silence the king—
    Till a youth, with an aspect unfearing but
        gentle,
'Mid the tremulous squires, stept out from the
        ring,
    Unbuckling his girdle, and doffing his mantle ;

And the murmuring crowd, as they parted asun-
    der,
On the stately boy cast their looks of wonder.


As he strode to the marge of the summit, and
    gave
  One glance on the gulf of that merciless main;
Lo! the wave that for ever devours the wave,
  Casts roaringly up the charybdis again;
And, as with the swell of the far thunder-boom,
Rushes foamingly forth from the heart of the
    gloom.


And it bubbles and seethes, and it hisses and
    roars,
  As when fire is with water commixed and con-
    tending;
And the spray of its wrath to the welkin up-soars,
  And flood upon flood hurries on, never ending.
And it never will rest, nor from travail be free,
Like a sea that is laboring the birth of a sea.


And at last there lay open the desolate realm!
  Through the breakers that whitened the waste
    of the swell,
Dark—dark yawned a cleft in the midst of the
    whelm,
  The path to the heart of that fathomless hell.
Round and round whirled the waves—deep and
    deeper still driven,
Like a gorge thro' the mountainous main thunder-
    riven.

The youth gave his trust to his Maker!  Before
  That path through the riven abyss closed
    again—
Hark! a shriek from the crowd rang aloft from
    the shore,
  And, behold! he is whirled in the grasp of the
    main!
And o'er him the breakers mysteriously rolled,
And the giant-mouth closed on the swimmer so
    bold.

O'er the surface grim silence lay dark and pro-
    found,
  But the deep from below murmured hollow and
    fell;
And the crowd, as it shuddered, lamented aloud—
  " Gallant youth—noble heart—fare-thee-well,
    fare-thee-well! "
And still ever deepening that wail as of woe,
More hollow the gulf sent its howl from below.

If thou should'st in those waters thy diadem fling,
  And cry, " Who may find it shall win it, and
    wear; "
God's wot, though the prize were the crown of a
    king—
  A crown at such hazard were valued too dear.
For never did lips of the living reveal,
What the deeps that howl yonder in terror con-
    ceal.

Oh many a ship, to that breast grappled fast,
  Has gone down to the fearful and fathomless
    grave;

Again crashed together, the keel and the mast,
  To be seen, tossed aloft in the glee of the
    wave.—
Like the growth of a storm ever louder and
  clearer,
Grows the roar of the gulf rising nearer and
  nearer.

And it bubbles and seethes, and it hisses and
  roars,
  As when fire is with water commixed and con-
    tending;
And the spray of its wrath to the welkin up-soars,
  And flood upon flood hurries on, never ending,
And, as with the swell of the far thunder-boom,
Rushes roaringly forth from the heart of the
  gloom.

And lo! from the heart of that far-floating gloom,
  What gleams on the darkness so swanlike and
    white?
Lo! an arm and a neck, glancing up from the
  tomb!—
  They battle—the Man with the Element's
    might.
It is he—it is he!—In his left hand behold,
As a sign—as a joy! shines the goblet of gold!

And he breathèd deep, and he breathèd long,
  And he greeted the heavenly delight of the day.
They gaze on each other—they shout as they
  throng—
  "He lives—lo, the ocean has rendered its prey!

And out of the grave where the Hell began,
His valor has rescued the living man!"


And he comes with the crowd in their clamor and
    glee,
    And the goblet his daring has won from the
    water,
He lifts to the king as he sinks on his knee;
    And the king from her maidens has beckoned
    his daughter,
And he bade her the wine to his cup-bearer bring,
And thus spake the Diver—" Long life to the
    king!


" Happy they whom the rose-hues of daylight re-
    joice,
    The air and the sky that to mortals are given!
May the horror below never more find a voice—
    Nor Man stretch too far the wide mercy of
    Heaven!
Never more—never more may he lift from the mir-
    ror,
The Veil which is woven with Night and with
    Terror!


" Quick-brightening like lightning—it tore me
    along,
    Down, down, till the gush of a torrent at play
In the rocks of its wilderness caught me—and
    strong
    As the wings of an eagle, it whirled me away.
Vain, vain were my struggles—the circle had won
    me,

Round and round in its dance the wild element
    spun me.

" And I called on my God, and my God heard my
    prayer,
  In the strength of my need, in the gasp of my
    breath—
And showed me a crag that rose up from the lair,
  And I clung to it, trembling—and baffled the
    death.
And, safe in the perils around me, behold
On the spikes of the coral the goblet of gold!

" Below, at the foot of that precipice drear,
  Spread the gloomy, and purple, and pathless ob-
    scure!
A silence of horror that slept on the ear,
  That the eye more appalled might the horror
    endure!
Salamander—snake—dragon—vast reptiles that
    dwell
In the deep—coiled about the grim jaws of their
    hell!

" Dark-crawled—glided dark the unspeakable
    swarms,
  Like masses unshapen, made life hideously;
Here clung and here bristled the fashionless
    forms,
  Here the Hammer-fish darkened the dark of the
    sea,
And with teeth grinning white, and a menacing
    motion,
Went the terrible Shark—the hyena of Ocean.
  4

"There I hung, and the awe gathered icily o'er
    me,
  So far from the earth where man's help there
    was none!
The one Human Thing, with the Goblins before
    me—
  Alone—in a loneness so ghastly—ALONE!
Fathom-deep from man's eye in the speechless pro-
    found,
With the death of the main and the monsters
    around.


"Methought, as I gazed through the darkness,
    that now
  A hundred-limbed creature caught sight of its
    prey,
And darted.—O God! from the far-flaming bough
  Of the coral, I swept on the horrible way;
And it seized me, the wave with its wrath and its
    roar,
It seized me to save—King, the danger is o'er!"


On the youth gazed the monarch, and marvelled—
    quoth he,
  "Bold Diver, the goblet I promised is thine,
And this ring will I give, a fresh guerdon to
    thee,
  Never jewels more precious shone up from the
    mine;
If thou'll bring me fresh tidings, and venture
    again,
To say what lies hid in the *innermost* main!"

Then outspake the daughter in tender emotion,
  "Ah! father, my father, what more can there
    rest?
Enough of this sport with the pitiless ocean—
  He has served thee as none would, thyself hast
    confest.
If nothing can slake thy wild thirst of desire,
Be your knights not, at least, put to shame by the
    squire!"

The king seized the goblet—he swung it on high,
  And whirling, it fell in the roar of the tide;
"But bring back that goblet again to my eye,
  And I'll hold thee the dearest that rides by my
    side,
And thine arms shall embrace as thy bride, I de-
    cree,
The maiden whose pity now pleadeth for thee."

In his heart, as he listened, there leapt the wild
    joy—
  And the hope and the love through his eyes
    spoke in fire,
On that bloom, on that blush, gazed, delighted, the
    boy;
  The maiden she faints at the feet of her sire!
Here the guerdon divine; there the danger be-
    neath;
He resolves!—To the strife with the life and the
    death!

They hear the loud surges sweep back in their
    swell;
  Their coming the thunder-sound heralds along!

Fond eyes yet are tracking the spot where he
        fell—
    They come, the wild waters, in tumult and
        throng,
Rearing up to the cliff—roaring back as before;
But no wave ever brought the lost youth to the
        shore.

From the German of JOHANN C. F. SCHILLER.

## GOD'S JUDGMENT ON A WICKED BISHOP.

[Hatto, Archbishop of Mentz, in the year 914, barbar-
ously murdered a number of poor people to prevent their
consuming a portion of the food during that year of
famine. He was afterwards devoured by rats in his tower
on an island in the Rhine.—OLD LEGEND.]

THE summer and autumn had been so wet,
That in winter the corn was growing yet:
'T was a piteous sight to see all around
The grain lie rotting on the ground.

Every day the starving poor
Crowded around Bishop Hatto's door;
For he had a plentiful last-year's store,
And all the neighborhood could tell
His granaries were furnished well.

At last Bishop Hatto appointed a day
To quiet the poor without delay;
He bade them to his great barn repair,
And they should have food for the winter there.

Rejoiced the tidings good to hear,
The poor folks flocked from far and near;

The great barn was full as it could hold
Of women and children, and young and old.

Then, when he saw it could hold no more,
Bishop Hatto he made fast the door;
And whilst for mercy on Christ they call,
He set fire to the barn, and burnt them all.

" I' faith, 't is an excellent bonfire! " quoth he;
" And the country is greatly obliged to me
For ridding it, in these times forlorn,
Of rats that only consume the corn."

So then to his palace returned he,
And he sate down to supper merrily,
And he slept that night like an innocent man;
But Bishop Hatto never slept again.

In the morning, as he entered the hall,
Where his picture hung against the wall,
A sweat like death all over him came,
For the rats had eaten it out of the frame.

As he looked, there came a man from his farm—
He had a countenance white with alarm:
" My lord, I opened your granaries this morn,
And the rats had eaten all your corn."

Another came running presently,
And he was pale as pale could be.
" Fly! my lord bishop, fly! " quoth he,
" Ten thousand rats are coming this way,—
The Lord forgive you for yesterday! "

" I 'll go to my tower in the Rhine," replied he;
" 'T is the safest place in Germany,—
The walls are high, and the shores are steep,
And the tide is strong, and the water deep."

Bishop Hatto fearfully hastened away;
And he crossed the Rhine without delay,
And reached his tower, and barred with care
All the windows, doors, and loop-holes there.

He laid him down and closed his eyes,
But soon a scream made him arise;
He started, and saw two eyes of flame
On his pillow, from whence the screaming came.

He listened and looked,—it was only the cat;
But the bishop he grew more fearful for that,
For she sate screaming, mad with fear,
At the army of rats that were drawing near.

For they have swum over the river so deep,
And they have climbed the shores so steep,
And now by thousands up they crawl
To the holes and the windows in the wall.

Down on his knees the bishop fell,
And faster and faster his beads did he tell,
As louder and louder, drawing near,
The saw of their teeth without he could hear.

And in at the windows, and in at the door,
And through the walls, by thousands they pour;
And down from the ceiling and up through the
     floor,

From the right and the left, from behind and be-
    fore,
From within and without, from above and be-
    low,—
And all at once to the bishop they go.


They have whetted their teeth against the stones,
And now they pick the bishop's bones;
They gnawed the flesh from every limb,
For they were sent to do judgment on him!

ROBERT SOUTHEY.

---

## COUNTESS LAURA.

It was a dreary day in Padua.
The Countess Laura, for a single year
Fernando's wife, upon her bridal bed,
Like an uprooted lily on the snow,
The withered outcast of a festival,
Lay dead. She died of some uncertain ill,
That struck her almost on her wedding day,
And clung to her, and dragged her slowly down,
Thinning her cheeks and pinching her full lips,
Till in her chance, it seemed that with a year
Full half a century was overpast.
In vain had Paracelsus taxed his art,
And feigned a knowledge of her malady;
In vain had all the doctors, far and near,
Gathered around the mystery of her bed,
Draining her veins, her husband's treasury,
And physic's jargon, in a fruitless quest
For causes equal to the dread result.

The Countess only smiled when they were gone,
Hugged her fair body with her little hands,
And turned upon her pillows wearily,
As though she fain would sleep no common sleep,
But the long, breathless slumber of the grave.
She hinted nothing.  Feeble as she was,
The rack could not have wrung her secret out.
The Bishop, when he shrived her, coming forth,
Cried, in a voice of heavenly ecstasy,
" O blessèd soul! with nothing to confess
Save virtues and good deeds, which she mistakes—
So humble is she—for our human sins!"
Praying for death, she tossed upon her bed
Day after day; as might a shipwrecked bark
That rocks upon one billow, and can make
No onward motion towards her port of hope.
At length, one morn, when those around her said,
" Surely the Countess mends, so fresh a light
Beams from her eyes and beautifies her face,"—
One morn in spring, when every flower of earth
Was opening to the sun, and breathing up
Its votive incense, her impatient soul
Opened itself, and so exhaled to heaven.
When the Count heard it, he reeled back a pace;
Then turned with anger on the messenger;
Then craved his pardon, and wept out his heart
Before the menial; tears, ah me! such tears
As love sheds only, and love only once.
Then he bethought him, " Shall this wonder die,
And leave behind no shadow? not a trace
Of all the glory that environed her,
That mellow nimbus circling round my star?"
So, with his sorrow glooming in his face,

He paced along his gallery of art,
And strode among the painters, where they stood,
With Carlo, the Venetian, at their head,
Studying the Masters by the dawning light
Of his transcendent genius. Through the groups
Of gayly vestured artists moved the Count,
As some lone cloud of thick and leaden hue,
Packed with the secret of a coming storm,
Moves through the gold and crimson evening
    mists,
Deadening their splendor. In a moment still
Was Carlo's voice, and still the prattling crowd;
And a great shadow overwhelmed them all,
As their white faces and their anxious eyes
Pursued Fernando in his moody walk.
He paused, as one who balances a doubt,
Weighing two courses, then burst out with this:
" Ye all have seen the tidings in my face;
Or has the dial ceased to register
The workings of my heart? Then hear the bell,
That almost cracks its frame in utterance;
The Countess,—she is dead!" "Dead!" Carlo
    groaned.
And if a bolt from middle heaven had struck
His splendid features full upon the brow,
He could not have appeared more scathed and
    blanched.
" Dead!—dead!" He staggered to his easel-
    frame,
And clung around it, buffeting the air
With one wild arm, as though a drowning man
Hung to a spar and fought against the waves.
The Count resumed: " I came not here to grieve,

Nor see my sorrow in another's eyes.
Who 'll paint the Countess, as she lies to-night
In state within the chapel?  Shall it be
That earth must lose her wholly? that no hint
Of her gold tresses, beaming eyes, and lips
That talked in silence, and the eager soul
That ever seemed outbreaking through her clay,
And scattering glory round it,—shall all these
Be dull corruption's heritage, and we,
Poor beggars, have no legacy to show
That love she bore us?  That were shame to love,
And shame to you, my masters."  Carlo stalked
Forth from his easel stiffly as a thing
Moved by mechanic impulse.  His thin lips,
And sharpened nostrils, and wan, sunken cheeks,
And the cold glimmer in his dusky eyes,
Made him a ghastly sight.  The throng drew back
As though they let a spectre through.  Then he,
Fronting the Count, and speaking in a voice
Sounding remote and hollow, made reply:
"Count, I shall paint the Countess.  'T is my
      fate,—
Not pleasure,—no, nor duty."  But the Count,
Astray in woe, but understood assent,
Not the strange words that bore it; and he flung
His arm round Carlo, drew him to his breast,
And kissed his forehead.  At which Carlo shrank;
Perhaps 't was at the honor.  Then the Count,
A little reddening at his public state,—
Unseemly to his near and recent loss,—
Withdrew in haste between the downcast eyes
That did him reverence as he rustled by.

Night fell on Padua.  In the chapel lay
The Countess Laura at the altar's foot.
Her coronet glittered on her pallid brows;
A crimson pall, weighed down with golden work,
Sown thick with pearls, and heaped with early
    flowers,
Draped her still body almost to the chin;
And over all a thousand candles flamed
Against the winking jewels, or streamed down
The marble aisle, and flashed along the guard
Of men-at-arms that slowly wove their turns,
Backward and forward, through the distant
    gloom.
When Carlo entered, his unsteady feet
Scarce bore him to the altar, and his head
Drooped down so low that all his shining curls
Poured on his breast, and veiled his countenance.
Upon his easel a half-finished work,
The secret labor of his studio,
Said from the canvas, so that none might err,
" I am the Countess Laura." Carlo kneeled,
And gazed upon the picture; as if thus,
Through those clear eyes, he saw the way to
    heaven.
Then he arose; and as a swimmer comes
Forth from the waves, he shook his locks aside,
Emerging from his dream, and standing firm
Upon a purpose with his sovereign will.
He took his palette, murmuring, " Not yet!"
Confidingly and softly to the corpse,
And as the veriest drudge, who plies his art
Against his fancy, he addressed himself
With stolid resolution to his task,

Turning his vision on his memory,
And shutting out the present, till the dead,
The gilded pall, the lights, the pacing guard,
And all the meaning of that solemn scene
Became as nothing, and creative Art
Resolved the whole to chaos, and reformed
The elements according to her law:
So Carlo wrought, as though his eye and hand
Were Heaven's unconscious instruments, and
    worked
The settled purpose of Omnipotence.
And it was wondrous how the red, the white,
The ochre, and the umber, and the blue,
From mottled blotches, hazy and opaque,
Grew into rounded forms and sensuous lines;
How just beneath the lucid skin the blood
Glimmered with warmth; the scarlet lips apart
Bloomed with the moisture of the dews of life;
How the light glittered through and underneath
The golden tresses, and the deep, soft eyes
Became intelligent with conscious thought,
And somewhat troubled underneath the arch
Of eyebrows but a little too intense
For perfect beauty; how the pose and poise
Of the lithe figure on its tiny foot
Suggested life just ceased from motion; so
That any one might cry, in marvelling joy,
" That creature lives,—has senses, mind, a soul
To win God's love or dare hell's subtleties!"
The artist paused. The ratifying " Good!"
Trembled upon his lips. He saw no touch
To give or soften. " It is done," he cried,—
" My task, my duty! Nothing now on earth

Can taunt me with a work left unfulfilled!"
The lofty flame, which bore him up so long,
Died in the ashes of humanity;
And the mere man rocked to and fro again
Upon the centre of his wavering heart.
He put aside his palette, as if thus
He stepped from sacred vestments, and assumed
A mortal function in the common world.
" Now for my rights!" he muttered, and ap-
    proached
The noble body. " O lily of the world!
So withered, yet so lovely! what wast thou
To those who came thus near thee—for I stood
Without the pale of thy half-royal rank—
When thou wast budding, and the streams of life
Made eager struggles to maintain thy bloom,
And gladdened heaven dropped down in gracious
    dews
On its transplanted darling? Hear me now!
I say this but in justice, not in pride,
Not to insult thy high nobility,
But that the poise of things in God's own sight
May be adjusted; and hereafter I
May urge a claim that all the powers of heaven
Shall sanction, and with clarions blow abroad.—
Laura you loved me! Look not so severe,
With your cold brows, and deadly, close-drawn
    lips!
You proved it, Countess, when you died for it,—
Let it consume you in the wearing strife
It fought with duty in your ravaged heart.
I knew it ever since that summer day
I painted Lilla, the pale beggar's child,

At rest beside the fountain; when I felt—
O Heaven!—the warmth and moisture of your
　　breath
Blow through my hair, as with your eager soul—
Forgetting soul and body go as one—
You leaned across my easel till our cheeks—
Ah me! 't was not your purpose—touched, and
　　clung!
Well, grant 't was genius; and is genius naught?
I ween it wears as proud a diadem—
Here, in this very world—as that you wear.
A king has held my palette, a grand-duke
Has picked my brush up, and a pope has begged
The favor of my presence in his Rome.
I did not go; I put my fortune by.
I need not ask you why: you knew too well.
It was but natural, it was no way strange,
That I should love you. Everything that saw,
Or had its other senses, loved you, sweet,
And I among them. Martyr, holy saint,—
I see the halo curving round your head,—
I loved you once; but now I worship you,
For the great deed that held my love aloof,
And killed you in the action! I absolve
Your soul from any taint. For from the day
Of that encounter by the fountain-side
Until this moment, never turned on me
Those tender eyes, unless they did a wrong
To nature by the cold, defiant glare
With which they chilled me. Never heard I word
Of softness spoken by those gentle lips;
Never received a bounty from that hand
Which gave to all the world. I know the cause.

You did your duty,--not for honor's sake,
Nor to save sin, or suffering, or remorse,
Or all the ghosts that haunt a woman's shame,
But for the sake of that pure, loyal love
Your husband bore you.  Queen, by grace of **God,**
I bow before the lustre of your throne!
I kiss the edges of your garment-hem,
And hold myself ennobled!  Answer me,--
If I had wronged you, you would answer me
Out of the dusty porches of the tomb:--
Is this a dream, a falsehood? or have I
Spoken the very truth?"  "The very truth!"
A voice replied; and at his side he saw
A form, half shadow and half substance, stand,
Or, rather, rest; for on the solid earth
It had no footing, more than some dense mist
That waves o'er the surface of the ground
It scarcely touches.  With a reverent look
The shadow's waste and wretched face was bent
Above the picture; as though greater awe
Subdued its awful being, and appalled,
With memories of terrible delight
And fearful wonder, its devouring gaze.
" You make what God makes,--beauty," said the
        shape.
" And might not this, this second Eve, console
The emptiest heart?  Will not this thing outlast
The fairest creature fashioned in the flesh?
Before that figure, Time, and Death himself,
Stand baffled and disarmed.  What would you
        ask
More than God's power, from nothing to create?"
The artist gazed upon the boding form,

And answered : " Goblin, if you had a heart,
That were an idle question.  What to me
Is my creative power, bereft of love?
Or what to God would be that self-same power,
If  so  bereaved?"   "And  yet  the  love,  thus
    mourned,
You calmly forfeited.  For had you said
To living Laura—in her burning ears—
One half that you professed to Laura dead,
She would have been your own.  These contraries
Sort not with my intelligence.  But speak,
Were Laura living, would the same stale play
Of raging passion tearing out its heart
Upon the rock of duty be performed? "
" The same, O phantom, while the heart I bear
Trembled, but turned not its magnetic faith
From God's fixed centre."   " If I wake for you
This Laura,—give her all the bloom and glow
Of that midsummer day you hold so dear,—
The smile, the motion, the impulsive soul,
The love of genius,—yea, the very love,
The mortal, hungry, passionate, hot love,
She bore you, flesh to flesh,—would you receive
That gift, in all its glory, at my hands? "
A smile of malice curled the tempter's lips,
And glittered in the caverns of his eyes,
Mocking the answer.  Carlo paled and shook;
A  woful  spasm  went  shuddering  through  his
    frame,
Curdling his blood, and twisting his fair face
With nameless torture.  But he cried aloud,
Out of the clouds of anguish, from the smoke
Of very martyrdom, " O God, she is thine!

Do with her at thy pleasure!" Something grand,
And radiant as a sunbeam, touched the head.
He bent in awful sorrow. " Mortal, see—"
" Dare not! As Christ was sinless, I abjure
These vile abominations! Shall she bear
Life's burden twice, and life's temptations twice,
While God is justice?" "Who has made you
        judge
Of what you call God's good, and what you think
God's evil? One to him, the source of both,
The God of good and of permitted ill.
Have you no dream of days that might have been,
Had you and Laura filled another fate?—
Some cottage on the sloping Apennines,
Roses and lilies, and the rest all love?
I tell you that this tranquil dream may be
Filled to repletion. Speak, and in the shade
Of my dark pinions I shall bear you hence,
And land you where the mountain-goat himself
Struggles for footing." He outspread his wings,
And all the chapel darkened, as though hell
Had swallowed up the tapers; and the air
Grew thick, and, like a current sensible,
Flowed round the person, with a wash and dash,
As of the waters of a nether sea.
Slowly and calmly through the dense obscure,
Dove-like and gentle, rose the artist's voice:
" I dare not bring her spirit to that shame!
Know my full meaning,—I who neither fear
Your mystic person nor your dreadful power.
Nor shall I now invoke God's potent name
For my deliverance from your toils. I stand
Upon the founded structure of his law,
    5

Established from the first, and thence defy
Your arts, reposing all my trust in that!"
The darkness eddied off; and Carlo saw
The figure gathering, as from outer space,
Brightness on brightness; and his former shape
Fell from him, like the ashes that fall off,
And show a core of mellow fire within.
Adown his wings there poured a lambent flood,
That seemed as molten gold, which plashing fell
Upon the floor, enringing him with flame;
And o'er the tresses of his beaming head
Arose a stream of many-colored light,
Like that which crowns the morning.  Carlo stood
Steadfast, for all the splendor, reaching up
The outstretched palms of his untainted soul
Towards heaven for strength.  A moment thus;
    then asked,
With reverential wonder quivering through
His sinking voice, "Who, spirit, and what, art
    thou?"
" I am that blessing which men fly from,—Death."
" Then take my hand, if so God orders it;
For Laura waits me."  "But, bethink thee, man,
What the world loses in the loss of thee!
What wondrous art will suffer with eclipse!
What unwon glories are in store for thee!
What fame, outreaching time and temporal
    shocks,
Would shine upon the letters of thy name
Graven in marble, or the brazen height
Of columns wise with memories of thee!"
" Take me!  If I outlived the Patriarchs,
I could but paint those features o'er and o'er:

Lo! that is done." A smile of pity lit
The seraph's features, as he looked to heaven,
With deep inquiry in his tender eyes.
The mandate came. He touched with downy wing
The sufferer lightly on his aching heart;
And gently, as the skylark settles down
Upon the clustered treasures of her nest,
So Carlo softly slid along the prop
Of his tall easel, nestling at the foot
As though he slumbered; and the morning broke
In silver whiteness over Padua.

GEORGE HENRY BOKER.

## OTHELLO'S REMORSE.

FROM " OTHELLO," ACT V. SC. 2.

BEHOLD, I have a weapon;
A better never did itself sustain
Upon a soldier's thigh: I have seen the day,
That, with this little arm and this good sword,
I have made my way through more impediments
Than twenty times your stop:—but, O vain boast!
Who can control his fate? 't is not so now.—
Be not afraid, though you do see me weaponed;
Here is my journey's end, here is my butt,
And very sea-mark of my utmost sail.
Do you go back dismayed? 't is a lost fear;
Man but a rush against Othello's breast,
And he retires:—where should Othello go?—
Now, how dost thou look now? O ill-starred
      wench!
Pale as thy smock! when we shall meet at compt,

This look of thine will hurl my soul from heaven,
And fiends will snatch at it.  Cold, cold, my girl?
Even like thy chastity—O, cursèd slave!—
Whip me, ye devils,
From the possession of this heavenly sight!
Blow me about in winds! roast me in sulphur!
Wash me in steep-down gulfs of liquid fire!—
O Desdemona! Desdemona! dead? O! O!

SHAKESPEARE.

---

## THE TRIAL OF BEATRICE.

FROM "THE CENCI," ACT V.

SCENE II.—*A  Hall  of  Justice.*  CAMILLO,
JUDGES, *etc., are discovered seated;* MARZIO *is
led in.*

FIRST JUDGE.—Accused, do you persist in your
        denial?
I ask you, are you innocent, or guilty?
I demand who were the participators
In your offence?  Speak truth and the whole
        truth.
    MARZIO.—My God!  I did not kill him; I know
        nothing;
Olimpio sold the robe to me from which
You would infer my guilt.
    SECOND JUDGE.—Away with him!
    FIRST JUDGE.—Dare you, with lips yet white
        from the rack's kiss
Speak false?  Is it so soft a questioner,

That you would bandy lovers' talk with it
Till it wind out your life and soul?  Away!
    MARZIO.—Spare me!  O, spare!  I will confess.
    FIRST JUDGE.—Then speak.
    MARZIO.—I strangled him in his sleep.
    FIRST JUDGE.—Who urged you to it?
    MARZIO.—His own son, Giacomo, and the young
       prelate
Orsino sent me to Petrella; there
The ladies Beatrice and Lucretia
Tempted me with a thousand crowns, and I
And my companion forthwith murdered him.
Now let me die.
    FIRST JUDGE.—This sounds as bad as truth.
       Guards, there,
Lead forth the prisoner!
*Enter* LUCRETIA, BEATRICE, *and* GIACOMO, *guarded.*
                Look upon this man;
When did you see him last?
    BEATRICE.—We never saw him.
    MARZIO.—You know me too well, Lady Beatrice.
    BEATRICE.—I know thee!  How? where? when?
    MARZIO.—You know 't was I
Whom you did urge with menaces and bribes
To kill your father.  When the thing was done
You clothed me in a robe of woven gold
And bade me thrive: how I have thriven, you see.
You, my Lord Giacomo, Lady Lucretia,
You know that what I speak is true.
(BEATRICE *advances towards him; he covers his*
      *face, and shrinks back.*)
                  O, dart
The terrible resentment of those eyes

On the dead earth! Turn them away from me!
They wound: 't was torture forced the truth.  My
    Lords,
Having said this let me be led to death.
    Beatrice.—Poor wretch, I pity thee: yet stay
      awhile.
      Camillo.—Guards, lead him not away.
      Beatrice.—Cardinal Camillo,
You have a good repute for gentleness
And wisdom: can it be that you sit here
To countenance a wicked farce like this?
When some obscure and trembling slave is
    dragged
From sufferings which might shake the sternest
    heart
And bade to answer, not as he believes,
But as those may suspect or do desire
Whose questions thence suggest their own reply:
And that in peril of such hideous torments
As merciful God spares even the damned.  Speak
    now
The thing you surely know, which is that you,
If your fine frame were stretched upon that wheel,
And you were told: " Confess that you did poison
Your little nephew; that fair blue-eyed child
Who was the lodestar of your life: "—and tho'
All see, since his most swift and piteous death,
That day and night, and heaven and earth, and
    time
And all the things hoped for or done therein
Are changed to you, thro' your exceeding grief,
Yet you would say, " I confess anything: "
And beg from your tormentors, like that slave,

The refuge of dishonorable death.
I pray thee, Cardinal, that thou assert
My innocence.

    CAMILLO (*much moved*).—What shall we think,
        my Lords?
Shame on these tears! I thought the heart was
        frozen
Which is their fountain. I would pledge my soul
That she is guiltless.

    JUDGE.—Yet she must be tortured.

    CAMILLO.—I would as soon have tortured mine
        own nephew
(If he now lived he would be just her age;
His hair, too, was her color, and his eyes
Like hers in shape, but blue and not so deep)
As that most perfect image of God's love
That ever came sorrowing upon the earth.
She is as pure as speechless infancy!

    JUDGE.—Well, be her purity on your head, my
        Lord,
If you forbid the rack. His Holiness
Enjoined us to pursue this monstrous crime
By the severest forms of law; nay even
To stretch a point against the criminals.
The prisoners stand accused of parricide
Upon such evidence as justifies
Torture.

    BEATRICE.—What evidence? This man's?

    JUDGE.—Even so.

    BEATRICE (*to* MARZIO).—Come near. And who
        art thou thus chosen forth
Out of the multitude of living men
To kill the innocent?

Marzio—I am Marzio,
Thy father's vassal.
    Beatrice.—Fix thine eyes on mine;
Answer to what I ask.

        (*Turning to the* Judges.)
I prithee mark
His countenance: unlike bold calumny
Which sometimes dares not speak the thing it
      looks,
He dares not look the thing he speaks, but bends
His gaze on the blind earth.
    (*To* Marzio.)  What! wilt thou say
That I did murder my own father?
    Marzio.—Oh!
Spare me!  My brain swims round . . . I can-
      not speak . . .
It was that horrid torture forced the truth.
Take me away!  Let her not look on me!
I am a guilty miserable wretch;
I have said all I know; now, let me die!
    Beatrice.—My Lords, if by my nature I had
      been
So stern, as to have planned the crime alleged,
Which your suspicions dictate to this slave,
And the rack makes him utter, do you think
I should have left this two-edged instrument
Of my misdeed; this man, this bloody knife
With my own name engraven on the heft,
Lying unsheathed amid a world of foes,
For my own death? That with such horrible need
For deepest silence, I should have neglected
So trivial a precaution, as the making

His tomb the keeper of a secret written
On a thief's memory? What is his poor life?
What are a thousand lives? A parricide
Had trampled them like dust; and, see, he lives!
(*Turning to* MARZIO.) And thou . . .

    MARZIO.—Oh, spare me! Speak to me no more!
That stern yet piteous look, those solemn tones,
Wound worse than torture.

    (*To the* JUDGES.) I have told it all;
For pity's sake lead me away to death.

    CAMILLO.—Guards, lead him nearer the Lady
        Beatrice;
He shrinks from her regard like autumn's leaf
From the keen breath of the serenest north.

    BEATRICE.—O thou who tremblest on the giddy
        verge
Of life and death, pause ere thou answerest me;
So mayst thou answer God with less dismay:
What evil have we done thee? I, alas!
Have lived but on this earth a few sad years
And so my lot was ordered, that a father
First turned the moments of awakening life
To drops, each poisoning youth's sweet hope; and
        then
Stabbed with one blow my everlasting soul;
And my untainted fame; and even that peace
Which sleeps within the core of the heart's heart;
But the wound was not mortal; so my hate
Became the only worship I could lift
To our great Father, who in pity and love,
Armed thee, as thou dost say, to cut him off;
And thus his wrong becomes my accusation;
And art thou the accuser? If thou hopest

Mercy in heaven, show justice upon earth:
Worse than a bloody hand is a hard heart.
If thou hast done murders, made thy life's path
Over the trampled laws of God and man,
Rush not before thy Judge, and say: " My maker,
I have done this and more; for there was one
Who was most pure and innocent on earth;
And because she endured what never any
Guilty or innocent endured before:
Because her wrongs could not be told, not
    thought;
Because thy hand at length did rescue her;
I with my words killed her and all her kin."
Think, I adjure you, what it is to slay
The reverence living in the minds of men
Towards our ancient house, and stainless fame!
Think what it is to strangle infant pity,
Cradled in the belief of guileless looks,
Till it become a crime to suffer.  Think
What 't is to blot with infamy and blood
All that which shows like innocence, and is,
 Hear me, great God! I swear, most innocent,
So that the world lose all discrimination
Between the sly, fierce, wild regard of guilt,
And that which now compels thee to reply
To what I ask: Am I, or am I not
A parricide?
   MARZIO.—Thou art not!
   JUDGE.—What is this?
   MARZIO.—I here declare those whom I did ac-
    cuse
Are innocent.  'T is I alone am guilty.
   JUDGE.—Drag him away to torments; let them
    be

Subtle and long drawn out, to tear the folds
Of the heart's inmost cell.  Unbind him not
Till he confess.

MARZIO.—Torture me as ye will:
A keener pain has wrung a higher truth
From my last breath.  She is most innocent!
Bloodhounds, not men, glut yourselves well with
  me;
I will not give you that fine piece of nature
To rend and ruin.

   (*Exit* MARZIO, *guarded.*)

CAMILLO.—What say ye now, my Lords?

JUDGE.—Let tortures strain the truth till it be
  white
As snow thrice sifted by the frozen wind.

CAMILLO.—Yet stained with blood.

JUDGE (*to* BEATRICE).—Know you this paper,
  Lady?

BEATRICE.—Entrap me not with questions.  Who
  stands here
As my accuser?  Ha! wilt thou be he,
Who art my judge?  Accuser, witness, judge,
What, all in one?  Here is Orsino's name;
Where is Orsino?  Let his eye meet mine.
What means this scrawl?  Alas! ye know not
  what,
And therefore on the chance that it may be
Some evil, will ye kill us?

   (*Enter an Officer.*)

OFFICER.—Marzio's dead.

JUDGE.—What did he say?

OFFICER.—Nothing.  As soon as we
Had bound him on the wheel, he smiled on us,

As one who baffles a deep adversary;
And holding his breath, died.

    JUDGE.—There remains nothing
But to apply the question to those prisoners,
Who yet remain stubborn.

    CAMILLO.—I overrule
Further proceedings, and in the behalf
Of these most innocent and noble persons
Will use my interest with the Holy Father.

    JUDGE.—Let the Pope's pleasure then be done.
        Meanwhile
Conduct these culprits each to separate cells;
And be the engines ready: for this night
If the Pope's resolution be as grave,
Pious, and just as once, I 'll wring the truth
Out of those nerves and sinews, groan by groan.

                (*Exeunt.*)

                    PERCY BYSSHE SHELLEY.

_____

### FRA GIACOMO.

ALAS, Fra Giacomo,
    Too late!—but follow me;
Hush! draw the curtain,—so!—
    She is dead, quite dead, you see.
Poor little lady! she lies
With the light gone out of her eyes,
But her features still wear that soft
    Gray meditative expression,
Which you must have noticed oft,
    And admired too, at confession.
How saintly she looks, and how meek!

Though this be the chamber of death,
   I fancy I feel her breath
As I kiss her on the cheek.
With that pensive religious face,
She has gone to a holier place!
And I hardly appreciated her,—
   Her praying, fasting, confessing,
Poorly, I own, I mated her;
I thought her too cold, and rated her
   For her endless image-caressing.
Too saintly for me by far,
As pure and as cold as a star,
   Not fashioned for kissing and pressing,—
But made for a heavenly crown.
Ay, father, let us go down,—
   But first, if you please, your blessing.

Wine? No? Come, come, you must!
   You 'll bless it with your prayers,
And quaff a cup, I trust,
   To the health of the saint up stairs?
My heart is aching so!
   And I feel so weary and sad,
   Through the blow that I have had,—
You 'll sit, Fra Giacomo?
My friend! (and a friend I rank you
   For the sake of that saint,)—nay, nay!
   Here 's the wine,—as you love me, stay!—
'T is Montepulciano!—Thank you.

Heigh-ho! 'T is now six summers
   Since I won that angel and married her:
   I was rich, not old, and carried her

Off in the face of all comers.
So fresh, yet so brimming with soul!
    A tenderer morsel, I swear,
Never made the dull black coal
    Of a monk's eye glitter and glare.
        Your pardon!—nay, keep your chair!
I wander a little, but mean
No offence to the gray gaberdine;
Of the church, Fra Giacomo,
I 'm a faithful upholder, you know,
But (humor me!) she was as sweet
    As the saints in your convent windows,
So gentle, so meek, so discreet,
    She knew not what lust does or sin does.
I 'll confess, though, before we were one,
    I deemed her less saintly, and thought
    The blood in her veins had caught
Some natural warmth from the sun.
I was wrong,—I was blind as a bat,—
    Brute that I was, how I blundered!
Though such a mistake as that
Might have occurred as pat
    To ninety-nine men in a hundred.
Yourself, for example? you 've seen her?
Spite her modest and pious demeanor,
And the manners so nice and precise,
    Seemed there not color and light,
    Bright motion and appetite,
That were scarcely consistent with *ice?*
Externals implying, you see,
    Internals less saintly than human?—
Pray speak, for between you and me
    You 're not a bad judge of a woman!

A jest,—but a jest!—Very true:
   'T is hardly becoming to jest,
   And that saint up stairs at rest,—
Her soul may be listening, too!
I was always a brute of a fellow!
Well may your visage turn yellow,—
To think how I doubted and doubted,
Suspected, grumbled at, flouted
That golden-haired angel,—and solely
Because she was zealous and holy!
Noon and night and morn
   She devoted herself to piety;
Not that she seemed to scorn
   Or dislike her husband's society;
But the claims of her *soul* superseded
All that I asked for or needed,
And her thoughts were far away
From the level of sinful clay,
And she trembled if earthly matters
Interfered with her *aves* and *paters*.
Poor dove, she so fluttered in flying
   Above the dim vapors of hell—
Bent on self-sanctifying—
That she never thought of trying
   To save her husband as well.
And while she was duly elected
   For place in the heavenly roll,
I (brute that I was!) suspected
   Her manner of saving her soul.
So, half for the fun of the thing,
What did I (blasphemer!) but fling
On my shoulders the gown of a monk—
   Whom I managed for that very day

To get safely out of the way—
And seat me, half sober, half drunk,
With the cowl thrown over my face,
In the father confessor's place.
*Eheu! benedicite!*
In her orthodox sweet simplicity,
With that pensive gray expression,
She sighfully knelt at confession,
While I bit my lips till they bled,
   And dug my nails in my hand,
And heard with averted head
   What I 'd guessed and could understand.
Each word was a serpent's sting,
   But, wrapt in my gloomy gown,
I sat, like a marble thing,
   As she told me all!—Sit down!

More wine, Fra Giacomo!
One cup,—if you love me! No?
What, have these dry lips drank
   So deep of the sweets of pleasure—
   *Sub rosa,* but quite without measure—
That Montepulciano tastes rank?
Come, drink! 't will bring the streaks
Of crimson back to your cheeks;
Come, drink again to the saint
Whose virtues you loved to paint,
Who, stretched on her wifely bed,
   With the tender, grave expression
   You used to admire at confession,
Lies poisoned, overhead!

Sit still,—or by heaven, you die!
Face to face, soul to soul, you and I

Have settled accounts, in a fine
Pleasant fashion, over our wine.
Stir not, and seek not to fly,—
Nay, whether or not, you are mine!
Thank Montepulciano for giving
 You death in such delicate sips;
'T is not every monk ceases living
 With so pleasant a taste on his lips;
But, lest Montepulciano unsurely should kiss,
 Take this! and this! and this!

Cover him over, Pietro,
And bury him in the court below,—
You can be secret, lad, I know!
And, hark you, then to the convent go,—
Bid every bell of the convent toll,
And the monks say mass for your mistress' soul.

ROBERT BUCHANAN.

---

## GINEVRA.

If thou shouldst ever come by choice or chance
To Modena, where still religiously
Among her ancient trophies is preserved
Bologna's bucket (in its chain it hangs
Within that reverend tower, the Guirlandina),
Stop at a palace near the Reggio gate,
Dwelt in of old by one of the Orsini.
Its noble gardens, terrace above terrace,
And rich in fountains, statues, cypresses,
Will long detain thee; through their archèd walks,
Dim at noonday, discovering many a glimpse
Of knights and dames, such as in old romance,

6

And lovers, such as in heroic song,
Perhaps the two, for groves were their delight,
That in the springtime, as alone they sat,
Venturing together on a tale of love,
Read only part that day.—A summer sun
Sets ere one half is seen; but ere thou go,
Enter the house—prythee, forget it not—
And look awhile upon a picture there.

'T is of a Lady in her earliest youth,
The last of that illustrious race;
Done by Zampieri—but I care not whom.
He who observes it, ere he passes on,
Gazes his fill, and comes and comes again,
That he may call it up when far away.

She sits inclining forward as to speak,
Her lips half open, and her finger up,
As though she said " Beware! " her vest of gold
Broidered with flowers, and clasped from head to
    foot,
An emerald stone in every golden clasp;
And on her brow, fairer than alabaster,
A coronet of pearls. But then her face,
So lovely, yet so arch, so full of mirth,
The overflowings of an innocent heart,—
It haunts me still, though many a year has fled,
Like some wild melody!
                          Alone it hangs
Over a moldering heirloom, its companion,
An oaken chest, half eaten by the worm,
But richly carved by Antony of Trent
With Scripture stories from the life of Christ;

A chest that came from Venice, and had held
The ducal robes of some old Ancestor,
That, by the way—it may be true or false—
But don't forget the picture; and thou wilt not
When thou hast heard the tale they told me there.

She was an only child; from infancy
The joy, the pride, of an indulgent Sire;
Her Mother dying of the gift she gave,
That precious gift, what else remained to him?
The young Ginevra was his all in life,
Still as she grew, for ever in his sight;
And in her fifteenth year became a bride,
Marrying an only son, Francesco Doria,
Her playmate from her birth, and her first love.

Just as she looks there in her bridal dress,
She was all gentleness, all gayety,
Her pranks the favorite theme of every tongue.
But now the day was come, the day, the hour;
Now, frowning, smiling, for the hundredth time,
The nurse, that ancient lady, preached decorum;
And, in the lustre of her youth, she gave
Her hand, with her heart in it, to Francesco.

Great was the joy; but at the Bridal-feast,
When all sate down, the bride was wanting there,
Nor was she to be found! Her Father cried,
" 'T is but to make a trial of our love!"
And filled his glass to all; but his hand shook,
And soon from guest to guest the panic spread.
'T was but that instant she had left Francesco,
Laughing and looking back, and flying still,
Her ivory tooth imprinted on his finger.

But now, alas, she was not to be found;
Nor from that hour could anything be guessed,
But that she was not!
                     Weary of his life,
Francesco flew to Venice, and, forthwith,
Flung it away in battle with the Turk.
Orsini lived,—and long mightst thou have seen
An old man wandering as in quest of something,
Something he could not find, he knew not what.
When he was gone, the house remained awhile
Silent and tenantless,—then went to strangers.

   Full fifty years were past, and all forgot,
When, on an idle day, a day of search
Mid the old lumber in the Gallery,
That moldering chest was noticed; and 't was
     said
By one as young, as thoughtless as Ginevra,
" Why not remove it from its lurking-place? "
'T was done as soon as said; but on the way
It burst, it fell; and lo, a skeleton,
With here and there a pearl, an emerald stone,
A golden clasp, clasping a shred of gold!
All else had perished,—save a nuptial-ring,
And a small seal, her mother's legacy,
Engraven with a name, the name of both,
" GINEVRA."
             There then had she found a grave!
Within that chest had she concealed herself,
Fluttering with joy, the happiest of the happy;
When a spring-lock, that lay in ambush there,
Fastened her down for ever!

                       SAMUEL ROGERS.

## BERNARDO DEL CARPIO.

THE warrior bowed his crested head, and tamed
    his heart of fire,
And sued the haughty king to free his long-im-
    prisoned sire;
" I bring thee here my fortress keys, I bring my
    captive train,
I pledge thee faith, my liege, my lord!—oh, break
    my father's chain ! "

" Rise, rise! even now thy father comes, a ran-
    somed man this day;
Mount thy good horse, and thou and I will meet
    him on his way."
Then lightly rose that loyal son, and bounded on
    his steed,
And urged, as if with lance in rest, the charger's
    foamy speed.

And lo! from far, as on they pressed, there came
    a glittering band,
With one that 'midst them stately rode, as a leader
    in the land;
" Now haste, Bernardo, haste! for there, in very
    truth, is he,
The father whom thy faithful heart hath yearned
    so long to see."

His dark eye flashed, his proud breast heaved, his
    cheek's blood came and went;
He reached that gray-haired chieftain's side, and
    there, dismounting, bent;

A lowly knee to earth he bent, his father's hand
    he took,—
What was there in its touch that all his fiery
    spirit shook?
That hand was cold,—a frozen thing,—it dropped
    from his like lead,—
He looked up to the face above,—the face was of
    the dead!
A plume waved o'er the noble brow,—the brow
    was fixed and white;—
He met at last his father's eyes,—but in them was
    no sight!

Up from the ground he sprung, and gazed, but
    who could paint that gaze?
They hushed their very hearts, that saw its horror
    and amaze;
They might have chained him, as before that stony
    form he stood,
For the power was stricken from his arm, and
    from his lip the blood.

"Father!" at length he murmured low, and wept
    like childhood then:
Talk not of grief till thou hast seen the tears of
    warlike men!
He thought on all his glorious hopes, and all his
    young renown;
He flung the falchion from his side, and in the
    dust sate down.

Then covering with his steel-gloved hands his
    darkly mournful brow,—
"No more, there is no more," he said, "to lift the
    sword for now;

My king is false, my hope betrayed; my father—
oh! the worth,
The glory, and the loveliness, are passed away
from earth!

" I thought to stand where banners waved, my
sire! beside thee yet,
I would that there our kindred blood on Spain's
free soil had met!
Thou wouldst have known my spirit then; for thee
my fields were won;
And thou hast perished in thy chains, as though
thou hadst no son!"

Then, starting from the ground once more, he
seized the monarch's rein,
Amidst the pale and wildered looks of all the
courtier train;
And with a fierce o'ermastering grasp, the raging
war-horse led,
And sternly set them face to face,—the king before the dead!

" Came I not forth upon thy pledge, my father's
hand to kiss?
Be still, and gaze thou on, false king, and tell me
what is this?
The voice, the glance, the heart I sought—give
answer, where are they?
If thou wouldst clear thy perjured soul, send life
through this cold clay!

" Into these glassy eyes put light;—be still! keep
down thine ire!
Bid these white lips a blessing speak,—this earth
is not my sire!

Give me back him for whom I strove, for whom
　　my blood was shed,
Thou canst not?—and a king!—his dust be moun-
　　tains on thy head!"

He loosed the steed; his slack hand fell; upon the
　　silent face
He cast one long, deep, troubled look,—then
　　turned from that sad place.
His hope was crushed, his after-fate untold in
　　martial strain:
His banner led the spears no more amidst the hills
　　of Spain.

FELICIA HEMANS.

---

## THE PRISONER OF CHILLON.

ETERNAL spirit of the chainless mind!
Brightest in dungeons, Liberty! thou art,
For there thy habitation is the heart,—
The heart which love of thee alone can bind;
And when thy sons to fetters are consigned,—
To fetters, and the damp vault's dayless gloom,—
Their country conquers with their martyrdom,
And Freedom's fame finds wings on every wind.
Chillon! thy prison is a holy place,
And thy sad floor an altar,—for 't was trod,
Until his very steps have left a trace
Worn, as if thy cold pavement were a sod,
By Bonnivard!—May none those marks efface!
For they appeal from tyranny to God.

---

My hair is gray, but not with years,
　　Nor grew it white
　　In a single night,
As men's have grown from sudden fears:
My limbs are bowed, though not with toil,
　　But rusted with a vile repose,
For they have been a dungeon spoil,
　　And mine has been the fate of those
To whom the goodly earth and air
Are banned, and barred,—forbidden fare;
But this was for my father's faith
I suffered chains and courted death;
That father perished at the stake
For tenets he would not forsake;
And for the same his lineal race
In darkness found a dwelling-place;
We were seven,—who now are one,
　　Six in youth, and one in age,
Finished as they had begun,
　　Proud of Persecution's rage;
One in fire, and two in field,
Their belief with blood have sealed!
Dying as their father died,
For the God their foes denied;
Three were in a dungeon cast,
Of whom this wreck is left the last.

There are seven pillars of Gothic mould
In Chillon's dungeons deep and old,
There are seven columns, massy and gray,
Dim with a dull imprisoned ray,—
A sunbeam which hath lost its way,
And through the crevice and the cleft

Of the thick wall is fallen and left,
Creeping o'er the floor so damp,
Like a marsh's meteor lamp,—
And in each pillar there is a ring,
    And in each ring there is a chain;
That iron is a cankering thing,
    For in these limbs its teeth remain
With marks that will not wear away,
Till I have done with this new day,
Which now is painful to these eyes,
Which have not seen the sun to rise
For years,—I cannot count them o'er,
I lost their long and heavy score
When my last brother drooped and died,
And I lay living by his side.

They chained us each to a column stone,
And we were three, yet each alone;
We could not move a single pace,
We could not see each other's face,
But with that pale and livid light
That made us strangers in our sight;
And thus together, yet apart,
Fettered in hand, but pined in heart;
'T was still some solace, in the dearth
Of the pure elements of earth,
To hearken to each other's speech,
And each turn comforter to each
With some new hope, or legend old,
Or song heroically bold;
But even these at length grew cold.
Our voices took a dreary tone,
An echo of the dungeon-stone,

A grating sound,—not full and free
As they of yore were wont to be;
It might be fancy,—but to me
They never sounded like our own.

I was the eldest of the three,
And to uphold and cheer the rest
I ought to do—and did—my best,
And each did well in his degree.
The youngest, whom my father loved,
Because our mother's brow was given
To him, with eyes as blue as heaven,—
For him my soul was sorely moved;
And truly might it be distrest
To see such bird in such a nest;
For he was beautiful as day
(When day was beautiful to me
As to young eagles, being free),—
A polar day, which will not see
A sunset till its summer's gone,
Its sleepless summer of long light,
The snow-clad offspring of the sun;
And thus he was as pure and bright,
And in his natural spirit gay,
With tears for naught but others' ills,
And then they flowed like mountain rills,
Unless he could assuage the woe
Which he abhorred to view below.

The other was as pure of mind,
But formed to combat with his kind;
Strong in his frame, and of a mood
Which 'gainst the world in war had stood,

And perished in the foremost rank
   With joy;—but not in chains to pine;
His spirit withered with their clank,
   I saw it silently decline,—
   And so perchance in sooth did mine;
But yet I forced it on to cheer
Those relics of a home so dear.
He was a hunter of the hills,
   Had followed there the deer and wolf;
   To him this dungeon was a gulf
And fettered feet the worst of ills.

Lake Leman lies by Chillon's walls:
A thousand feet in depth below
Its massy waters meet and flow;
Thus much the fathom-line was sent
From Chillon's snow-white battlement,
   Which round about the wave inthralls;
And double dungeon wall and wave
Have made,—and like a living grave.
Below the surface of the lake
The dark vault lies wherein we lay,
We heard it ripple night and day;
   Sounding o'er our heads it knocked;
And I have felt the winter's spray
Wash through the bars when winds were high
And wanton in the happy sky;
   And then the very rock hath rocked,
   And I have felt it shake, unshocked,
Because I could have smiled to see
The death that would have set me free.

I said my nearer brother pined,
I said his mighty heart declined,

He loathed and put away his food;
It was not that 't was coarse and rude,
For we were used to hunter's fare,
And for the like had little care;
The milk drawn from the mountain goat
Was changed for water from the moat.
Our bread was such as captives' tears
Have moistened many a thousand years,
Since man first pent his fellow-men
Like brutes within an iron den;
But what were these to us or him?
These wasted not his heart or limb;
My brother's soul was of that mould
Which in a palace had grown cold,
Had his free breathing been denied
The range of the steep mountain's side;
But why delay the truth?—he died.
I saw, and could not hold his head,
Nor reach his dying hand—nor dead—
Though hard I strove, but strove in vain,
To rend and gnash my bonds in twain.
He died,—and they unlocked his chain,
And scooped for him a shallow grave
Even from the cold earth of our cave.
I begged them, as a boon, to lay
His corse in dust whereon the day
Might shine,—it was a foolish thought,
But then within my brain it wrought,
That even in death his free-born breast
In such a dungeon could not rest.
I might have spared my idle prayer,—
They coldly laughed, and laid him there.
The flat and turfless earth above

The being we so much did love;
His empty chain above it leant,
Such murder's fitting monument!

But he, the favorite and the flower,
Most cherished since his natal hour,
His mother's image in fair face,
The infant love of all his race,
His martyred father's dearest thought,
My latest care, for whom I sought
To hoard my life, that his might be
Less wretched now, and one day free;
He, too, who yet had held untired
A spirit natural or inspired,—
He, too, was struck, and day by day
Was withered on the stalk away.
O God! it is a fearful thing
To see the human soul take wing
In any shape, in any mood:—
I 've seen it rushing forth in blood,
I 've seen it on the breaking ocean
Strive with a swoln convulsive motion,
I 've seen the sick and ghastly bed
Of Sin delirious with its dread:
But these were horrors,—this was woe
Unmixed with such,—but sure and slow:
He faded, and so calm and meek,
So softly worn, so sweetly weak,
So tearless, yet so tender—kind,
And grieved for those he left behind;
With all the while a cheek whose bloom
Was as a mockery of the tomb,
Whose tints as gently sunk away
As a departing rainbow's ray,—

An eye of most transparent light,
That almost made the dungeon bright,
And not a word of murmur,—not
A groan o'er his untimely lot,—
A little talk of better days,
A little hope my own to raise,
For I was sunk in silence,—lost
In this last loss, of all the most;
And then the sighs he would suppress
Of fainting nature's feebleness,
More slowly drawn, grew less and less:
I listened, but I could not hear,—
I called, for I was wild with fear;
I knew 't was hopeless, but my dread
Would not be thus admonishèd;
I called, and thought I heard a sound,—
I burst my chain with one strong bound,
And rushed to him:—I found him not,
*I* only stirred in this black spot,
*I* only lived,—*I* only drew
The accursed breath of dungeon-dew;
The last—the sole—the dearest link
Between me and the eternal brink,
Which bound me to my failing race,
Was broken in this fatal place.
One on the earth, and one beneath—
My brothers—both had ceased to breathe.
I took that hand which lay so still,
Alas! my own was full as chill;
I had not strength to stir or strive,
But felt that I was still alive,—
A frantic feeling when we know
That what we love shall ne'er be so.

I know not why
I could not die,
I had no earthly hope—but faith,
And that forbade a selfish death.

What next befell me then and there
    I know not well—I never knew.
First came the loss of light and air,
    And then of darkness too;
I had no thought, no feeling—none:
Among the stones I stood a stone,
And was, scarce conscious what I wist,
As shrubless crags within the mist;
For all was blank and bleak and gray;
It was not night,—it was not day;
It was not even the dungeon-light,
So hateful to my heavy sight;
But vacancy absorbing space,
And fixedness, without a place:
There were no stars—no earth—no time—
No check—no change—no good—no crime:
But silence, and a stirless breath
Which neither was of life nor death:—
A sea of stagnant idleness,
Blind, boundless, mute, and motionless!

A light broke in upon my brain,—
    It was the carol of a bird;
It ceased, and then it came again,—
    The sweetest song ear ever heard,
And mine was thankful till my eyes
Ran over with the glad surprise,
And they that moment could not see

I was the mate of misery;
But then by dull degrees came back
My senses to their wonted track,
I saw the dungeon walls and floor
Close slowly round me as before,
I saw the glimmer of the sun
Creeping as it before had done,
But through the crevice where it came
That bird was perched, as fond and tame,
   And tamer than upon the tree;
A lovely bird, with azure wings,
And song that said a thousand things,
   And seemed to say them all for me!
I never saw its like before,
I ne'er shall see its likeness more.
It seemed, like me, to want a mate,
But was not half so desolate,
And it was come to love me when
None lived to love me so again,
And cheering from my dungeon's brink,
Had brought me back to feel and think.
I know not if it late were free,
   Or broke its cage to perch on mine,
But knowing well captivity,
   Sweet bird! I could not wish for thine!
Or if it were, in wingèd guise,
A visitant from Paradise:
For—Heaven forgive that thought! the while
Which made me both to weep and smile—
I sometimes deemed that it might be
My brother's soul come down to me;
But then at last away it flew,
And then 't was mortal,—well I knew,
7

For he would never thus have flown,
And left me twice so doubly lone,—
Lone—as the corse within its shroud,
Lone—as a solitary cloud,
  A single cloud on a sunny day,
While all the rest of heaven is clear,
A frown upon the atmosphere
That hath no business to appear
  When skies are blue and earth is gay.

A kind of change came in my fate,
My keepers grew compassionate;
I know not what had made them so,
They were inured to sights of woe,
But so it was:—my broken chain
With links unfastened did remain,
And it was liberty to stride
Along my cell from side to side,
And up and down, and then athwart,
And tread it over every part;
And round the pillars one by one,
Returning where my walk begun,
Avoiding only, as I trod,
  My brothers' graves without a sod;
For if I thought with heedless tread
My step profaned their lowly bed,
My breath came gaspingly and thick,
And my crushed heart fell blind and sick.

I made a footing in the wall,
  It was not therefrom to escape,
For I had buried one and all
  Who loved me in a human shape:

And the whole earth would henceforth be
A wider prison unto me:
No child,—no sire,—no kin had I,
No partner in my misery;
I thought of this and I was glad,
For thought of them had made me mad;
But I was curious to ascend
To my barred windows, and to bend
Once more, upon the mountains high,
The quiet of a loving eye.

I saw them,—and they were the same,
They were not changed like me in frame;
I saw their thousand years of snow
On high,—their wide long lake below,
And the blue Rhone in fullest flow;
I heard the torrents leap and gush
O'er channelled rock and broken bush;
I saw the white-walled distant town,
And whiter sails go skimming down;
And then there was a little isle,
Which in my very face did smile,
    The only one in view;
A small green isle, it seemed no more,
Scarce broader than my dungeon floor,
But in it there were three tall trees,
And o'er it blew the mountain breeze,
And by it there were waters flowing,
And on it there were young flowers growing,
    Of gentle breath and hue.
The fish swam by the castle wall,
And they seemed joyous each and all;
The eagle rode the rising blast,—

Methought he never flew so fast
As then to me he seemed to fly,
And then new tears came in my eye,
And I felt troubled,—and would fain
I had not left my recent chain;
And when I did descend again,
The darkness of my dim abode
Fell on me as a heavy load;
It was as in a new-dug grave
Closing o'er one we sought to save,
And yet my glance, too much oppressed,
Had almost need of such a rest.

It might be months, or years, or days,
    I kept no count,—I took no note,
I had no hope my eyes to raise,
    And clear them of their dreary mote;
At last men came to set me free,
    I asked not why and recked not where,
It was at length the same to me,
Fettered or fetterless to be,
    I learned to love despair.
And thus when they appeared at last,
And all my bonds aside were cast,
These heavy walls to me had grown
A hermitage, and all my own!
And half I felt as they were come
To tear me from a second home;
With spiders I had friendship made,
And watched them in their sullen trade,
Had seen the mice by moonlight play,
And why should I feel less than they?
We were all inmates of one place,

And I, the monarch of each race,
Had power to kill,—yet, strange to tell;
In quiet we had learned to dwell,—
My very chains and I grew friends,
So much a long communion tends
To make us what we are:—even I
Regained my freedom with a sigh.

LORD BYRON.

## BEFORE SEDAN.

"The dead hand clasped a letter."
—SPECIAL CORRESPONDENT.

HERE in this leafy place,
    Quiet he lies,
Cold, with his sightless face
    Turned to the skies;
'T is but another dead;—
All you can say is said.

Carry his body hence,—
    Kings must have slaves;
Kings climb to eminence
    Over men's graves.
So this man's eye is dim;—
Throw the earth over him.

What was the white you touched,
    There at his side?
Paper his hand had clutched
    Tight ere he died;
Message or wish, may be:—
Smooth out the folds and see.

Hardly the worst of us
　Here could have smiled!—
Only the tremulous
　Words of a child:—
Prattle, that had for stops
Just a few ruddy drops.

Look.　She is sad to miss,
　Morning and night,
His—her dead father's—kiss,
　Tries to be bright,
Good to mamma, and sweet.
That is all.　"*Marguerite.*"

Ah, if beside the dead
　Slumbered the pain!
Ah, if the hearts that bled
　Slept with the slain!
If the grief died!—But no:—
Death will not have it so.

AUSTIN DOBSON.

# IVÀN IVÀNOVITCH.

EARLY one winter morn, in such a village as this,
Snow-whitened everywhere except the middle road
Ice-roughed by track of sledge, there worked by his
　　abode
Ivàn Ivànovitch, the carpenter, employed
On a huge shipmast trunk; his axe now trimmed
　　and toyed
With branch and twig, and now some chop
　　athwart the bole

Changed bole to billets, bared at once the sap and
　　soul.
About him, watched the work his neighbors sheep-
　　skin-clad;
Each bearded mouth puffed steam, each gray eye
　　twinkled glad
To see the sturdy arm which, never stopping play,
Proved strong man's blood still boils, freeze winter
　　as he may.
Sudden, a burst of bells.　Out of the road, on edge
Of the hamlet—horse's hoofs galloping.　" How, a
　　sledge?
What 's here? " cried all as—in, up to the open
　　space,
Workyard and market-ground, folk's common
　　meeting-place,—
Stumbled on, till he fell, in one last bound for life,
A horse; and, at his heels, a sledge held—" Dmì-
　　tri's wife!
Back without Dmìtri too! and children—where
　　are they?
Only a frozen corpse! "

　　　　　　　　They drew it forth: then—" Nay,
Not dead, though like to die! Gone hence a month
　　ago:
Home again, this rough jaunt—alone through
　　night and snow—
What can the cause be? Hark—Droug, old horse,
　　how he groans:
His day 's done! Chafe away, keep chafing, for
　　she moans:
She 's coming to!　Give here: see, motherkin, your
　　friends!

Cheer up, all safe at home!  Warm inside makes
    amends
For outside cold,—sup quick!  Don't look as we
    were bears!
What is it startles you?  What strange adven-
    ture stares
Up at us in your face?  You know friends—which
    is which?
I 'm Vàssili, he 's Sergeì, Ivàn Ivànovitch "—


At the word, the woman's eyes, slow-wandering
    till they neared
The blue eyes o'er the bush of honey-colored beard,
Took in full light and sense and—torn to rags,
    some dream
Which hid the naked truth—O loud and long the
    scream
She gave, as if all power of voice within her throat
Poured itself wild away to waste in one dread
    note!
Then followed gasps and sobs, and then the steady
    flow
Of kindly tears: the brain was saved, a man might
    know.
Down fell her face upon the good friend's propping
    knee;
His broad hands smoothed her head, as fain to
    brush it free
From fancies, swarms that stung like bees un-
    hived.  He soothed—
" Loukèria,   Loùscha! " — still   he,   fondling,
    smoothed and smoothed.
At last her lips formed speech.

"Iván, dear—you indeed?
You, just the same dear you! While I . . . Oh,
    intercede,
Sweet Mother, with thy Son Almighty—let his
    might
Bring yesterday once more, undo all done last
    night!
But this time yesterday, Iván, I sat like you,
A child on either knee, and, dearer than the
    two,
A babe inside my arms, close to my heart—that 's
    lost
In morsels o'er the snow! Father, Son, Holy
    Ghost,
Cannot you bring again my blessèd yesterday?"

When no more tears would flow, she told her tale:
    this way.

"Maybe, a month ago,—was it not?—news came
    here,
They wanted, deeper down, good workmen fit to
    rear
A church and roof it in. 'We'll go,' my husband
    said:
'None understands like me to melt and mould
    their lead.'
So, friends here helped us off—Iván, dear, you the
    first!
How gay we jingled forth, all five—(my heart will
    burst)—
While Dmìtri shook the reins, urged Droug upon
    his track!

" Well, soon the month ran out, we just were com-
    ing back,
When yesterday—behold, the village was on fire!
Fire ran from house to house.  What help, as,
    nigh and nigher,
The flames came furious?  ' Haste,' cried Dmìtri,
    ' men must do
The little good man may: to sledge and in with
    you,
You and our three!  We check the fire by laying
    flat
Each building in its path,—I needs must stay for
    that,—
But you . . . no time for talk!  Wrap round you
    every rug,
Cover the couple close,—you 'll have the babe to
    hug.
No care to guide old Droug, he knows his way, by
    guess,
Once start him on the road: but chirrup, none the
    less!
The snow lies glib as glass and hard as steel, and
    soon
You 'll have rise, fine and full, a marvel of a moon.
Hold straight up, all the same, this lighted twist
    of pitch!
Once home and with our friend Ivàn Ivànovitch,
All 's safe: I have my pay in pouch, all 's right
    with me,
So I but find as safe you and our precious three!
Off, Droug!'—because the flames had reached us,
    and the men
Shouted, ' But lend a hand, Dmìtri—as good as
    ten!'

" So, in we bundled—I and those God gave me
    once ;
Old Droug, that 's stiff at first, seemed youthful
    for the nonce :
He understood the case, galloping straight ahead.
Out came the moon : my twist soon dwindled,
    feebly red
In that unnatural day—yes, daylight bred between
Moonlight and snow-light, lamped those grotto-
    depths which screen
Such devils from God's eye. Ah, pines, how
    straight you grow,
Nor bend one pitying branch, true breed of brutal
    snow !
Some undergrowth had served to keep the devils
    blind
While we escaped outside their border !

                   " Was that—wind ?
Anyhow, Droug starts, stops, back go his ears, he
    snuffs,
Snorts,—never such a snort ! then plunges, knows
    the sough 's
Only the wind : yet, no—our breath goes up too
    straight !
Still the low sound,—less low, loud, louder, at a
    rate
There 's no mistaking more ! Shall I lean out—
    look—learn
The truth whatever it be ? Pad, pad ! At last, I
    turn—

" 'T is the regular pad of the wolves in pursuit of
    the life in the sledge !

An army they are: close-packed they press like the
    thrust of a wedge:
They increase as they hunt: for I see, through the
    pine-trunks ranged each side,
Slip forth new fiend and fiend, make wider and
    still more wide
The four-footed steady advance.  The foremost—
    none may pass:
They are the elders and lead the line, eye and eye
    —green-glowing brass!
But a long way distant still.  Droug, save us!
    He does his best:
Yet they gain on us, gain, till they reach,—one
    reaches . . .  How utter the rest?
O that Satan-faced first of the band!  How he lolls
    out the length of his tongue,
How he laughs and lets gleam his white teeth!
    He is on me, his paws pry among
The wraps and the rugs!  O my pair, my twin-
    pigeons, lie still and seem dead!
Stepàn, he shall never have you for a meal,—
    here's your mother instead!
No, he will not be counselled—must cry, poor
    Stiòpka, so foolish! though first
Of my boy-brood, he was not the best: nay, neigh-
    bors called him the worst:
He was puny, an undersized slip,—a darling to
    me, all the same!
But little there was to be praised in the boy, and
    a plenty to blame.
I loved him with heart and soul, yes—but, deal
    him a blow for a fault,

He would sulk for whole days. 'Foolish boy!
    lie still or the villain will vault,
Will snatch you from over my head!' No use! he
    cries, he screams,—who can hold
Fast a boy in frenzy of fear! It follows—as I
    foretold!
The Satan-face snatched and snapped: I tugged,
    I tore, and then
His brother too needs must shriek! If one must
    go, 't is men
The Tsar needs, so we hear, not ailing boys! Per-
    haps
My hands relaxed their grasp, got tangled in the
    wraps:
God, he was gone! I looked: there tumbled the
    cursed crew,
Each fighting for a share: too busy to pursue!
That 's so far gain at least: Droug, gallop another
    verst
Or two, or three—God sends we beat them, arrive
    the first!
A mother who boasts two boys was ever accounted
    rich:
Some have not a boy: some have, but lose him,—
    God knows which
Is worse: how pitiful to see your weakling pine
And pale and pass away! Strong brats, this pair
    of mine!

"O misery! for while I settle to what near
    seems
Content, I am 'ware again of the tramp, and again
    there gleams—

Point and point—the line, eyes, levelled green
    brassy fire!
So soon is resumed your chase?   Will nothing ap-
    pease, naught tire
The furies?   And yet I think—I am certain the
    race is slack,
And the numbers are nothing like.   Not a quarter
    of the pack!
Feasters and those full-fed are staying behind . . .
    Ah, why?
We 'll sorrow for that too soon!   Now,—gallop,
    reach home and die,
Nor ever again leave house, to trust our life in the
    trap
For life—we call a sledge!   Teriòscha, in my lap!
Yes, I 'll lie down upon you, tight-tie you with the
    strings
Here—of my heart!   No fear, this time, your
    mother flings . . .
Flings?   I flung?   Never!   But think!—a wo-
    man, after all,
Contending with a wolf!   Save you I must and
    shall,
Terentiì!

" How now?   What, you still head the race,
Your eyes and tongue and teeth crave fresh food,
        Satan-face?
        Flash again?
There and there!   Plain I struck green fire out!
All a poor fist can do to damage eyes proves vain!
My fist—why not crunch that?   He is wanton
    for . . . O God,

Why give this wolf his taste?  Common wolves
　　scrape and prod
The earth till out they scratch some corpse—mere
　　putrid flesh!
Why must this glutton leave the faded, choose
　　the fresh?
Terentiì—God, feel!—his neck keeps fast thy bag
Of holy things, saints' bones, this Satan-face will
　　drag
Forth, and devour along with him, our Pope de-
　　clared
The relics were to save from danger!

　　　　　　　　　" Spurned, not spared!
'T was through my arms, crossed arms, he—nuz-
　　zling now with snout,
Now ripping, tooth and claw—plucked, pulled
　　Terentiì out,
A prize indeed!  I saw—how could I else but
　　see?—
My precious one—I bit to hold back—pulled from
　　me!
Up came the others, fell to dancing—did the
　　imps!—
Skipped as they scampered round.  There 's one
　　is gray, and limps:
Who knows but old bad Màrpha—she always
　　owed me spite
And envied me my births—skulks out of doors at
　　night
And turns into a wolf, and joins the sisterhood,
And laps the youthful life, then slinks from out
　　the wood,

Squats down at the door by dawn, spins there de-
    mure as erst
—No strength, old crone—not she!—to crawl
    forth half a verst!


"Well, I escaped with one: 'twixt one and none
    there lies
The space 'twixt heaven and hell.   And see, a rose-
    light dyes
The endmost snow: 't is dawn, 't is day, 't is safe
    at home!
We have outwitted you!   Ay, monsters, snarl and
    foam,
Fight each the other fiend, disputing for a share,—
Forgetful in your greed, our finest off we bear,
Tough Droug and I,—my babe, my boy that shall
    be man,
My man that shall be more, do all a hunter can
To trace and follow and find and catch and cru-
    cify
Wolves, wolfkins, all your crew!   A thousand
    deaths shall die
The whimperingest cub that ever squeezed the
    teat!
'Take that!' we 'll stab you with,—' the tender-
    ness we met
When, wretches, you danced round,—not this,
    thank God—not this!
Hellhounds, we balk you!'


"But—Ah, God above!—Bliss, bliss,—
Not the band, no!   And yet—yes, for Droug
    knows him!   One—

This only of them all has said ' She saves a son ! '
His fellows disbelieve such luck : but he believes,
He lets them pick the bones, laugh at him in their
      sleeves :
He 's off and after us,—one speck, one spot, one
      ball
Grows bigger, bound on bound,—one wolf as good
      as all !
Oh, but I know the trick ! Have at the snaky
      tongue !
That 's the right way with wolves ! Go, tell your
      mates I wrung
The panting morsel out, left you to howl your
      worst !
Now for it—now ! Ah me, I know him—thrice-
      accurst
Satan-face,—him to the end my foe !

                  " All fight 's in vain :
This time the green brass points pierce to my very
      brain.
I fall—fall as I ought—quite on the babe I guard :
I overspread with flesh the whole of him. Too
      hard
To die this way, torn piecemeal ? Move hence ?
      Not I—one inch !
Gnaw through me, through and through : flat thus
      I lie nor flinch !
O God, the feel of the fang furrowing my shoul-
      der !—see !
It grinds—it grates the bone. O Kìrill under me,
Could I do more ? Besides he knew the wolf's way
      to win :

8

I clung, closed round like wax: yet in he wedged
    and in,
Past my neck, past my breasts, my heart, until
    . . . how feels
The onion-bulb your knife parts, pushing through
    its peels,
Till out you scoop its clove wherein lie stalk and
    leaf
And bloom and seed unborn?


              " That slew me: yes, in brief,
I died then, dead I lay doubtlessly till Droug
    stopped
Here, I suppose.   I come to life, I find me propped
Thus,—how or when or why—I know not.   Tell
    me, friends,
All was a dream: laugh quick and say the night-
    mare ends!
Soon I shall find my house: 't is over there: in
    proof,
Save for that chimney heaped with snow, you'd
    see the roof
Which holds my three—my two—my one—not
    one?

                    " Life 's mixed
With misery, yet we live—must live.   The Satan
    fixed
His face on mine so fast, I took its print as pitch
Takes what it cools beneath.   Ivàn Ivànovitch,
'T is you unharden me, you thaw, disperse the
    thing!
Only keep looking kind, the horror will not cling,

Your face smooths fast away each print of Satan.
    Tears
—What good they do! Life's sweet, and all its
    after-years,
Ivàn Ivànovitch, I owe you! Yours am I!
May God reward you, dear!"

                    Down she sank.  Solemnly
Ivàn rose, raised his axe,—for fitly as she knelt,
Her head lay: well apart, each side, her arms
    hung,—dealt
Lightning-swift thunder-strong one blow—no need
    of more!
Headless she knelt on still: that pine was sound
    of core
(Neighbors used to say)—cast-iron-kernelled—
    which
Taxed for a second stroke Ivàn Ivànovitch.

The man was scant of words as strokes.  "It had
    to be:
I could no other: God it was, bade 'Act for me!'"
Then stooping, peering round—what is it now he
    lacks?
A proper strip of bark wherewith to wipe his axe,
Which done, he turns, goes in, closes the door be-
    hind.
The others mute remain, watching the blood-
    snake wind
Into a hiding-place among the splinter-heaps⸻

At length, still mute, all move: one lifts—from
    where it steeps

Redder each ruddy rag of pine—the head: two
    more
Take up the dripping body: then, mute still as be-
    fore,
Move in a sort of march, march on till marching
    ends
Opposite to the church; where halting,—who sus-
    pends,
By its long hair, the thing, deposits in its place
The piteous head: once more the body shows no
    trace
Of harm done: there lies whole the Loùscha, maid
    and wife
And mother, loved until this latest of her life.
Then all sit on the bank of snow which bounds a
    space
Kept free before the porch of judgment: just the
    place!

Presently all the souls, man, woman, child which
    make
The village up, are found assembling for the sake
Of what is to be done.   The very Jews are there:
A Gypsy-troop, though bound with horses for the
    Fair,
Squats with the rest.   Each heart with its con-
    ception seethes
And simmers, but no tongue speaks: one may say,
    —none breathes.

Anon from out the church totters the Pope—the
    priest—
    Hardly alive, so old, a hundred years at least.

With him, the Commune's head, a hoary senior
　　too,
Stàrosta, that 's his style,—like Equity Judge with
　　you,—
Natural Jurisconsult: then, fenced about with
　　furs,
Pomeschik—Lord of the Land, who wields—and
　　none demurs—
A power of life and death.  They stoop, survey the
　　corpse.

Then, straightened on his staff, the Stàrosta—the
　　thorpe's
Sagaciousest old man—hears what you just have
　　heard,
From Droug's first inrush, all, up to Ivàn's last
　　word—
" God bade me act for him: I dared not disobey! "

Silence—the Pomeschik broke with " A wild
　　wrong way
Of righting wrong—if wrong there were, such
　　wrath to rouse!
Why was not law observed?

　　.　　.　　.　　.　　.　　.

Ivàn Ivànovitch has done a deed that 's named
Murder by law and me: who doubts, may speak un-
　　blamed! "

All turned to the old Pope.  " Ay, children, I am
　　old—
How old, myself have got to know no longer.
　　Rolled
Quite round, my orb of life, from infancy to age,

Seems passing back again to youth.  A certain
    stage
At least I reach, or dream I reach, where I dis-
    cern
Truer truths, laws behold more lawlike than we
    learn
When first we set our foot to tread the course I
    trod
With man to guide my steps: who leads me now is
    God.
' Your young men shall see visions: ' and in my
    youth I saw
And paid obedience to man's visionary law:
' Your old men shall dream dreams.'  And, in my
    age, a hand
Conducts me through the cloud round law to
    where I stand
Firm on its base,—know cause, who, before, knew
    effect.

.    .    .    .    .    .

                       I hold he saw
The unexampled sin, ordained the novel law,
Whereof first instrument was first intelligence
Found loyal here.  I hold that, failing human
    sense,
The very earth had oped, sky fallen, to efface
Humanity's new wrong, motherhood's first dis-
    grace.
Earth oped not, neither fell the sky, for prompt
    was found
A man and man enough, head-sober and heart-
    sound
Ready to hear God's voice, resolute to obey.

Ivàn Ivànovitch, I hold, has done, this day,
No otherwise than did, in ages long ago,
Moses when he made known the purport of that flow
Of fire athwart the law's twain-tables ! I pro-
claim
Ivàn Ivànovitch God's servant ! "

　　.　　.　　.　　.　　.

When the Amen grew dull
And died away and left acquittal plain adjudged,
" Amen ! " last sighed the lord. " There's none
shall say I grudged
Escape from punishment in such a novel case.
Deferring to old age and holy life,—be grace
Granted ! say I. No less, scruples might shake a
sense
Firmer than I boast mine. Law's law, and evi-
dence
Of breach therein lies plain,—blood-red-bright—all
may see !
Yet all absolve the deed : absolved the deed must
be ! "

　　.　　.　　.　　.　　.

So, while the youngers raised the corpse, the elders
trooped
Silently to the house : where halting, some one
stooped,
Listened beside the door ; all there was silent too.
Then they held counsel ; then pushed door and,
passing through,
Stood in the murderer's presence.
Ivàn Ivànovitch
Knelt, building on the floor that Kremlin rare and
rich

He deftly cut and carved on lazy winter nights.
Some five young faces watched, breathlessly, as, to
    rights,
Piece upon piece, he reared the fabric nigh com-
    plete.
Stèscha, Ivàn's old mother, sat spinning by the
    heat
Of the oven where his wife Kàtia stood baking
    bread.
Ivàn's self, as he turned his honey-colored head,
Was just in the act to drop, 'twixt fir-cones,—each
    a dome,
The scooped-out yellow gourd presumably the
    home
Of Kolokol the Big : the bell, therein to hitch,
—An acorn-cup—was ready : Ivàn Ivànovitch
Turned with it in his mouth.

                  They told him he was free
As air to walk abroad.  " How otherwise ? " asked
    he.

                       ROBERT BROWNING.

---

## A DAGGER OF THE MIND.

FROM " MACBETH," ACT II. SC. 1.

[MACBETH, before the murder of Duncan, meditating alone,
  sees the image of a dagger in the air, and thus solilo-
  quizes :]

    Is this a dagger which I see before me,
The handle toward my hand ?  Come, let me clutch
    thee :—

I have thee not, and yet I see thee still.
Art thou not, fatal vision, sensible
To feeling as to sight? or art thou but
A dagger of the mind, a false creation,
Proceeding from the heat-oppressèd brain?
I see thee yet, in form as palpable
As this which now I draw.
Thou marshal'st me the way that I was going;
And such an instrument I was to use.
Mine eyes are made the fools o' the other senses,
Or else worth all the rest: I see thee still;
And on thy blade and dudgeon gouts of blood,
Which was not so before.—There's no such thing:
It is the bloody business, which informs
Thus to mine eyes.—Now o'er the one half world
Nature seems dead, and wicked dreams abuse
The curtained sleep; witchcraft celebrates
Pale Hecate's offerings; and withered murder,
Alarumed by his sentinel, the wolf,
Whose howl's his watch, thus with his stealthy
        pace,
With Tarquin's ravishing strides, towards his de-
        sign
Moves like a ghost.—Thou sure and firm-set earth,
Hear not my steps, which way they walk, for fear
The very stones prate of my whereabout,
And take the present horror from the time,
Which now suits with it.—Whiles I threat, he
        lives:
Words to the heat of deeds too cold breath gives.

(*A bell rings.*)

I go, and it is done; the bell invites me.

Hear it not, Duncan; for it is a knell
That summons thee to heaven or to hell.

SHAKESPEARE.

---

## THE MURDER.

FROM " MACBETH," ACT II. SC. 2.

SCENE *in the Castle.  Enter* LADY MACBETH.

LADY MACBETH.—That which hath made them
    drunk hath made me bold,
What hath quenched them hath given me fire.
    Hark!—Peace!
It was the owl that shrieked, the fatal bellman,
Which gives the stern'st good night.   He is about
    it :
The doors are open; and the surfeited grooms
Do mark their charge with snores: I have drugged
    their possets,
That death and nature do contend about them,
Whether they live or die.
    MACBETH (*within*).—Who's there?  What, ho!
    LADY MACBETH.—Alack, I am afraid they have
    awaked
And 't is not done:—the attempt and not the deed
Confounds us.—Hark!—I laid their daggers
    ready;
He could not miss them.—Had he not resembled
My father, as he slept, I had done 't.—My hus-
    band!

(Enter MACBETH.)

    MACBETH.—I have done the deed.  Didst thou
    not hear a noise?

LADY MACBETH.—I heard the owl scream, and
the crickets cry.

Did not you speak?

MACBETH.—When?

LADY MACBETH.—        Now.

MACBETH.—                As I descended?

LADY MACBETH.—Ay.

MACBETH.—Hark!—

Who lies i' the second chamber?

LADY MACBETH.—              Donalbain.

MACBETH (*looking on his hands*).—This is a
sorry sight.

LADY MACBETH.—A foolish thought, to say a
sorry sight.

MACBETH.—There 's one did laugh in 's sleep,
and one cried, " Murder ! "

That they did wake each other : I stood and heard
them :

But they did say their prayers, and addressed
them

Again to sleep.

LADY MACBETH.—There are two lodged together.

MACBETH.—One cried, " God bless us ! " and,
" Amen," the other;

As they had seen me with these hangman's hands.
Listening their fear, I could not say, " Amen,"
When they did say, " God bless us."

LADY MACBETH.—Consider it not so deeply.

MACBETH.—But wherefore could not I pronounce " Amen " ?

I had most need of blessing, and " Amen "
Stuck in my throat.

LADY MACBETH.—These deeds must not be
    thought
After these ways; so, it will make us mad.
    MACBETH.—Methought I heard a voice cry,
        " Sleep no more!
Macbeth does murder sleep,"—the innocent sleep,
Sleep that knits up the ravelled sleave of care,
The death of each day's life, sore labor's bath,
Balm of hurt minds, great nature's second course,
Chief nourisher in life's feast,—
    LADY MACBETH.—             What do you mean?
    MACBETH.—Still it cried, " Sleep no more!" to
        all the house:
" Glamis hath murdered sleep; and therefore Caw-
        dor
Shall sleep no more,—Macbeth shall sleep no
        more!"
    LADY MACBETH.—Who was it that thus cried?
        Why, worthy thane,
You do unbend your noble strength, to think
So brainsickly of things.—Go, get some water,
And wash this filthy witness from your hand.
Why did you bring these daggers from the place?
They must lie there: go carry them; and smear
The sleepy grooms with blood.
    MACBETH.—                    I 'll go no more!
I am afraid to think what I have done;
Look on 't again, I dare not.
    LADY MACBETH. —              Infirm of purpose!
Give me the daggers: the sleeping, and the dead,
Are but as pictures: 't is the eye of childhood
That fears a painted devil.  If he do bleed,
I 'll gild the faces of the grooms withal;

For it must seem their guilt.

              [*Exit. Knocking within.*

MACBETH.—Whence is that knocking?
How is 't with me, when every noise appalls me?
What hands are here! Ha! they pluck out mine
    eyes!
Will all great Neptune's ocean wash this blood
Clean from my hand? No; this my hand will
    rather
The multitudinous seas incarnadine,
Making the green—one red.

        (*Re-enter* LADY MACBETH.)

LADY MACBETH.—My hands are of your color;
    but I shame
To wear a heart so white. (*Knocking.*) I hear a
    knocking
At the south entry:—retire we to our chamber:
A little water clears us of this deed:
How easy is it then! Your constancy
Hath left you unattended. (*Knocking.*) Hark,
    more knocking.
Get on your nightgown, lest occasion call us,
And show us to be watchers:—be not lost
So poorly in your thoughts.

    MACBETH.—To know my deed, 't were best not
    know myself. (*Knocking.*)
Wake Duncan with thy knocking! I would thou
    couldst.

                  SHAKESPEARE.

## THE TWA CORBIES.

As I was walking all alane,
I heard two corbies making a mane;
The tane unto the t'other say,
" Where sall we gang and dine to-day? "

" In behint yon auld fail dyke,
I wot there lies a new-slain knight;
And nae body kens that he lies there,
But his hawk, his hound, and lady fair.

" His hound is to the hunting gane,
His hawk to fetch the wild-fowl hame,
His lady's ta'en another mate,
So we may make our dinner sweet.

" Ye 'll sit on his white hause bane,
And I 'll pike out his bonny blue een:
Wi' ae lock o' his gowden hair,
We 'll theek our nest when it grows bare.

" Mony a one for him makes mane,
But nane sall ken whare he is gane;
O'er his white banes, when they are bare,
The wind sall blaw for evermair."

ANONYMOUS.

## THE SACK OF BALTIMORE.

[Baltimore is a small seaport in the barony of Carbery,
in South Munster. It grew up around a castle of O'Driscoll's, and was, after his ruin, colonized by the English.
On the 20th of June, 1631, the crews of two Algerine
galleys landed in the dead of the night, sacked the town,
and bore off into slavery all who were not too old, or too
young, or too fierce, for their purpose. The pirates were
steered up the intricate channel by one Hackett, a Dungarvan fisherman, whom they had taken at sea for the
purpose. Two years later, he was convicted of the crime
and executed. Baltimore never recovered from this.]

THE summer sun is falling soft on Carbery's
    hundred isles,
The summer sun is gleaming still through Ga-
    briel's rough defiles,—
Old Inisherkin's crumbled fane looks like a moult-
    ing bird;
And in a calm and sleepy swell the ocean tide is
    heard:
The hookers lie upon the beach; the children cease
    their play;
The gossips leave the little inn; the households
    kneel to pray;
And full of love and peace and rest,—its daily
    labor o'er,—
Upon that cosy creek there lay the town of Balti-
    more.

A deeper rest, a starry trance, has come with mid-
    night there;
No sound, except that throbbing wave, in earth or
    sea or air.

The massive capes and ruined towers seem con-
    scious of the calm;
The fibrous sod and stunted trees are breathing
    heavy balm.
So still the night, these two long barks round
    Dunashad that glide
Must trust their oars—methinks not few—against
    the ebbing tide.
O, some sweet mission of true love must urge
    them to the shore,—
They bring some lover to his bride, who sighs in
    Baltimore!


All, all asleep within each roof along that rocky
    street,
And these must be the lover's friends, with gently
    gliding feet.
A stifled gasp! a dreamy noise! The roof is in
    a flame!
From out their beds, and to their doors, rush maid
    and sire and dame,
And meet upon the threshold stone, the gleaming
    sabre's fall,
And o'er each black and bearded face the white
    or crimson shawl.
The yell of "Allah!" breaks above the prayer and
    shriek and roar—
O blessèd God! the Algerine is lord of Balti-
    more!
Then flung the youth his naked hand against the
    shearing sword;
Then sprung the mother on the brand with which
    her son was gored;

Then sunk the grandsire on the floor, his grand-
    babes clutching wild;
Then fled the maiden moaning faint, and nestled
    with the child.
But see, yon pirate strangling lies, and crushed
    with splashing heel,
While o'er him in an Irish hand there sweeps his
    Syrian steel;
Though virtue sink, and courage fail, and misers
    yield their store,
There 's *one* hearth well avenged in the sack of
    Baltimore!

Midsummer morn, in woodland nigh, the birds
    begin to sing;
They see not now the milking-maids, deserted is
    the spring!
Midsummer day, this gallant rides from the dis-
    tant Bandon's town,
These hookers crossed from stormy Skull, that
    skiff from Affadown.
They only found the smoking walls with neigh-
    bors' blood besprent,
And on the strewed and trampled beach awhile
    they wildly went,
Then dashed to sea, and passed Cape Clear, and
    saw, five leagues before,
The pirate-galleys vanishing that ravaged Balti-
    more.

O, some must tug the galley's oar, and some must
    tend the steed,—
This boy will bear a Scheik's chibouk, and that
    a Bey's jerreed.

9

O, some are for the arsenals by beauteous Darda-
    nelles,
And some are in the caravan to Mecca's sandy
    dells.
The maid that Bandon gallant sought is chosen
    for the Dey,
She 's safe,—she 's dead,—she stabbed him in the
    midst of his Serai;
And when to die a death of fire that noble maid
    they bore,
She only smiled,—O'Driscoll's child,—she thought
    of Baltimore.


'T is two long years since sunk the town beneath
    that bloody band,
And all around its trampled hearth a larger con-
    course stand,
Where high upon a gallows-tree a yelling wretch
    is seen,—
'T is Hackett of Dungarvan,—he who steered the
    Algerine!
He fell amid a sullen shout, with scarce a passing
    prayer,
For he had slain the kith and kin of many a hun-
    dred there:
Some muttered of MacMorrogh, who had brought
    the Norman o'er,
Some cursed him with Iscariot, that day in Balti-
    more.

THOMAS OSBORNE DAVIS.

## THE ROSE AND THE GAUNTLET.

Low spake the knight to the peasant-girl:
" I tell thee sooth, I am belted earl;
Fly with me from this garden small,
And thou shalt sit in my castle's hall;

"Thou shalt have pomp, and wealth, and pleasure,
Joys beyond thy fancy's measure;
Here with my sword and horse I stand,
To bear thee away to my distant land.

" Take, thou fairest! this full-blown rose,
A token of love that as ripely blows."
With his glove of steel he plucked the token,
But it fell from his gauntlet crushed and broken.

The maiden exclaimed, " Thou seest, sir knight,
Thy fingers of iron can only smite;
And, like the rose thou hast torn and scattered,
I in thy grasp should be wrecked and shattered."

She trembled and blushed, and her glances fell;
But she turned from the knight, and said, " Fare-
    well!"
" Not so," he cried, " will I lose my prize;
I heed not thy words, but I read thine eyes."

He lifted her up in his grasp of steel,
And he mounted and spurred with furious heel;
But her cry drew forth her hoary sire,
Who snatched his bow from above the fire.

Swift from the valley the warrior fled,
Swifter the bolt of the crossbow sped;
And the weight that pressed on the fleet-foot horse
Was the living man, and the woman's corse.

That morning the rose was bright of hue;
That morning the maiden was fair to view;
But the evening sun its beauty shed
On the withered leaves, and the maiden dead.

JOHN STERLING.

## THE YOUNG GRAY HEAD.

GRIEF hath been known to turn the young head
    gray,—
To silver over in a single day
The bright locks of the beautiful, their prime
Scarcely o'erpast; as in the fearful time
Of Gallia's madness, that discrownèd head
Serene, that on the accursèd altar bled
Miscalled of Liberty.  O martyred Queen!
What must the sufferings of that night have
    been—
*That one*—that sprinkled thy fair tresses o'er
With time's untimely snow!  But now no more,
Lovely, august, unhappy one! of thee—
I have to tell a humbler history;
A village tale, whose only charm, in sooth
(If any), will be sad and simple truth.

" Mother," quoth Ambrose to his thrifty dame,—
So oft our peasant's use his wife to name,
" Father " and " Master " to himself applied,

As life's grave duties matronize the bride,—
" Mother," quoth Ambrose, as he faced the north
With hard-set teeth, before he issued forth
To his day labor, from the cottage door,—
" I 'm thinking that, to-night, if not before,
There 'll be wild work.   Dost hear old Chewton*
     roar?
It 's brewing up, down westward; and look there,
One of those sea-gulls! ay, there goes a pair;
And such a sudden thaw!   If rain comes on,
As threats, the waters will be out anon.
That path by the ford 's a nasty bit of way,—
Best let the young ones bide from school to-day."

" Do, mother, do! " the quick-eared urchins cried;
Two little lasses to the father's side
Close clinging, as they looked from him, to spy
The answering language of the mother's eye.
*There* was denial, and she shook her head:
" Nay, nay,—no harm will come to them," she
     said,
" The mistress lets them off these short dark days
An hour the earlier; and our Liz, she says,
May quite be trusted—and I know 't is true—
To take care of herself and Jenny too.
And so she ought,—she 's seven come first of
     May,—
Two years the oldest; and they give away
The Christmas bounty at the school to-day."

The mother's will was law (alas, for her
That hapless day, poor soul!)—*she* could not err,

* A fresh-water spring rushing into the sea, called
Chewton Bunny.

Thought Ambrose; and his little fair-haired Jane
(Her namesake) to his heart he hugged again.
When each had had her turn; she clinging so
As if that day she could not let him go.
But Labor's sons must snatch a hasty bliss
In nature's tenderest mood.   One last fond kiss.
"God bless my little maids!" the father said,
And cheerily went his way to win their bread.
Then might be seen, the playmate parent gone,
What looks demure the sister pair put on,—
Not of the mother as afraid, or shy,
Or questioning the love that could deny;
But simply, as their simple training taught,
In quiet, plain straightforwardness of thought
(Submissively resigned the hope of play)
Towards the serious business of the day.

To me there 's something touching, I confess,
In the grave look of early thoughtfulness,
Seen often in some little childish face
Among the poor.   Not that wherein we trace
(Shame to our land, our rulers, and our race!)
The unnatural sufferings of the factory child,
But a staid quietness, reflective, mild,
Betokening, in the depths of those young eyes,
Sense of life's cares, without its miseries.
So to the mother's charge, with thoughtful brow,
The docile Lizzy stood attentive now,
Proud of her years and of the imputed sense,
And prudence justifying confidence,—
And little Jenny, more demurely still,
Beside her waited the maternal will.
So standing hand in hand, a lovelier twain

Gainsborough ne'er painted: no—nor he of Spain,
Glorious Murillo!—and by contrast shown
More beautiful.  The younger little one,
With large blue eyes and silken ringlets fair,
By nut-brown Lizzy, with smooth parted hair,
Sable and glossy as the raven's wing,
And lustrous eyes as dark.

　　　　　　　　" Now, mind and bring
Jenny safe home," the mother said,—" don't stay
To pull a bough or berry by the way:
And when you come to cross the ford, hold fast
Your little sister's hand, till you 're quite past,—
That plank 's so crazy, and so slippery
(If not o'erflowed) the stepping-stones will be.
But you 're good children—steady as old folk—
I 'd trust ye anywhere."  Then Lizzy's cloak,
A good gray duffle, lovingly she tied,
And ample little Jenny's lack supplied
With her own warmest shawl.  " Be sure," said
　　　she,
" To wrap it round and knot it carefully
(Like this), when you come home, just leaving
　　　free
One hand to hold by.  Now, make haste away—
Good will to school, and then good right to play."


Was there no sinking at the mother's heart
When, all equipt, they turned them to depart?
When down the lane she watched them as they
　　　went
Till out of sight, was no forefeeling sent
Of coming ill?  In truth I cannot tell:
Such warnings *have been* sent, we know full well

And must believe—believing that they are—
In mercy then—to rouse, restrain, prepare.

And now I mind me, something of the kind
Did surely haunt that day the mother's mind,
Making it irksome to bide all alone
By her own quiet hearth.   Though never known
For idle gossipry was Jenny Gray,
Yet so it was, that morn she could not stay
At home with her own thoughts, but took her way
To her next neighbor's, half a loaf to borrow,—
Yet might her store have lasted out the morrow,—
And with the loan obtained, she lingered still.
Said she, " My master, if he 'd had his will,
Would have kept back our little ones from school
This dreadful morning; and I 'm such a fool,
Since they 've been gone, I 've wished them back.
    But then
It won't do in such things to humor men,—
Our Ambrose specially.   If let alone
He 'd spoil those wenches.   But it 's coming on,
That storm he said was brewing, sure enough,—
Well! what of that?   To think what idle stuff
Will come into one's head!   And here with you
I stop, as if I 'd nothing else to do—
And they 'll come home, drowned rats.   I must
    be gone
To get dry things, and set the kettle on."

His day's work done, three mortal miles and
    more,
Lay between Ambrose and his cottage-door.
A weary way, God wot, for weary wight!

But yet far off the curling smoke in sight
From his own chimney, and his heart felt light.
How pleasantly the humble homestead stood,
Down the green lane, by sheltering Shirley wood!
How sweet the wafting of the evening breeze,
In spring-time, from his two old cherry-trees,
Sheeted with blossom!  And in hot July,
From the brown moor-track, shadowless and dry,
How grateful the cool covert to regain
Of his own avenue,—that shady lane,
With the white cottage, in the slanting glow
Of sunset glory, gleaming bright below,
And Jasmine porch, his rustic portico!

With what a thankful gladness in his face,
  (Silent heart-homage,—plant of special grace!)
At the lane's entrance, slackening oft his pace,
Would Ambrose send a loving look before,
Conceiting the caged blackbird at the door;
The very blackbird strained its little throat,
In welcome, with a more rejoicing note;
And honest Tinker, dog of doubtful breed,
All bristle, back, and tail, but " good at need,"
Pleasant his greeting to the accustomed ear;
But of all welcomes pleasantest, most dear,
The ringing voices, like sweet silver bells,
Of his two little ones.  How fondly swells
The father's heart, as, dancing up the lane,
Each clasps a hand in her small hand again,
And each must tell her tale and " say her say,"
Impeding as she leads with sweet delay
(Childhood's blest thoughtlessness!) his onward
    way.

And when the winter day closed in so fast;
Scarce for his task would dreary daylight last;
And in all weathers—driving sleet and snow—
Home by that bare, bleak moor-track must he go,
Darkling and lonely.  O, the blessèd sight
(His polestar) of that little twinkling light
From one small window, through the leafless
    trees,—
Glimmering so fitfully; no eye but his
Had spied it so far off.   And sure was he,
Entering the lane, a steadier beam to see,
Ruddy and broad as peat-fed hearth could pour,
Streaming to meet him from the open door.
Then, though the blackbird's welcome was un-
    heard,—
Silenced by winter,—note of summer bird
Still hailed him from no mortal fowl alive,
But from the cuckoo clock just striking five.
And Tinker's ear and Tinker's nose were keen,—
Off started he, and then a form was seen
Darkening the doorway; and a smaller sprite,
And then another, peered into the night,
Ready to follow free on Tinker's track,
But for the mother's hand that held her back:
And yet a moment—a few steps—and there,
Pulled o'er the threshold by that eager pair,
He sits by his own hearth, in his own chair;
Tinker takes post beside with eyes that say,
" Master, we 've done our business for the day."
The kettle sings, the cat in chorus purrs,
The busy housewife with her tea-things stirs;
The door 's made fast, the old stuff curtain drawn;
How the hail clatters!   Let it clatter on!

How the wind raves and rattles! What cares he?
Safe housed and warm beneath his own roof-tree,
With a wee lassie prattling on each knee.

Such was the hour—hour sacred and apart—
Warmed in expectancy the poor man's heart.
Summer and winter, as his toil he plied,
To him and his the literal doom applied,
Pronounced on Adam. But the bread was sweet
So earned, for such dear mouths. The weary feet,
Hope-shod, stept lightly on the homeward way;
So specially it fared with Ambrose Gray
That time I tell of. He had worked all day
At a great clearing; vigorous stroke on stroke
Striking, till, when he stopt, his back seemed
        broke,
And the strong arms dropt nerveless. What of
        that?
There was a treasure hidden in his hat,—
A plaything for the young ones. He had found
A dormouse nest; the living ball coiled round
For its long winter sleep; and all his thought,
As he trudged stoutly homeward, was of naught
But the glad wonderment in Jenny's eyes,
And graver Lizzy's quieter surprise,
When he should yield, by guess and kiss and
        prayer
Hard won, the frozen captive to their care.

'T was a wild evening,—wild and rough. "I
        knew,"
Thought Ambrose, "those unlucky gulls spoke
        true,—

And Gaffer Chewton never growls for naught,—
I should be mortal 'mazed now if I thought
My little maids were not safe housed before
That blinding hail-storm,—ay, this hour and
        more,—
Unless by that old crazy bit of board,
They 've not passed dry-foot over Shallow ford,
That I 'll be bound for,—swollen as it must be—
Well! if my mistress had been ruled by me—"
But, checking the half-thought as heresy,
He looked out for the Home Star.   There it shone,
And with a gladdened heart he hastened on.

He 's in the lane again,—and there below,
Streams from the open doorway that red glow,
Which warms him but to look at.   For his prize
Cautious he feels,—all safe and snug it lies,—
" Down, Tinker! down, old boy!—not quite so
        free,—
The thing thou sniffest is no game for thee.—
But what 's the meaning? no lookout to-night!
No living soul astir!   Pray God, all 's right!
Who 's flittering round the peat-stack in such
        weather?
Mother!" you might have felled him with a
        feather,
When the short answer to his loud " Hillo!"
And hurried question, " Are they come?" was
        " No."

To throw his tools down, hastily unhook
The old cracked lantern from its dusty nook,
And, while he lit it, speak a cheering word,

That almost choked him, and was scarcely heard,
Was but a moment's act, and he was gone
To where a fearful foresight led him on.
Passing a neighbor's cottage in his way,—
Mark Fenton's,—him he took with short delay
To bear him company,—for who could say
What need might be? They struck into the track
The children should have taken coming back
From school that day; and many a call and shout
Into the pitchy darkness they sent out,
And, by the lantern light, peered all about,
In every roadside thicket, hole, nook,
Till suddenly—as nearing now the brook—
Something brushed past them. That was Tinker's
    bark,—
Unheeded, he had followed in the dark,
Close at his master's heels; but, swift as light,
Darted before them now.  " Be sure he 's right,—
He 's on the track," cried Ambrose.  " Hold the
    light
Low down,—he 's making for the water.  Hark!
I know that whine,—the old dog 's found them,
    Mark."
So speaking, breathlessly he hurried on
Toward the old crazy foot-bridge.  It was gone!
And all his dull contracted light could show
Was the black void and dark swollen stream be-
    low.
" Yet there 's life somewhere,—more than Tinker's
    whine,—
That 's sure," said Mark.  " So, let the lantern
    shine
Down yonder.  There 's the dog,—and, hark!"
" O dear!"

And a low sob came faintly on the ear,
Mocked by the sobbing gust.  Down, quick as
    thought,
Into the stream leapt Ambrose, where he caught
Fast hold of something,—a dark huddled heap,—
Half in the water, where 't was scarce knee-deep
For a tall man, and half above it, propped
By some old ragged side-piles, that had stopt
Endways the broken plank, when it gave way
With the two little ones that luckless day!
" My babes!—my lambkins! " was the father's
    cry.
*One little voice* made answer, " Here am I ! "
'T was Lizzy's.  There she crouched with face as
    white,
More ghastly by the flickering lantern-light
Than sheeted corpse.  The pale blue lips drawn
    tight,
Wide parted, showing all the pearly teeth,
And eyes on some dark object underneath,
Washed by the turbid water, fixed as stone,—
One arm and hand stretched out, and rigid
    grown,
Grasping, as in the death-gripe, Jenny's frock.
There she lay drowned.  Could he sustain that
    shock,
The doting father?  Where 's the unriven rock
Can bide such blasting in its flintiest part
As that soft sentient thing,—the human heart?

They lifted her from out her watery bed,—
Its covering gone, the lovely little head
Hung like a broken snowdrop all aside;

And one small hand,—the mother's shawl was
    tied,
Leaving *that* free, about the child's small form,
As was her last injunction—"*fast* and warm "—
Too well obeyed,—too fast! A fatal hold
Affording to the scrag by a thick fold
That caught and pinned her in the river's bed,
While through the reckless water overhead
Her life-breath bubbled up.
                 " She might have lived,
Struggling like Lizzy," was the thought that rived
The wretched mother's heart, when she knew all,
" But for my foolishness about that shawl!
And Master would have kept them back the day;
But I was wilful,—driving them away
In such wild weather! "
               Thus the tortured heart
Unnaturally against itself takes part,
Driving the sharp edge deeper of a woe
Too deep already. They had raised her now,
And parting the wet ringlets from her brow,
To that, and the cold cheek, and lips as cold,
The father glued his warm ones, ere they rolled
Once more the fatal shawl—her winding-sheet—
About the precious clay. One heart still beat,
Warmed by his heart's blood. To his only child
He turned him, but her piteous moaning mild
Pierced him afresh,—and now she knew him not.
" Mother! " she murmured, " who says I forgot?
Mother! indeed, indeed, I kept fast hold,
And tied the shawl quite close—she can't be cold—
But she won't move—we slipt—I don't know
    how—

But I held on—and I'm so weary now—
And it's so dark and cold! O dear! O dear!—
And she won't move;—if daddy was but here!"

.      .      .      .      .

Poor lamb! she wandered in her mind, 't was
      clear;
But soon the piteous murmur died away,
And quiet in her father's arms she lay,—
They their dead burden had resigned, to take
The living, so near lost.  For her dear sake,
And one at home, he armed himself to bear
His misery like a man,—with tender care
Doffing his coat her shivering form to fold
(His neighbor bearing that which felt no cold),
He clasped her close, and so, with little said,
Homeward they bore the living and the dead.


From Ambrose Gray's poor cottage all that night
Shone fitfully a little shifting light,
Above, below,—for all were watchers there,
Save one sound sleeper.  Her, parental care,
Parental watchfulness, availed not now.
But in the young survivor's throbbing brow,
And wandering eyes, delirious fever burned;
And all night long from side to side she turned,
Piteously plaining like a wounded dove,
With now and then the murmur, " She won't
      move."
And lo! when morning, as in mockery, bright
Shone on that pillow, passing strange the sight,—
That young head's raven hair was streaked with
      white!

No idle fiction this. Such things have been,
We know. And now *I tell what I have seen.*

Life struggled long with death in that small frame,
But it was strong, and conquered. All became
As it had been with the poor family,—
All, saving that which nevermore might be:
There was an empty place,—they were but three.

CAROLINE BOWLES SOUTHEY.

## HIGH-TIDE ON THE COAST OF LINCOLN-SHIRE. [TIME, 1571.]

THE old mayor climbed the belfry tower,
 The ringers rang by two, by three;
" Pull! if ye never pulled before;
 Good ringers, pull your best," quoth he.
" Play uppe, play uppe, O Boston bells!
Ply all your changes, all your swells!
 Play uppe *The Brides of Enderby!* "

Men say it was a " stolen tyde,"—
 The Lord that sent it, he knows all,
But in myne ears doth still abide
 The message that the bells let fall;
And there was naught of strange, beside
The flights of mews and peewits pied,
 By millions crouched on the old sea-wall.

I sat and spun within the doore;
 My thread brake off, I raised myne eyes:
The level sun, like ruddy ore,
 Lay sinking in the barren skies;
10

And dark against day's golden death
She moved where Lindis wandereth,—
My sonne's faire wife, Elizabeth.

" Cusha! Cusha! Cusha!" calling,
Ere the early dews were falling,
Farre away I heard her song.
" Cusha! Cusha!" all along;
Where the reedy Lindis floweth,
     Floweth, floweth,
From the meads where melick groweth,
Faintly came her milking-song.

" Cusha! Cusha! Cusha!" calling,
" For the dews will soone be falling;
Leave your meadow grasses mellow,
     Mellow, mellow!
Quit your cowslips, cowslips yellow!
Come uppe, Whitefoot! come uppe, Lightfoot!
Quit the stalks of parsley hollow,
     Hollow, hollow!
Come uppe, Jetty! rise and follow;
From the clovers lift your head!
Come uppe, Whitefoot! come uppe, Lightfoot!
Come uppe, Jetty! rise and follow,
Jetty, to the milking-shed."

If it be long—ay, long ago—
  When I beginne to think howe long,
Againe I hear the Lindis flow,
  Swift as an arrowe, sharpe and strong;
And all the aire, it seemeth mee,
Bin full of floating bells (sayth shee),
That ring the tune of *Enderby.*

Alle fresh the level pasture lay,
   And not a shadowe mote be seene,
Save where, full fyve good miles away,
   The steeple towered from out the greene.
And lo! the great bell farre and wide
Was heard in all the country side
That Saturday at eventide.

The swannerds, where their sedges are,
   Moved on in sunset's golden breath;
The shepherde lads I heard afarre,
   And my sonne's wife, Elizabeth;
Till, floating o'er the grassy sea,
Came downe that kyndly message free,
*The Brides of Mavis Enderby.*

Then some looked uppe into the sky,
   And all along where Lindis flows
To where the goodly vessels lie,
   And where the lordly steeple shows.
They sayde, " And why should this thing be,
What danger lowers by land or sea?
They ring the tune of *Enderby.*

"For evil news from Mablethorpe,
   Of pyrate galleys, warping down,—
For shippes ashore beyond the scorpe,
   They have not spared to wake the towne;
But while the west bin red to see,
And storms be none, and pyrates flee,
Why ring *The Brides of Enderby?* "

I looked without, and lo! my sonne
   Came riding downe with might and main;

He raised a shout as he drew on,
   Till all the welkin rang again:
" Elizabeth! Elizabeth!"
(A sweeter woman ne'er drew breath
Than my sonne's wife, Elizabeth.)

" The olde sea-wall (he cryed) is downe!
   The rising tide comes on apace;
And boats adrift in yonder towne
   Go sailing uppe the market-place!"
He shook as one that looks on death:
" God save you, mother!" straight he sayth;
" Where is my wife, Elizabeth?"

" Good sonne, where Lindis winds away
   With her two bairns I marked her long;
And ere yon bells beganne to play,
   Afar I heard her milking-song."
He looked across the grassy sea,
To right, to left, *Ho, Enderby!*
They rang *The Brides of Enderby.*

With that he cried and beat his breast;
   For lo! along the river's bed
A mighty eygre reared his crest,
   And uppe the Lindis raging sped.
It swept with thunderous noises loud,—
Shaped like a curling snow-white cloud,
Or like a demon in a shroud.

And rearing Lindis, backward pressed,
   Shook all her trembling bankes amaine;
Then madly at the eygre's breast
   Flung uppe her weltering walls again.

Then bankes came downe with ruin and rout,—
Then beaten foam flew round about,—
Then all the mighty floods were out.

So farre, so fast, the eygre drave,
    The heart had hardly time to beat
Before a shallow seething wave
    Sobbed in the grasses at oure feet:
The feet had hardly time to flee
Before it brake against the knee,—
And all the world was in the sea.

Upon the roofe we sate that night;
    The noise of bells went sweeping by;
I marked the lofty beacon light
    Stream from the church-tower, red and high,—
A lurid mark, and dread to see;
And awsome bells they were to mee,
That in the dark rang *Enderby.*

They rang the sailor lads to guide,
    From roofe to roofe who fearless rowed;
And I,—my sonne was at my side,
    And yet the ruddy beacon glowed;
And yet he moaned beneath his breath,
" O, come in life, or come in death!
O lost! my love, Elizabeth!"

And didst thou visit him no more?
    Thou didst, thou didst, my daughter deare?
The waters laid thee at his doore
    Ere yet the early dawn was clear:
Thy pretty bairns in fast embrace,

The lifted sun shone on thy face,
Downe drifted to thy dwelling-place.

That flow strewed wrecks about the grass,
    That ebbe swept out the flocks to sea,—
A fatal ebbe and flow, alas!
    To manye more than myne and mee;
But each will mourne his own (she sayth)
And sweeter woman ne'er drew breath
Than my sonne's wife, Elizabeth.

I shall never hear her more
By the reedy Lindis shore,
"Cusha! Cusha! Cusha!" calling,
Ere the early dews be falling;
I shall never hear her song,
"Cusha! Cusha!" all along,
Where the sunny Lindis floweth,
        Goeth, floweth,
From the meads where melick groweth,
Where the water, winding down,
Onward floweth to the town.

I shall never see her more,
Where the reeds and rushes quiver,
        Shiver, quiver,
Stand beside the sobbing river,—
Sobbing, throbbing, in its falling,
To the sandy, lonesome shore;
I shall never hear her calling,
"Leave your meadow grasses mellow,
        Mellow, mellow!
Quit your cowslips, cowslips yellow!

Come uppe, Whitefoot! come uppe, Lightfoot!
Quit your pipes of parsley hollow,
    Hollow, hollow!
Come uppe, Lightfoot! rise and follow;
    Lightfoot! Whitefoot!
From your clovers lift the head;
Come uppe, Jetty! follow, follow,
Jetty, to the milking-shed!"

JEAN INGELOW.

---

## RIZPAH.

### 17—.

### I.

Wailing, wailing, wailing, the wind over land and
    sea—
And Willy's voice in the wind, "O mother, come
    out to me."
Why should he call me to-night, when he knows
    that I cannot go?
For the downs are as bright as day, and the full
    moon stares at the snow.

### II.

We should be seen, my dear; they would spy us
    out of the town.
The loud black nights for us, and the storm rush-
    ing over the down,
When I cannot see my own hand, but am led by
    the creak of the chain,
And grovel and grope for my son till I find myself
    drenched with the rain.

### III.

Anything fallen again? nay—what was there left
    to fall?
I have taken them home, I have numbered the
    bones, I have hidden them all.
What am I saying? and what are *you?* do you
    come as a spy?
Falls? what falls? who knows?   As the tree falls
    so must it lie.

### IV.

Who let her in? how long has she been? you—
    what have you heard?
Why did you sit so quiet? you never have spoken
    a word.
O—to pray with me—yes—a lady—none of their
    spies—
But the night has crept into my heart, and begun
    to darken my eyes.

### V.

Ah—you, that have lived so soft, what should *you*
    know of the night,
The blast and the burning shame and the bitter
    frost and the fright?
I have done it, while you were asleep—you were
    only made for the day.
I have gathered my baby together—and now you
    may go your way.

### VI.

Nay—for it's kind of you, Madam, to sit by an old
    dying wife.
But say nothing hard of my boy, I have only an
    hour of life.

I kissed my boy in the prison, before he went out
    to die.
" They dared me to do it," he said, and he never
    has told me a lie.
I whipt Lim for robbing an orchard once when
    he was but a child—
" The farmer dared me to do it," he said; he was
    always so wild—
And idle—and couldn't be idle—my Willy—he
    never could rest.
The King should have made him a soldier, he
    would have been one of his best.

### VII.

But he lived with a lot of wild mates, and they
    never would let him be good;
They swore that he dare not rob the mail, and he
    swore that he would:
And he took no life, but he took one purse, and
    when all was done
He flung it among his fellows—I'll none of it,
    said my son.

### VIII.

I came into court to the Judge and the lawyers.
    I told them my tale,
God's own truth—but they killed him, they killed
    him for robbing the mail.
They hanged him in chains for a show—we had
    always borne a good name—
To be hanged for a thief—and then put away—
    isn't that enough shame?

Dust to dust—low down—let us hide! but they
    set him so high
That all the ships of the world could stare at him,
    passing by.
God 'ill pardon the hell-black raven and horrible
    fowls of the air,
But not the black heart of the lawyer who killed
    him and hanged him there.

### IX.

And the jailer forced me away.  I had bid him
    my last good-bye;
They had fastened the door of his cell.  "O
    mother!" I heard him cry.
I couldn't get back tho' I tried, he had something
    further to say,
And now I never shall know it.   The jailer forced
    me away.

### X.

Then since I couldn't but hear that cry of my boy
    that was dead,
They seized me and shut me up: they fastened me
    down on my bed.
"Mother, O mother!"—he called in the dark to
    me year after year—
They beat me for that, they beat me—you know
    that I couldn't but hear;
And then at the last they found I had grown so
    stupid and still
They let me abroad again—but the creatures had
    worked their will.

XI.

Flesh of my flesh was gone, but bone of my bone
was left—
I stole them all from the lawyers—and you, will
you call it a theft?—
My baby, the bones that had sucked me, the bones
that had laughed and had cried—
Theirs? O no! they are mine—not theirs—they
had moved in my side.

XII.

Do you think I was scared by the bones? I
kissed 'em, I buried 'em all—
I can't dig deep, I am old—in the night by the
churchyard wall.
My Willy 'ill rise up whole when the trumpet of
judgment 'ill sound,
But I charge you never to say that I laid him in
holy ground.

XIII.

They would scratch him up—they would hang him
again on the cursèd tree.
Sin? O yes—we are sinners, I know—let all that
be,
And read me a Bible verse of the Lord's good will
toward men—
" Full of compassion and mercy, the Lord "—let
me hear it again;
" Full of compassion and mercy—long-suffering."
Yes, O yes!
For the lawyer is born but to murder—the
Saviour lives but to bless.

*He* 'll never put on the black cap except for the worst of the worst,

And the first may be last—I have heard it in church—and the last may be first.

Suffering—O long-suffering—yes, as the Lord must know,

Year after year in the mist and the wind and the shower and the snow.

### XIV.

Heard, have you? what? they have told you he never repented his sin.

How do they know it? are *they* his mother? are you of his kin?

Heard! have you ever heard, when the storm on the downs began,

The wind that 'ill wail like a child and the sea that 'ill moan like a man?

### XV.

Election, Election and Reprobation—it 's all very well.

But I go to-night to my boy, and I shall not find him in Hell.

For I cared so much for my boy that the Lord has looked into my care,

And He means me I'm sure to be happy with Willy, I know not where.

### XVI.

And if *he* be lost—but to save *my* soul, that is all your desire :

Do you think that I care for *my* soul if my boy be gone to the fire?

I have been with God in the dark—go, go, you may
    leave me alone—
You never have borne a child—you are just as
    hard as a stone.

XVII.

Madam, I beg your pardon! I think that you
    mean to be kind,
But I cannot hear what you say for my Willy's
    voice in the wind—
The snow and the sky so bright—he used but to
    call in the dark,
And he calls to me now from the church and not
    from the gibbet—for hark!
Nay—you can hear it yourself—it is coming—
    shaking the walls—
Willy—the moon's in a cloud—Good night. I am
    going. He calls.

ALFRED, LORD TENNYSON.

## THE DREAM OF EUGENE ARAM.

'T was in the prime of summer time,
    An evening calm and cool,
And four-and-twenty happy boys
    Came bounding out of school;
There were some that ran, and some that leapt
    Like troutlets in a pool.

Away they sped with gamesome minds
    And souls untouched by sin;
To a level mead they came, and there
    They drave the wickets in:

Pleasantly shone the setting sun
  Over the town of Lynn.

Like sportive deer they coursed about,
  And shouted as they ran,
Turning to mirth all things of earth
  As only boyhood can;
But the usher sat remote from all,
  A melancholy man!

His hat was off, his vest apart,
  To catch heaven's blessèd breeze;
For a burning thought was in his brow,
  And his bosom ill at ease;
So he leaned his head on his hands, and read
  The book between his knees.

Leaf after leaf he turned it o'er,
  Nor ever glanced aside,—
For the peace of his soul he read that book
  In the golden eventide;
Much study had made him very lean,
  And pale, and leaden-eyed.

At last he shut the ponderous tome;
  With a fast and fervent grasp
He strained the dusky covers close,
  And fixed the brazen hasp:
"O God! could I so close my mind,
  And clasp it with a clasp!"

Then leaping on his feet upright,
  Some moody turns he took,—

Now up the mead, then down the mead,
    And past a shady nook,—
And, lo! he saw a little boy
    That pored upon a book.


" My gentle lad, what is 't you read,—
    Romance or fairy fable?
Or is it some historic page,
    Of kings and crowns unstable? "
The young boy gave an upward glance,—
    " It is ' The Death of Abel.' "


The usher took six hasty strides,
    As smit with sudden pain,—
Six hasty strides beyond the place,
    Then slowly back again;
And down he sat beside the lad,
    And talked with him of Cain;


And, long since then, of bloody men,
    Whose deeds tradition saves;
And lonely folk cut off unseen,
    And hid in sudden graves;
And horrid stabs, in groves forlorn;
    And murders done in caves;


And how the sprites of injured men
    Shriek upward from the sod;
Ay, how the ghostly hand will point
    To show the burial clod;
And unknown facts of guilty acts
    Are seen in dreams from God.

He told how murderers walk the earth
   Beneath the curse of Cain,—
With crimson clouds before their eyes,
   And flames about their brain;
For blood has left upon their souls
   Its everlasting stain!

" And well," quoth he, " I know for truth
   Their pangs must be extreme—
Woe, woe, unutterable woe!—
   Who spill life's sacred stream.
For why? Methought, last night I wrought
   A murder, in a dream!

" One that had never done me wrong,—
   A feeble man and old;
I led him to a lonely field,—
   The moon shone clear and cold:
Now here, said I, this man shall die,
   And I will have his gold!

" Two sudden blows with a raggèd stick,
   And one with a heavy stone,
One hurried gash with a hasty knife,—
   And then the deed was done:
There was nothing lying at my feet
   But lifeless flesh and bone!

" Nothing but lifeless flesh and bone,
   That could not do me ill;
And yet I feared him all the more
   For lying there so still:
There was a manhood in his look
   That murder could not kill!

" And, lo! the universal air
   Seemed lit with ghastly flame,—
Ten thousand thousand dreadful eyes
   Were looking down in blame;
I took the dead man by his hand,
   And called upon his name.

" O God! it made me quake to see
   Such sense within the slain;
But, when I touched the lifeless clay,
   The blood gushed out amain!
For every clot a burning spot
   Was scorching in my brain!

" My head was like an ardent coal,
   My heart as solid ice;
My wretched, wretched soul, I knew,
   Was at the Devil's price.
A dozen times I groaned,—the dead
   Had never groaned but twice.

" And now, from forth the frowning sky,
   From heaven's topmost height,
I heard a voice,—the awful voice
   Of the blood-avenging sprite:
' Thou guilty man! take up thy dead,
   And hide it from my sight!'

" And I took the dreary body up,
   And cast it in a stream,—
The sluggish water black as ink,
   The depth was so extreme:—
My gentle boy, remember, this
   Is nothing but a dream!

11

" Down went the corse with a hollow plunge,
   And vanished in the pool;
Anon I cleansed my bloody hands,
   And washed my forehead cool,
And sat among the urchins young,
   That evening, in the school.

" O Heaven! to think of their white souls,
   And mine so black and grim!
I could not share in childish prayer,
   Nor join in evening hymn;
Like a devil of the pit I seemed,
   Mid holy cherubim!

" And peace went with them, one and all,
   And each calm pillow spread;
But Guilt was my grim chamberlain,
   That lighted me to bed,
And drew my midnight curtains round
   With fingers bloody red!

" All night I lay in agony,
   In anguish dark and deep;
My fevered eyes I dared not close,
   But stared aghast at Sleep;
For Sin had rendered unto her
   The keys of hell to keep!

" All night I lay in agony,
   From weary chime to chime;
With one besetting horrid hint
   That racked me all the time,—
A mighty yearning, like the first
   Fierce impulse unto crime,—

" One stern tyrannic thought, that made
   All other thoughts its slave!
Stronger and stronger every pulse
   Did that temptation crave,—
Still urging me to go and see
   The dead man in his grave!

" Heavily I rose up, as soon
   As light was in the sky,
And sought the black accursed pool
   With a wild, misgiving eye;
And I saw the dead in the river-bed,
   For the faithless stream was dry.

" Merrily rose the lark, and shook
   The dew-drop from its wing;
But I never marked its morning flight,
   I never heard it sing,
For I was stooping once again
   Under the horrid thing.

" With breathless speed, like a soul in chase,
   I took him up and ran;
There was no time to dig a grave
   Before the day began,—
In a lonesome wood with heaps of leaves,
   I hid the murdered man!

" And all that day I read in school,
   But my thought was otherwhere;
As soon as the midday task was done,
   In secret I was there,—
And a mighty wind had swept the leaves,
   And still the corse was bare!

" Then down I cast me on my face,
　　And first began to weep,
For I knew my secret then was one
　　That earth refused to keep,—
Or land or sea, though he should be
　　Ten thousand fathoms deep.

" So wills the fierce avenging sprite,
　　Till blood for blood atones!
Ay, though he 's buried in a cave,
　　And trodden down with stones,
And years have rotted off his flesh,—
　　The world shall see his bones!

" O God! that horrid, horrid dream
　　Besets me now awake!
Again—again, with dizzy brain,
　　The human life I take;
And my red right hand grows raging hot,
　　Like Cranmer's at the stake.

" And still no peace for the restless clay
　　Will wave or mold allow;
The horrid thing pursues my soul,—
　　It stands before me now!"
The fearful boy looked up, and saw
　　Huge drops upon his brow.

That very night, while gentle sleep
　　The urchin's eyelids kissed,
Two stern-faced men set out from Lynn
　　Through the cold and heavy mist;
And Eugene Aram walked between,
　　With gyves upon his wrist.

THOMAS HOOD.

## IN THE ENGINE–SHED.

THROUGH air made heavy with vapors murk,
  O'er slack and cinders in heaps and holes,
The engine-driver came to his work,
  Burly and bluff as a bag of coals;
With a thick gold chain where he bulged the most,
And a beard like a brush, and a face like a toast,
And a hat half-eaten by fire and frost;
And a diamond pin in the folded dirt
Of the shawl that served him for collar and shirt.
  Whenever he harnessed his steed of mettle:—
The shovel-fed monster that could not tire,
With limbs of steel and entrails of fire;
  Above us it sang like a tea-time kettle.

He came to his salamander toils
  In what seemed a devil's cast-off suit,
All charred, and discolored with rain and oils,
  And smeared and sooted from muffler to boot.
Some wiping—it struck him—his paws might suf-
    fer
With a wisp of thread he found on the buffer
(The improvement effected was not very great);
Then he spat, and passed his pipe to his mate.

And his whole face laughed with an honest mirth,
As any extant on this grimy earth,
  Welcoming me to his murky region;
And had you known him, I tell you this—
Though your bright hair shiver and sink at its
    roots,
    O piano-fingering fellow-collegian—

You would have returned no cold salutes
  To the cheery greeting of old Chris,
  But locked your hand in the vise of his.

For at night when the sleet-storm shatters and
    scatters,
And clangs on the pane like a pile of fetters,
He flies through it all with the world's love-let-
    ters:
The master of mighty leviathan motions,
  That make for him storm when the nights are
    fair,
  And cook him with fire and carve him with
    air,
While we sleep soft on the carriage cushions,
And he looks sharp for the signals, blear-eyed.
  Often had Chris over England rolled me;
  You shall hear a story he told me—
A dream of his rugged watch unwearied.

### THE STORY.

We were driving the down express;
  Will at the steam, and I at the coal;
Over the valleys and villages,
  Over the marshes and coppices,
Over the river, deep and broad;
Through the mountain, under the road,
      Flying along,
      Tearing along.
Thunderbolt engine, swift and strong,
  Fifty tons she was, whole and sole!

I had been promoted to the express:
I warrant I was proud and gay.

It was the evening that ended May,
　And the sky was a glory of tenderness.
We were thundering down to a midland town,—
　It doesn't matter about the name,
For we didn't stop there, or anywhere
　For a dozen miles on either side.
　Well, as I say, just there you slide,
With your steam shut off and your brakes in
　　hand,
Down the steepest and longest grade in the land,
At a pace that, I promise you, is grand.
　We were just there with the express,
　　When I caught sight of a girl's white dress
On the bank ahead; and as we passed—
You have no notion how fast—
She sank back scared from our baleful blast.

We were going—a mile and a quarter a minute—
　With vans and carriages—down the incline!
But I saw her face, and the sunshine in it;
　I looked in her eyes, and she looked in mine
As the train went by, like a shot from a mortar:
　A roaring hell-breath of dust and smoke.
　And it was a minute before I woke,
When she lay behind us—a mile and a quarter.

And the years went on, and the express
Leaped in her black resistlessness,
　Evening by evening, England through.—
　　Will—God rest him!—was found—a mash
　　Of bleeding rags, in a fearful smash
　He made of Christmas train at Crewe.
It chanced I was ill the night of the mess,
　Or I shouldn't now be here alive;

But thereafter, the five o'clock out express,
  Evening by evening, I used to drive.


And often I saw her: that lady, I mean,
  That I spoke of before.  She often stood
Atop of the bank;—it was pretty high,
  Say, twenty feet, and backed by a wood.—
She would pick daisies out of the green
  To fling down at us as we went by.
We had grown to be friends, too, she and I.
Though I was a stalwart, grimy chap,
And she a lady! I 'd wave my cap
  Evening by evening, when I 'd spy
That she was there, in the summer air,
  Watching the sun sink out of the sky.


Oh, I didn't see her every night:
  Bless you! no; just now and then,
And not at all for a twelvemonth quite.
  Then, one evening, I saw her again,
Alone, as ever—but wild and pale—
Climbing down on the line, on the very rail,
While a light as of hell from our wild wheels
      broke,
    Tearing down the slope with their devilish
      clamors
    And deafening din, as of giant hammers
That smote in a whirlwind of dust and smoke
  All the instant or so that we sped to meet her.
    Never, O never, had she seemed sweeter!—
I let yell the whistle, reversing the stroke,
Down that awful incline; and signalled the guard
To put on his brakes at once, and HARD!—

Though we couldn't have stopped. We tattered
    the rail
Into splinters and sparks, but without avail.
We couldn't stop; and she wouldn't stir,
    Saving to turn us her eyes, and stretch
    Her arms to us:—and the desperate wretch
I pitied, comprehending her.
So the brakes let off, and the steam full again,
Sprang down on the lady the terrible train.—
She never flinched. We beat her down,
And ran on through the lighted length of the town
    Before we could stop to see what was done.

    Yes, I 've run over more than one!
Full a dozen, I should say; but none
That I pitied as I pitied her.
If I could have stopped—with all the spur
Of the train's weight on, and cannily—
But it never would do with a lad like me
And she a lady,—or had been.—Sir?—
We won't say any more of her;
    The world is hard. But I 'm her friend,
Right through—down to the world's end.
It is a curl of her sunny hair
Set in this locket that I wear;
I picked it off the big wheel there.—
Time 's up, Jack—Stand clear, sir. Yes,
We 're going out with the express.

                WILLIAM WILKINS.

## REVELRY OF THE DYING.

[Supposed to be written in India, while the plague was raging, and playing havoc among the British residents and troops stationed there.]

WE meet 'neath the sounding rafter,
    And the walls around are bare;
As they shout to our peals of laughter,
    It seems that the dead are there.
But stand to your glasses, steady!
    We drink to our comrades' eyes;
Quaff a cup to the dead already—
    And hurrah for the next that dies!

Not here are the goblets glowing,
    Not here is the vintage sweet;
'T is cold, as our hearts are growing,
    And dark as the doom we meet.
But stand to your glasses, steady!
    And soon shall our pulses rise;
A cup to the dead already—
    Hurrah for the next that dies!

Not a sigh for the lot that darkles,
    Not a tear for the friends that sink;
We'll fall, midst the wine-cup's sparkles,
    As mute as the wine we drink.
So stand to your glasses, steady!
    'T is this that the respite buys;
One cup to the dead already—
    Hurrah for the next that dies!

Time was when we frowned at others;
   We thought we were wiser then;
Ha! ha! let those think of their mothers,
   Who hope to see them again.
No! stand to your glasses, steady!
   The thoughtless are here the wise;
A cup to the dead already—
   Hurrah for the next that dies!

There's many a hand that's shaking,
   There's many a cheek that's sunk;
But soon, though our hearts are breaking,
   They'll burn with the wine we've drunk.
So stand to your glasses, steady!
   'T is here the revival lies;
A cup to the dead already—
   Hurrah for the next that dies!

There's a mist on the glass congealing,
   'T is the hurricane's fiery breath;
And thus does the warmth of feeling
   Turn ice in the grasp of Death.
Ho! stand to your glasses, steady!
   For a moment the vapor flies;
A cup to the dead already—
   Hurrah for the next that dies!

Who dreads to the dust returning?
   Who shrinks from the sable shore,
Where the high and haughty yearning
   Of the soul shall sting no more!
Ho! stand to your glasses, steady!
   The world is a world of lies;

A cup to the dead already—
  Hurrah for the next that dies!

Cut off from the land that bore us,
  Betrayed by the land we find,
Where the brightest have gone before us,
  And the dullest remain behind—
Stand, stand to your glasses, steady!
  'T is all we have left to prize;
A cup to the dead already—
  And hurrah for the next that dies!

BARTHOLOMEW DOWLING.

## THE DRUMMER-BOY'S BURIAL.

ALL day long the storm of battle through the
  startled valley swept;
All night long the stars in heaven o'er the slain
  sad vigils kept.

O, the ghastly upturned faces gleaming whitely
  through the night!
O, the heaps of mangled corses in that dim sepul-
  chral light!

One by one the pale stars faded, and at length
  the morning broke;
But not one of all the sleepers on that field of
  death awoke.

Slowly passed the golden hours of that long
  bright summer day,
And upon that field of carnage still the dead
  unburied lay.

Lay there stark and cold, but pleading with a
    dumb, unceasing prayer,
For a little dust to hide them from the staring
    sun and air.

But the foeman held possession of that hard-won
    battle-plain,
In unholy wrath denying even burial to our slain.

Once again the night dropped round them,—
    night so holy and so calm
That the moonbeams hushed the spirit, like the
    sound of prayer or psalm.

On a couch of trampled grasses, just apart from
    all the rest,
Lay a fair young boy, with small hands meekly
    folded on his breast.

Death had touched him very gently, and he lay
    as if in sleep;
Even his mother scarce had shuddered at that
    slumber calm and deep.

For a smile of wondrous sweetness lent a radi-
    ance to the face,
And the hand of cunning sculptor could have
    added naught of grace

To the marble limbs so perfect in their passion-
    less repose,
Robbed of all save matchless purity by hard,
    unpitying foes.

And the broken drum beside him all his life's short
story told:
How he did his duty bravely till the death-tide
o'er him rolled.

Midnight came with ebon garments and a diadem
of stars,
While right upward in the zenith hung the fiery
planet Mars.

Hark! a sound of stealthy footsteps and of voices
whispering low,
Was it nothing but the young leaves, or the
brooklet's murmuring flow?

Clinging closely to each other, striving never to
look round
As they passed with silent shudder the pale corses
on the ground,

Came two little maidens,—sisters, with a light
and hasty tread,
And a look upon their faces, half of sorrow, half
of dread.

And they did not pause nor falter till, with throbbing hearts, they stood
Where the drummer-boy was lying in that partial
solitude.

They had brought some simple garments from
their wardrobe's scanty store,
And two heavy iron shovels in their slender
hands they bore.

Then they quickly knelt beside him, crushing
    back the pitying tears,
For they had no time for weeping, nor for any
    girlish fears.

And they robed the icy body, while no glow of
    maiden shame
Changed the pallor of their foreheads to a flush
    of lambent flame.

For their saintly hearts yearned o'er it in that
    hour of sorest need,
And they felt that Death was holy, and it sanc-
    tified the deed.

But they smiled and kissed each other when
    their new strange task was o'er,
And the form that lay before them its unwonted
    garments wore.

Then with slow and weary labor a small grave
    they hollowed out,
And they lined it with the withered grass and
    leaves that lay about.

But the day was slowly breaking ere their holy
    work was done,
And in crimson pomp the morning heralded again
    the sun.

Gently then those little maidens—they were chil-
    dren of our foes—
Laid the body of our drummer-boy to undisturbed
    repose.

ANONYMOUS.

## RAMON.

REFUGIO MINE, NORTHERN MEXICO.

DRUNK and senseless in his place,
Prone and sprawling on his face,
More like brute than any man
    Alive or dead,—
  By his great pump out of gear,
  Lay the peon engineer,
  Waking only just to hear,
    Overhead,
  Angry tones that called his name,
  Oaths and cries of bitter blame,—
Woke to hear all this, and waking, turned and
    fled!


  " To the man who 'll bring to me,"
  Cried Intendant Harry Lee,—
Harry Lee, the English foreman of the mine,—
  " Bring the sot alive or dead,
  I will give to him," he said,
  " Fifteen hundred *pesos* down,
  Just to set the rascal's crown
Underneath this heel of mine :
    Since but death
  Deserves the man whose deed,
  Be it vice or want of heed,
  Stops the pumps that give us breath,—
  Stops the pumps that suck the death
From the poisoned lower level of the mine!"

No one answered, for a cry
From the shaft rose up on high;
And shuffling, scrambling, tumbling from below,
  Came the miners each, the bolder
  Mounting on the weaker's shoulder,
  Grappling, clinging to their hold or
    Letting go,
  As the weaker gasped and fell
  From the ladder to the well,—
  To the poisoned pit of hell
    Down below!

  " To the man who sets them free,"
  Cried the foreman, Harry Lee,—
Harry Lee, the English foreman of the mine,—
  " Brings them out and sets them free,
  I will give that man," said he,
  " Twice that sum, who with a rope
  Face to face with death shall cope:
  Let him come who dares to hope!"
  " Hold your peace!" some one replied,
  Standing by the foreman's side;
" There has one already gone, whoe'er he be!"

  Then they held their breath with awe,
  Pulling on the rope, and saw
  Fainting figures reappear,
  On the black ropes swinging clear,
Fastened by some skilful hand from below;
  Till a score the level gained,
  And but one alone remained,—
  He the hero and the last,
  He whose skilful hand made fast
  12

The long line that brought them back to hope and
        cheer!

    Haggard, gasping, down dropped he
    At the feet of Harry Lee,—
Harry Lee, the English foreman of the mine;
    " I have come," he gasped, " to claim
    Both rewards, Señor,—my name
        Is Ramon!
    I 'm the drunken engineer,—
    I 'm the coward, Señor—"    Here
    He fell over, by that sign
        Dead as stone!

                              BRET HARTE.

_____


## AT THE CEDARS.

    You had two girls—Baptiste—
    One is Virginie—
    Hold hard—Baptiste!
    Listen to me.

    The whole drive was jammed,
    In that bend at the Cedars;
    The rapids were dammed
    With the logs tight rammed
    And crammed; you might know
    The devil had clinched them below.

    We worked three days—not a budge!
    " She 's as tight as a wedge
    On the ledge,"
    Says our foreman:

" Mon Dieu! boys, look here,
We must get this thing clear."
He cursed at the men,
And we went for it then;
With our cant-dogs arow,
We just gave he-yo-ho,
When she gave a big shove
From above.

The gang yelled, and tore
For the shore;
The logs gave a grind,
Like a wolf's jaws behind,
And as quick as a flash,
With a shove and a crash,
They were down in a mash.
But I and ten more,
All but Isaàc Dufour,
Were ashore.

He leaped on a log in the front of the rush,
And shot out from the bind
While the jam roared behind;
As he floated along
He balanced his pole
And tossed us a song.
But, just as we cheered,
Up darted a log from the bottom,
Leaped thirty feet fair and square,
And came down on his own.

He went up like a block
With the shock;
And when he was there,

In the air,
Kissed his hand
To the land.
When he dropped
My heart stopped,
For the first log had caught him
And crushed him;
When he rose in his place
There was blood on his face.

There were some girls, Baptiste,
Picking berries on the hillside,
Where the river curls, Baptiste,
You know,—on the still side.
One was down by the water,
She saw Isaàc
Fall back.

She did not scream, Baptiste,
She launched her canoe;
It did seem, Baptiste,
That she wanted to die too,
For before you could think
The birch cracked like a shell
In the rush of hell,
And I saw them both sink—

Baptiste!
He had two girls,
One is Virginie;
What God calls the other
Is not known to me.

                    DUNCAN CAMPBELL SCOTT.

## THE SANDS O' DEE.

" O MARY, go and call the cattle home,
  And call the cattle home,
  And call the cattle home,
 ·Across the sands o' Dee! "
The western wind was wild and dank wi' foam,
  And all alone went she.

The creeping tide came up along the sand,
  And o'er and o'er the sand,
  And round and round the sand,
 As far as eye could see;
The blinding mist came down and hid the land:
  And never home came she.

" O, is it weed, or fish, or floating hair,—
  A tress o' golden hair,
  O' drownèd maiden's hair,—
 Above the nets at sea?
Was never salmon yet that shone so fair,
  Among the stakes on Dee."

They rowed her in across the rolling foam,—
  The cruel, crawling foam,
  The cruel, hungry foam,—
 ·To her grave beside the sea;
But still the boatmen hear her call the cattle home
  Across the sands o' Dee.
       CHARLES KINGSLEY.

## ON THE LOSS OF THE ROYAL GEORGE.

WRITTEN WHEN THE NEWS ARRIVED; 1782.

TOLL for the brave,—
　The brave that are no more!
All sunk beneath the wave,
　Fast by their native shore.

Eight hundred of the brave,
　Whose courage well was tried,
Had made the vessel heel,
　And laid her on her side.

A land-breeze shook the shrouds,
　And she was overset;
Down went the Royal George,
　With all her crew complete.

Toll for the brave!
　Brave Kempenfelt is gone;
His last sea-fight is fought,
　His work of glory done.

It was not in the battle;
　No tempest gave the shock;
She sprang no fatal leak;
　She ran upon no rock.

His sword was in its sheath,
　His fingers held the pen,
When Kempenfelt went down
　With twice four hundred men.

Weigh the vessel up,
　Once dreaded by our foes!
And mingle with our cup
　The tear that England owes.

Her timbers yet are sound,
　And she may float again,
Full charged with England's thunder,
　And plough the distant main.

But Kempenfelt is gone;
　His victories are o'er;
And he and his eight hundred
　Shall plough the wave no more.

WILLIAM COWPER.

## THE THREE FISHERS.

THREE fishers went sailing out into the west,—
　Out into the west as the sun went down;
Each thought of the woman who loved him the
　　best,
　And the children stood watching them out of
　　the town;
For men must work, and women must weep;
And there's little to earn, and many to keep,
　Though the harbor bar be moaning.

Three wives sat up in the light-house tower,
　And trimmed the lamps as the sun went down;
And they looked at the squall, and they looked at
　　the shower,
　And the rack it came rolling up, ragged and
　　brown;

But men must work, and women must weep,
Though storms be sudden, and waters deep,
   And the harbor bar be moaning.

Three corpses lay out on the shining sands
  In the morning gleam as the tide went down,
And the women are watching and wringing their
    hands,
  For those who will never come back to the
    town;
For men must work, and women must weep,—
And the sooner it's over, the sooner to sleep,—
   And good-bye to the bar and its moaning.

CHARLES KINGSLEY.

## CASABIANCA.

[Young Casabianca, a boy about thirteen years old, son
of the Admiral of the Orient, remained at his post (in the
Battle of the Nile) after the ship had taken fire and all the
guns had been abandoned, and perished in the explosion
of the vessel, when the flames had reached the powder.]

  The boy stood on the burning deck,
    Whence all but him had fled;
  The flame that lit the battle's wreck
    Shone round him o'er the dead.

  Yet beautiful and bright he stood,
    As born to rule the storm;
  A creature of heroic blood,
    A proud though childlike form.

  The flames rolled on; he would not go
    Without his father's word;

That father, faint in death below,
    His voice no longer heard.

He called aloud, " Say, father, say,
    If yet my task be done!"
He knew not that the chieftain lay
    Unconscious of his son.

" Speak, father!" once again he cried,
    " If I may yet be gone!"
And but the booming shots replied,
    And fast the flames rolled on.

Upon his brow he felt their breath,
    And in his waving hair,
And looked from that lone post of death
    In still yet brave despair;

And shouted but once more aloud,
    " My father! must I stay?"
While o'er him fast, through sail and shroud,
    The wreathing fires made way.

They wrapt the ship in splendor wild,
    They caught the flag on high,
And streamed above the gallant child,
    Like banners in the sky.

There came a burst of thunder sound;
    The boy,—Oh! where was *he?*
Ask of the winds, that far around
    With fragments strewed the sea,—

With shroud and mast and pennon fair,
　　That well had borne their part,—
But the noblest thing that perished there
　　Was that young, faithful heart.

FELICIA HEMANS.

---

## THE WRECK OF THE HESPERUS.

It was the schooner Hesperus
　　That sailed the wintry sea;
And the skipper had taken his little daughter,
　　To bear him company.

Blue were her eyes as the fairy flax,
　　Her cheeks like the dawn of day,
And her bosom white as the hawthorn buds,
　　That ope in the month of May.

The skipper he stood beside the helm;
　　His pipe was in his mouth;
And he watched how the veering flaw did blow
　　The smoke, now west, now south.

Then up and spake an old sailor,
　　Had sailed the Spanish main:
" I pray thee, put into yonder port,
　　For I fear a hurricane.

" Last night the moon had a golden ring,
　　And to-night no moon we see!"
The skipper he blew a whiff from his pipe,
　　And a scornful laugh laughed he.

Colder and louder blew the wind,
　　A gale from the northeast;
The snow fell hissing in the brine,
　　And the billows frothed like yeast.

Down came the storm, and smote amain
　　The vessel in its strength;
She shuddered and paused like a frighted steed,
　　Then leaped her cable's length.

" Come hither! come hither my little daughter,
　　And do not tremble so;
For I can weather the roughest gale
　　That ever wind did blow."

He wrapped her warm in his seaman's coat
　　Against the stinging blast;
He cut a rope from a broken spar,
　　And bound her to the mast.

" O father! I hear the church-bells ring;
　　Oh say, what may it be?"
" 'T is a fog-bell on a rock-bound coast!"
　　And he steered for the open sea.

" O father! I hear the sound of guns;
　　Oh say, what may it be?"
" Some ship in distress, that cannot live
　　In such an angry sea!"

" O father! I see a gleaming light!
　　Oh say, what may it be?"
But the father answered never a word—
　　A frozen corpse was he.

Lashed to the helm, all stiff and stark,
  With his face turned to the skies,
The lantern gleamed through the gleaming snow
  On his fixed and glassy eyes.

Then the maiden clasped her hands and prayed
  That savèd she might be!
And she thought of Christ, who stilled the wave
  On the Lake of Galilee.

And fast through the midnight dark and drear,
  Through the whistling sleet and snow,
Like a sheeted ghost, the vessel swept
  Towards the reef of Norman's Woe.

And ever, the fitful gusts between,
  A sound came from the land;
It was the sound of the trampling surf
  On the rocks and the hard sea-sand.

The breakers were right beneath her bows;
  She drifted a dreary wreck;
And a whooping billow swept the crew,
  Like icicles, from her deck.

She struck where the white and fleecy waves
  Looked soft as carded wool;
But the cruel rocks they gored her side
  Like the horns of an angry bull.

Her rattling shrouds, all sheathed in ice,
  With the mast went by the board;
Like a vessel of glass, she stove and sank—
  Ho! ho! the breakers roared!

At daybreak, on the bleak sea-beach,
   A fisherman stood aghast,
To see the form of a maiden fair,
   Lashed close to a drifting mast.

The salt sea was frozen on her breast,
   The salt tears in her eyes;
And he saw her hair, like the brown sea-weed,
   On the billows fall and rise.

Such was the wreck of the Hesperus,
   In the midnight and the snow;
Christ save us all from a death like this,
   On the reef of Norman's Woe!

        HENRY WADSWORTH LONGFELLOW.

---

## THE SECOND MATE.

" Ho, there!  Fisherman, hold your hand!
   Tell me, what is that far away,—
There, where over the isle of sand
   Hangs the mist-cloud sullen and gray?
See! it rocks with a ghastly life,
   Rising and rolling through clouds of spray,
Right in the midst of the breakers' strife,—
   Tell me what is it, Fisherman, pray?"

" That, good sir, was a steamer stout
   As ever paddled around Cape Race;
And many 's the wild and stormy bout
   She had with the winds, in that self-same place;
But her time was come; and at ten o'clock
   Last night she struck on that lonesome shore;

And her sides were gnawed by the hidden rock,
　　And at dawn this morning she was no more."


" Come, as you seem to know, good man,
　　The terrible fate of this gallant ship,
Tell me about her all that you can;
　　And here 's my flask to moisten your lip.
Tell me how many she had aboard,—
　　Wives, and husbands, and lovers true,—
How did it fare with her human hoard?
　　Lost she many, or lost she few? "


" Master, I may not drink of your flask,
　　Already too moist I feel my lip;
But I 'm ready to do what else you ask,
　　And spin you my yarn about the ship.
'T was ten o'clock, as I said, last night,
　　When she struck the breakers and went ashore;
And scarce had broken the morning's light
　　When she sank in twelve feet of water or more.


" But long ere this they knew her doom,
　　And the captain called all hands to prayer;
And solemnly over the ocean's boom
　　Their orisons wailed on the troublous air.
And round about the vessel there rose
　　Tall plumes of spray as white as snow,
Like angels in their ascension clothes,
　　Waiting for those who prayed below.


" So these three hundred people clung
　　As well as they could, to spar and rope;

With a word of prayer upon every tongue,
  Nor on any face a glimmer of hope.
But there was no blubbering weak and wild,—
  Of tearful faces I saw but one,
A rough old salt, who cried like a child,
  And not for himself, but the captain's son.

" The captain stood on the quarter-deck,
  Firm but pale with trumpet in hand;
Sometimes he looked at the breaking wreck,
  Sometimes he sadly looked to land;
And often he smiled to cheer the crew—
  But, Lord! the smile was terrible grim—
Till over the quarter a huge sea flew;
  And that was the last they saw of him.

" I saw one young fellow with his bride,
  Standing amidships upon the wreck;
His face was white as the boiling tide,
  And she was clinging about his neck.
And I saw them try to say good-bye,
  But neither could hear the other speak;
So they floated away through the sea to die—
  Shoulder to shoulder and cheek to cheek.

" And there was a child, but eight at best,
  Who went his way in a sea she shipped,
All the while holding upon his breast
  A little pet parrot whose wings were clipped.
And, as the boy and the bird went by,
  Swinging away on a tall wave's crest,
They were gripped by a man, with a drowning cry,
  And together the three went down to rest.

" And so the crew went one by one,
　Some with gladness, and few with fear,—
Cold and hardship such work had done
　That few seemed frightened when death was
　　near.
Thus every soul on board went down,—
　Sailor and passenger, little and great;
The last that sank was a man of my town,
　A capital swimmer,—the second mate."

" Now, lonely fisherman, who are you
　That say you saw this terrible wreck?
How do I know what you say is true,
　When every mortal was swept from the deck?
Where were you in that hour of death?
　How did you learn what you relate?"
His answer came in an under-breath
　" Master, I was the second mate!"

FITZ-JAMES O'BRIEN.

---

## A SEA STORY.

Silence.　A while ago
　　Shrieks went up piercingly;
But now is the ship gone down;
　　Good ship, well manned, was she.
There's a raft that's a chance of life for one,
　　This day upon the sea.

A chance for one of two
　　Young, strong, are he and he,
Just in the manhood prime,
　　The comelier, verily,

For the wrestle with wind and weather and
    wave,
      In the life upon the sea.

One of them has a wife
      And little children three ;
Two that can toddle and lisp,
      And a suckling on the knee :
Naked they 'll go, and hunger sore,
      If he be lost at sea.

One has a dream of home,
      A dream that well may be :
He never has breathed it yet ;
      She never has known it, she.
But some one will be sick at heart
      If he be lost at sea.

" Wife and kids at home ! —
      Wife, kids, nor home has he ! —
Give us a chance, Bill ! "  Then,
      " All right, Jem ! "  Quietly
A man gives up his life for a man,
      This day upon the sea.

                  EMILY HENRIETTA HICKEY.

13

# HUMOROUS POEMS.

# HUMOROUS POEMS.

## I.

## WOMAN.

### WOMAN.

WHEN Eve brought *woe* to all mankind
Old Adam called her *wo-man;*
But when she *woo*ed with love so kind,
He then pronounced her *woo-man.*
But now, with folly and with pride,
Their husbands' pockets trimming,
The women are so full of *whims*
That men pronounce them *wimmen!*

ANONYMOUS.

### THE WOMEN FO'K.*

O, SAIRLY may I rue the day
I fancied first the womenkind;

---

* The air of this song is my own. It was first set to
music by Heather, and most beautifully set too. It was
afterwards set by Dewar, whether with the same accom-
paniments or not, I have forgot. It is my own favorite
humorous song, when forced to sing by ladies against my
will, which too frequently happens; and, notwithstanding
my wood-notes wild, it will never be sung by any so well
again.—THE AUTHOR.

For aye sinsyne I ne'er can hae
    Ae quiet thought or peace o' mind!
They hae plagued my heart an' pleased my e'e,
    An' teased an' flattered me at will,
But aye for a' their witcherye,
    The pawky things I lo'e them still.

> *O the women fo'k! O the women fo'k!*
>     *But they hae been the wreck o' me;*
> *O weary fa' the women fo'k,*
>     *For they winna let a body be!*

I hae thought an' thought, but darena tell,
    I 've studied them wi' a' my skill,
I 've lo'd them better than mysell,
    I 've tried again to like them ill.
Wha sairest strives, will sairest rue,
    To comprehend what nae man can;
When he has done what man can do,
    He 'll end at last where he began.
    *O the women fo'k, etc.*

That they hae gentle forms an' meet,
    A man wi' half a look may see;
An gracefu' airs, an' faces sweet,
    An' waving curls aboon the bree;
An' smiles as soft as the young rosebud,
    And een sae pawky, bright, an' rare,
Wad lure the laverock frae the cludd,—
    But, laddie, seek to ken nae mair!
    *O the women fo'k, etc.*

Even but this night nae farther gane,
    The date is neither lost nor lang,

I tak ye witness ilka ane,
   How fell they fought, and fairly dang.
Their point they 've carried right or wrang,
   Without a reason, rhyme, or law,
An' forced a man to sing a sang,
   That ne'er could sing a verse ava.

> *O the women fo'k! O the women fo'k!*
>    *But they hae been the wreck o' me;*
> *O weary fa' the women fo'k,*
>    *For they winna let a body be!*

JAMES HOGG.

---

## OF A CERTAINE MAN.

THERE was (not certaine when) a certaine
   preacher,
That never learned, and yet became a teacher,
Who having read in Latine thus a text
Of *erat quidam homo*, much perplext,
He seemed the same with studie great to scan,
In English thus, *There was a certaine man.*
But now (quoth he), good people, note you this,
He saith there was, he doth not say there is;
For in these daies of ours it is most plaine
Of promise, oath, word, deed, no man 's certaine;
Yet by my text you see it comes to passe
That surely once a certaine man there was:
   But yet, I think, in all your Bible no man
   Can finde this text, *There was a certaine wo-*
     *man.*

SIR JOHN HARRINGTON.

## WOMEN'S CHORUS.

They 're always abusing the women,
   As a terrible plague to men :
They say we 're the root of all evil,
   And repeat it again and again ;
Of war, and quarrels, and bloodshed,
   All mischief, be what it may !
And pray, then, why do you marry us,
   If we 're all the plagues you say?
And why do you take such care of us,
   And keep us so safe at home,
And are never easy a moment
   If ever we chance to roam?
When you ought to be thanking heaven
   That your Plague is out of the way,
You all keep fussing and fretting—
   " Where is *my* Plague to-day? "
If a Plague peeps out of the window,
   Up go the eyes of men ;
If she hides, then they all keep staring
   Until she looks out again.

From the Greek of ARISTOPHANES.<br>Translation of WILLIAM COLLINS.

## THE WIVES OF WEINSBERG.

Which way to Weinsberg? neighbor, say !
   'T is sure a famous city :
It must have cradled, in its day,
Full many a maid of noble clay,
   And matrons wise and witty ;

And if ever marriage should happen to me,
A Weinsberg dame my wife shall be.

King Conrad once, historians say,
   Fell out with this good city;
So down he came, one luckless day,—
Horse, foot, dragoons,—in stern array,—
   And cannon,—more 's the pity!
Around the walls the artillery roared,
And bursting bombs their fury poured.

But naught the little town could scare;
   Then, red with indignation,
He bade the herald straight repair
Up to the gates, and thunder there
   The following proclamation:—
" Rascals! when I your town do take,
No living thing shall save its neck!"

Now, when the herald's trumpet sent
   These tidings through the city,
To every house a death knell went;
Such murder-cries the hot air rent
   Might move the stones to pity.
Then bread grew dear, but good advice
Could not be had for any price.

Then, " Woe is me!" " O misery!"
   What shrieks of lamentation!
And " Kyrie Eleison!" cried
The pastors, and the flock replied,
   " Lord! save us from starvation!"
" Oh, woe is me, poor Corydon—
My neck,—my neck!   I 'm gone,—I 'm gone!"

Yet oft, when counsel, deed, and prayer
   Had all proved unavailing,
When hope hung trembling on a hair,
How oft has woman's wit been there!—
   A refuge never failing;
For woman's wit and Papal fraud,
Of olden time, were famed abroad.

A youthful dame, praised be her name!—
   Last night had seen her plighted,—
Whether in waking hour or dream,
Conceived a rare and novel scheme,
   Which all the town delighted;
Which you, if you think otherwise,
Have leave to laugh at and despise.

At midnight hour, when culverin
   And gun and bomb were sleeping,
Before the camp with mournful mien,
The loveliest embassy were seen,
   All kneeling low and weeping.
So sweetly, plaintively they prayed,
But no reply save this was made:—

" The women have free leave to go,
   Each with her choicest treasure;
But let the knaves their husbands know
That unto them the King will show
   The weight of his displeasure."
With these sad terms the lovely train
Stole weeping from the camp again.

But when the morning gilt the sky,
   What happened?   Give attention:—

The city gates wide open fly,
And all the wives come trudging by,
  Each bearing—need I mention?—
Her own dear husband on her back,
All snugly seated in a sack!

Full many a sprig of court, the joke
  Not relishing, protested,
And urged the King; but Conrad spoke:—
" A monarch's word must not be broke!"
  And here the matter rested.
" Bravo!" he cried, " Ha, ha!  Bravo!
Our lady guessed it would be so."

He pardoned all, and gave a ball
  That night at royal quarters.
The fiddles squeaked, the trumpets blew,
And up and down the dancers flew,
  Court sprigs with city daughters.
The mayor's wife—O rarest sight!—
Danced with the shoemaker that night!

Ah, where is Weinsberg, sir, I pray?
  'T is sure a famous city:
It must have cradled in its day
Full many a maid of noble clay,
  And matrons wise and witty;
And if ever marriage should happen to me,
A Weinsberg dame my wife shall be.

From the German of GOTTFRIED AUGÜST BÜRGER.
Translation of CHARLES TIMOTHY BROOKS.

## SORROWS OF WERTHER.

Werther had a love for Charlotte
    Such as words could never utter;
Would you know how first he met her?
    She was cutting bread and butter.

Charlotte was a married lady,
    And a moral man was Werther,
And for all the wealth of Indies
    Would do nothing for to hurt her.

So he sighed and pined and ogled,
    And his passion boiled and bubbled,
Till he blew his silly brains out,
    And no more was by it troubled.

Charlotte, having seen his body
    Borne before her on a shutter,
Like a well-conducted person,
    Went on cutting bread and butter.

             WILLIAM MAKEPEACE THACKERAY.

---

## THE WELL OF ST. KEYNE.

"In the parish of St. Neots, Cornwall, is a well arched over with the robes of four kinds of trees,—withy, oak, elm, and ash,—and dedicated to St. Keyne. The reported virtue of the water is this, that; whether husband or wife first drink thereof, they get the mastery thereby."

             —FULLER.

A well there is in the West country,
    And a clearer one never was seen;

There is not a wife in the West country
  But has heard of the Well of St. Keyne.

An oak and an elm tree stand beside,
  And behind does an ash-tree grow,
And a willow from the bank above
  Droops to the water below.

A traveller came to the Well of St. Keyne;
  Pleasant it was to his eye,
For from cock-crow he had been travelling,
  And there was not a cloud in the sky.

He drank of the water so cool and clear,
  For thirsty and hot was he,
And he sat down upon the bank,
  Under the willow-tree.

There came a man from the neighboring town
  At the well to fill his pail,
On the well-side he rested it,
  And bade the stranger hail.

" Now art thou a bachelor, stranger? " quoth he,
  " For an if thou hast a wife,
The happiest draught thou hast drank this day
  That ever thou didst in thy life.

" Or has your good woman, if one you have,
  In Cornwall ever been?
For an if she have, I 'll venture my life
  She has drunk of the Well of St. Keyne."

" I have left a good woman who never was here,"
  The stranger he made reply;
" But that my draught should be better for that,
  I pray you answer me why."

" St. Keyne," quoth the countryman, " many a
    time
  Drank of this crystal well,
And before the angel summoned her
  She laid on the water a spell.

" If the husband of this gifted well
  Shall drink before his wife,
A happy man thenceforth is he,
  For he shall be master for life.

" But if the wife should drink of it first,
  Heaven help the husband then!"
The stranger stooped to the Well of St. Keyne,
  And drank of the waters again.

" You drank of the well, I warrant, betimes?"
  He to the countryman said.
But the countryman smiled as the stranger spake,
  And sheepishly shook his head.

" I hastened, as soon as the wedding was done,
  And left my wife in the porch.
But i' faith, she had been wiser than me,
  For she took a bottle to church."

ROBERT SOUTHEY.

## THE BELLE OF THE BALL.

YEARS, years ago, ere yet my dreams
　Had been of being wise or witty,
Ere I had done with writing themes,
　Or yawned o'er this infernal Chitty,—
Years, years ago, while all my joys
　Were in my fowling-piece and filly;
In short, while I was yet a boy,
　I fell in love with Laura Lilly.


I saw her at the county ball;
　There, when the sounds of flute and fiddle
Gave signal sweet in that old hall
　Of hands across and down the middle,
Hers was the subtlest spell by far
　Of all that sets young hearts romancing:
She was our queen, our rose, our star;
　And then she danced,—O Heaven! her dancing.


Dark was her hair; her hand was white;
　Her voice was exquisitely tender;
Her eyes were full of liquid light;
　I never saw a waist so slender;
Her every look, her every smile,
　Shot right and left a score of arrows:
I thought 't was Venus from her isle,
　And wondered where she 'd left her sparrows.


She talked of politics or prayers,
　Of Southey's prose or Wordsworth's sonnets,

Of danglers or of dancing bears,
  Of battles or the last new bonnets;
By candle-light, at twelve o'clock,—
  To me it mattered not a tittle,—
If those bright lips had quoted Locke,
  I might have thought they murmured Little.

Through sunny May, through sultry June,
  I loved her with a love eternal;
I spoke her praises to the moon,
  I wrote them to the Sunday Journal.
My mother laughed; I soon found out
  That ancient ladies have no feeling:
My father frowned; but how should gout
  See any happiness in kneeling?

She was the daughter of a dean,—
  Rich, fat, and rather apoplectic;
She had one brother just thirteen,
  Whose color was extremely hectic;
Her grandmother for many a year
  Had fed the parish with her bounty;
Her second cousin was a peer,
  And lord-lieutenant of the county.

But titles and the three-per-cents,
  And mortgages, and great relations,
And India bonds, and tithes and rents,
  O, what are they to love's sensations?
Black eyes, fair forehead, clustering locks,—
  Such wealth, such honors Cupid chooses;
He cares as little for the stocks
  As Baron Rothschild for the muses.

She sketched; the vale, the wood, the beach,
    Grew lovelier from her pencil's shading:
She botanized; I envied each
    Young blossom in her boudoir fading:
She warbled Handel; it was grand,—
    She made the Catilina jealous:
She touched the organ; I could stand
    For hours and hours to blow the bellows.

She kept an album too, at home,
    Well filled with all an album's glories,—
Paintings of butterflies and Rome,
    Patterns for trimmings, Persian stories,
Soft songs to Julia's cockatoo,
    Fierce odes to famine and to slaughter,
And autographs of Prince Leeboo,
    And recipes for elder-water.

And she was flattered, worshipped, bored;
    Her steps were watched, her dress was noted;
Her poodle-dog was quite adored;
    Her sayings were extremely quoted.
She laughed,—and every heart was glad,
    As if the taxes were abolished;
She frowned,—and every look was sad,
    As if the opera were demolished.

She smiled on many just for fun,—
    I knew that there was nothing in it;
I was the first, the only one,
    Her heart had thought of for a minute.
I knew it, for she told me so,
    In phrase which was divinely moulded;
14

She wrote a charming hand,—and O,
　　How sweetly all her notes were folded!

Our love was most like other loves,—
　　A little glow, a little shiver,
A rosebud and a pair of gloves,
　　And " Fly Not Yet," upon the river;
Some jealousy of some one's heir,
　　Some hopes of dying broken-hearted;
A miniature, a lock of hair,
　　The usual vows,—and then we parted.

We parted: months and years rolled by;
　　We met again four summers after.
Our parting was all sob and sigh,
　　Our meeting was all mirth and laughter!
For in my heart's most secret cell
　　There had been many other lodgers;
And she was not the ball-room's belle,
　　But only Mrs.—Something—Rogers!

　　　　　　　WINTHROP MACKWORTH PRAED.

　　　　　　　———

## ECHO AND THE LOVER.

*Lover.*　Echo! mysterious nymph, declare
　　Of what you 're made, and what you are.
*Echo.*　　　　　　　　　　　Air!
*Lover.*　Mid airy cliffs and places high,
　　Sweet Echo! listening love, you lie.
*Echo.*　　　　　　　　　　You lie!
*Lover.*　Thou dost resuscitate dead sounds,—
　　Hark! how my voice revives, resounds!
*Echo.*　　　　　　　　　　Zounds!

*Lover.*    I 'll question thee before I go,—
        Come, answer me more apropos!
*Echo.*                          Poh! poh!
*Lover.*    Tell me, fair nymph, if e'er you saw
        So sweet a girl as Phœbe Shaw.
*Echo.*                          Pshaw!
*Lover.*    Say, what will turn that frisking coney
        Into the toils of matrimony?
*Echo.*                          Money!
*Lover.*    Has Phœbe not a heavenly brow?
        Is not her bosom white as snow?
*Echo.*                          Ass! No!
*Lover.*    Her eyes! was ever such a pair?
        Are the stars brighter than they are?
*Echo.*                          They are!
*Lover.*    Echo, thou liest, but can't deceive me.
*Echo.*                          Leave me!
*Lover.*    But come, thou saucy, pert romancer,
        Who is as fair as Phœbe? Answer!
*Echo.*                          Ann, sir.

                  ANONYMOUS.

---

## ECHO.

I ASKED of Echo, t' other day,
  (Whose words are few and often funny,)
What to a novice she could say
  Of courtship, love, and matrimony.
  Quoth Echo, plainly,—" Matter-o'-money!"


Whom should I marry?—should it be
  A dashing damsel, gay and pert,

A pattern of inconstancy;
  Or selfish, mercenary flirt?
    Quoth Echo, sharply,—" Nary flirt!"

What if, aweary of the strife
  That long has lured the dear deceiver,
She promise to amend her life,
  And sin no more; can I believe her?
    Quoth Echo, very promptly,—" Leave her!"

But if some maiden with a heart
  On me should venture to bestow it,
Pray, should I act the wiser part
  To take the treasure or forego it?
    Quoth Echo, with decision,—" Go it!"

But what if, seemingly afraid
  To bind her fate in Hymen's fetter,
She vow she means to die a maid,
  In answer to my loving letter?
    Quoth Echo, rather coolly,—" Let her!"

What if, in spite of her disdain,
  I find my heart intwined about
With Cupid's dear delicious chain
  So closely that I can't get out?
    Quoth Echo, laughingly,—" Get out!"

But if some maid with beauty blest,
  As pure and fair as Heaven can make her,
Will share my labor and my rest
  Till envious Death shall overtake her?
    Quoth Echo (*sotto voce*),—" Take her!"

JOHN GODFREY SAXE.

## "NOTHING TO WEAR."

Miss Flora McFlimsey, of Madison Square,
   Has made three separate journeys to Paris,
And her father assures me, each time she was
     there,
   That she and her friend Mrs. Harris
(Not the lady whose name is so famous in history,
But plain Mrs. H., without romance or mys-
     tery)
Spent six consecutive weeks without stopping
In one continuous round of shopping,—
Shopping alone, and shopping together,
At all hours of the day, and in all sorts of
     weather,
For all manner of things that a woman can put
On the crown of her head or the sole of her foot,
Or wrap round her shoulders, or fit round her
     waist,
Or that can be sewed on, or pinned on, or laced,
Or tied on with a string, or stitched on with a
     bow,
In front or behind, above or below;
For bonnets, mantillas, capes, collars, and shawls;
Dresses for breakfasts and dinners and balls;
Dresses to sit in and stand in and walk in;
Dresses to dance in and flirt in and talk in;
Dresses in which to do nothing at all;
Dresses for Winter, Spring, Summer, and Fall;
All of them different in color and shape,
Silk, muslin, and lace, velvet, satin, and crape,

Brocade, and broadcloth, and other material,
Quite as expensive and much more ethereal;
In short, for all things that could ever be thought
        of,
Or milliner, *modiste,* or tradesman be bought of,
    From ten-thousand-francs robe to twenty-sous
        frills;
In all quarters of Paris, and to every store,
While McFlimsey in vain stormed, scolded, and
        swore,
    They footed the streets, and he footed the bills!

The last trip, their goods shipped by the steamer
        Arago,
Formed, McFlimsey declares, the bulk of her
        cargo,
Not to mention a quantity kept from the rest,
Sufficient to fill the largest-sized chest,
Which did not appear on the ship's manifest,
But for which the ladies themselves manifested
Such particular interest, that they invested
Their own proper persons in layers and rows
Of muslins, embroideries, worked under-clothes,
Gloves, handkerchiefs, scarfs, and such trifles as
        those;
Then, wrapped in great shawls, like Circassian
        beauties,
Gave *good-bye* to the ship, and *go-by* to the duties.
Her relations at home all marvelled, no doubt,
Miss Flora had grown so enormously stout
    For an actual belle and a possible bride;
But the miracle ceased when she turned inside
        out,

And the truth came to light, and the dry-goods
    beside,
Which, in spite of Collector and Custom-House
    sentry,
Had entered the port without any entry,

And yet, though scarce three months have passed
    since the day
This merchandise went, on twelve carts, up Broad-
    way,
This same Miss McFlimsey, of Madison Square,
The last time we met was in utter despair,
Because she had nothing whatever to wear!

NOTHING TO WEAR! Now, as this is a true ditty,
    I do not assert—this, you know, is between us—
That she's in a state of absolute nudity,
    Like Powers' Greek Slave, or the Medici Venus;
But I do mean to say, I have heard her declare,
    When, at the same moment, she had on a dress
    Which cost five hundred dollars, and not a cent
        less,
    And jewelry worth ten times more, I should
        guess,
That she had not a thing in the wide world to
    wear!

I should mention just here, that out of Miss
    Flora's
Two hundred and fifty or sixty adorers,
I had just been selected as he who should throw
    all
The rest in the shade, by the gracious bestowal

On myself after twenty or thirty rejections,
Of those fossil remains which she called her " af-
fections,"
And that rather decayed, but well-known work of
art,
Which Miss Flora persisted in styling her
" heart."
So we were engaged. Our troth had been plighted,
Not by moonbeam or starbeam, by fountain or
grove,
But in a front parlor, most brilliantly lighted,
    Beneath the gas-fixtures we whispered our love,
Without any romance or raptures or sighs,
Without any tears in Miss Flora's blue eyes,
Or blushes, or transports, or such silly actions,
It was one of the quietest business transactions,
With a very small sprinkling of sentiment, if any,
And a very large diamond imported by Tiffany.
On her virginal lips while I printed a kiss,
She exclaimed, as a sort of parenthesis,
And by way of putting me quite at my ease,
" You know, I 'm to polka as much as I please,
And flirt when I like,—now, stop, don't you
speak,—
And you must not come here more than twice in
the week,
Or talk to me either at party or ball,
But always be ready to come when I call;
So don't prose to me about duty and stuff,
If we don't break this off, there will be time
enough
For that sort of thing; but the bargain must be
That, as long as I choose, I am perfectly free,

For this is a kind of engagement, you see,
Which is binding on you but not binding on me."

Well, having thus wooed Miss McFlimsey and
    gained her,
With the silks, crinolines, and hoops that con-
    tained her,
I had, as I thought, a contingent remainder
At least in the property, and the best right
To appear as its escort by day and by night;
And it being the week of the STUCKUPS' grand
    ball,—
    Their cards had been out a fortnight or so,
    And set all the Avenue on the tiptoe,—
I considered it only my duty to call,
    And see if Miss Flora intended to go.
I found her,—as ladies are apt to be found,
When the time intervening between the first sound
Of the bell and the visitor's entry is shorter
Than usual,—I found; I won't say—I caught
    her,
Intent on the pier-glass, undoubtedly meaning
To see if perhaps it didn't need cleaning.
She turned as I entered,—" Why, Harry, you sin-
    ner,
I thought that you went to the Flashers' to din-
    ner!"
" So I did," I replied; " but the dinner is swal-
    lowed
    And digested, I trust, for 't is now nine and
    more,
So being relieved from that duty, I followed
    Inclination, which led me, you see, to your
    door;

And now will your ladyship so condescend
As just to inform me if you intend
Your beauty and graces and presence to lend
(All of which, when I own, I hope no one will
      borrow)
To the STUCKUPS, whose party, you know, is to-
      morrow? "
The fair Flora looked up with a pitiful air,
And answered quite promptly, " Why, Harry, *mon
      cher,*
I should like above all things to go with you
      there,
But really and truly—I 've nothing to wear."
" Nothing to wear! go just as you are;
Wear the dress you have on, and you 'll be by
      far,
I engage, the most bright and particular star
  On the Stuckup horizon—" I stopped—for her
      eye,
Notwithstanding this delicate onset of flattery,
Opened on me at once a most terrible battery
  Of scorn and amazement.   She made no reply,
But gave a slight turn to the end of her nose—
  That pure Grecian feature—as much as to say,
" How absurd that any sane man should sup-
      pose
That a lady would go to a ball in the clothes,
  No matter how fine, that she wears every day! "

So I ventured again: " Wear your crimson bro-
      cade "
(Second turn-up of nose)—" That 's too dark by
  a shade."

" Your blue silk "—" That 's too heavy." " Your
    pink "—" That 's too light."
" Wear tulle over satin "—" I can't endure white."
" Your rose-colored, then, the best of the batch "—
" I haven't a thread of point-lace to match."
" Your brown *moire antique* "—" Yes, and look
    like a Quaker."
" The pearl-colored "—" I would, but that plaguey
    dressmaker
Has had it a week." " Then that exquisite lilac
In which you would melt the heart of a Shylock "
(Here the nose took again the same elevation)—
" I wouldn't wear that for the whole of creation."
    " Why not? It 's my fancy, there 's nothing
    could strike it
As more *comme il faut* "—" Yes, but, dear me!
    that lean
Sophronia Stuckup has got one just like it,
And I won't appear dressed like a chit of sixteen."
" Then that splendid purple, that sweet Mazarine,
That superb *point d'aiguille*, that imperial green,
That zephyr-like tarlatan, that rich *grenadine* "—
" Not one of all which is fit to be seen,"
Said the lady, becoming excited and flushed.
" Then wear," I exclaimed, in a tone which quite
    crushed
    Opposition, " that gorgeous *toilette* which you
    sported
In Paris last spring, at the grand presentation,
When you quite turned the head of the head of the
    nation ;
    And by all the grand court were so very much
    courted."

The end of the nose was portentously tipped up,
And both the bright eyes shot forth indignation,
As she burst upon me with the fierce exclamation,
" I have worn it three times at the least calcula-
        tion,
    And that and most of my dresses are ripped
        up ! "
Here I *ripped out* something, perhaps rather rash,
    Quite innocent, though ; but, to use an expres-
        sion
More striking than classic, it " settled my hash,"
    And proved very soon the last act of our ses-
        sion.
" Fiddlesticks, is it, sir?   I wonder the ceiling
    Doesn't fall down and crush you—you men have
        no feeling ;
You selfish, unnatural, illiberal creatures,
Who set yourselves up as patterns and preachers,
    Your silly pretence—why, what a mere guess it
        is !
Pray, what do you know of a woman's necessities?
I have told you and showed you I 've nothing to
        wear,
And it 's perfectly plain you not only don't care,
But you do not believe me "—(here the nose went
        still higher)—
" I suppose, if you dared, you would call me a
        liar.
Our engagement is ended, sir—yes, on the spot ;
You 're a brute, and a monster, and—I don't know
        what."
I mildly suggested the words—Hottentot,
Pickpocket, and cannibal, Tartar, and thief,

As gentle expletives which might give relief;
But this only proved as a spark to the powder,
And the storm I had raised came faster and
     louder;
It blew and it rained, thundered, lightened, and
     hailed
Interjections, verbs, pronouns, till language quite
     failed
To express the abusive, and then its arrears
Were brought up all at once by a torrent of tears,
And my last faint, despairing attempt at an obs-
Ervation was lost in a tempest of sobs.

Well, I felt for the lady, and felt for my hat, too,
Improvised on the crown of the latter a tattoo,
In lieu of expressing the feelings which lay
Quite too deep for words, as Wordsworth would
     say;
Then, without going through the form of a bow,
Found myself in the entry—I hardly knew how,—
On doorstep and sidewalk, past lamp-post and
     square,
At home and up-stairs, in my own easy-chair;
   Poked my feet into slippers, my fire into blaze,
And said to myself, as I lit my cigar,
" Supposing a man had the wealth of the Czar
   Of the Russias to boot, for the rest of his days,
On the whole, do you think he would have much
     to spare,
If he married a woman with nothing to wear? "

Since that night, taking pains that it should not
     be bruited

Abroad in society, I 've instituted
A course of inquiry, extensive and thorough,
On this vital subject, and find, to my horror,
That the fair Flora's case is by no means sur-
      prising,
   But that there exists the greatest distress
In our female community, solely arising
   From this unsupplied destitution of dress,
Whose unfortunate victims are filling the air
With the pitiful wail of " Nothing to wear."
Researches in some of the " Upper Ten " districts
Reveal the most painful and startling statistics,
Of which let me mention only a few:
In one single house, on the Fifth Avenue,
Three young ladies were found, all below twenty-
      two,
Who have been three whole weeks without any-
      thing new
In the way of flounced silks, and thus left in the
      lurch
Are unable to go to ball, concert, or church.
In another large mansion, near the same place,
Was found a deplorable, heart-rending case
Of entire destitution of Brussels point-lace.
In a neighboring block there was found, in three
      calls,
Total want, long continued, of camel's-hair
      shawls;
And a suffering family, whose case exhibits
The most pressing need of real ermine tippets;
One deserving young lady almost unable
To survive for the want of a new Russian sable;

Still another, whose tortures have been most ter-
    rific
Ever since the sad loss of the steamer Pacific,
In which were engulfed, not friend or relation
(For whose fate she perhaps might have found
    consolation,
Or borne it, at least, with serene resignation),
But the choicest assortment of French sleeves and
    collars
Ever sent out from Paris, worth thousands of
    dollars,
And all as to style most *recherché* and rare,
The want of which leaves her with nothing to
    wear,
And renders her life so drear and dyspeptic
That she 's quite a recluse, and almost a sceptic;
For she touchingly says that this sort of grief
Cannot find in Religion the slightest relief,
And Philosophy has not a maxim to spare
For the victim of such overwhelming despair.
But the saddest by far of all these sad features
Is the cruelty practised upon the poor creatures
By husbands and fathers, real Bluebeards and
    Timons,
Who resist the most touching appeals made for
    diamonds
By their wives and their daughters, and leave them
    for days
Unsupplied with new jewelry, fans, or bouquets,
Even laugh at their miseries whenever they have
    a chance,
And deride their demands as useless extravagance.

One case of a bride was brought to my view,
Too sad for belief, but, alas! 't was too true,
Whose husband refused, as savage as Charon,
To permit her to take more than ten trunks to
    Sharon.
The consequence was, that when she got there,
At the end of three weeks she had nothing to
    wear,
And when she proposed to finish the season
At Newport, the monster refused out and out,
For his infamous conduct alleging no reason,
Except that the waters were good for his gout;
Such treatment as this was too shocking, of
    course,
And proceedings are now going on for divorce.

But why harrow the feelings by lifting the cur-
    tain
From these scenes of woe?  Enough, it is certain
Has here been disclosed to stir up the pity
Of every benevolent heart in the city,
And spur up Humanity into a canter
To rush and relieve these sad cases instanter.
Won't somebody, moved by this touching descrip-
    tion,
Come forward to-morrow and head a subscription?
Won't some kind philanthropist, seeing that aid is
So needed at once by these indigent ladies,
Take charge of the matter? Or won't Peter
    Cooper
The corner-stone lay of some new splendid super-
Structure, like that which to-day links his name
In the Union unending of Honor and Fame;

And found a new charity just for the care
Of these unhappy women with nothing to wear,
Which, in view of the cash which would daily be
    claimed,
The *Laying-out* Hospital well might be named?
Won't Stewart, or some of our dry-goods im-
    porters,
Take a contract for clothing our wives and our
    daughters?
Or, to furnish the cash to supply these distresses,
And life's pathway strew with shawls, collars, and
    dresses,
For poor womankind, won't some venturesome
    lover
A new California somewhere discover?

O ladies, dear ladies, the next sunny day
Please trundle your hoops just out of Broadway,
From its whirl and its bustle, its fashion and
    pride,
And temples of Trade which tower on each side,
To the alleys and lanes, where Misfortune and
    Guilt
Their children have gathered, their city have built;
Where Hunger and Vice, like twin beasts of prey,
    Have hunted their victims to gloom and de-
    spair;
Raise the rich, dainty dress, and the fine broi-
    dered skirt,
Pick your delicate way through the dampness and
    dirt,
    Grope through the dark dens, climb the rickety
    stair
15

To the garret, where wretches, the young and the
    old,
Half starved and half naked, lie crouched from the
    cold.
See those skeleton limbs, those frost-bitten feet,
All bleeding and bruised by the stones of the
    street;
Hear the sharp cry of childhood, the deep groans
    that swell
    From the poor dying creature who writhes on
      the floor;
Hear the curses that sound like the echoes of Hell,
    As you sicken and shudder and fly from the
      door;
Then home to your wardrobes, and say, if you
    dare—
Spoiled children of Fashion—you've nothing to
    wear!

And O, if perchance there should be a sphere
Where all is made right which so puzzles us here,
Where the glare and the glitter and tinsel of Time
Fade and die in the light of that region sublime,
Where the soul, disenchanted of flesh and of sense,
Unscreened by its trappings and shows and pre-
    tence,
Must be clothed for the life and the service above,
With purity, truth, faith, meekness, and love;
O daughters of Earth! foolish virgins, beware!
Lest in that upper realm you have nothing to
    wear!

               WILLIAM ALLEN BUTLER.

## THE SEA.

SHE was rich and of high degree;
A poor and unknown artist he.
" Paint me," she said, " a view of the sea."

So he painted the sea as it looked the day
That Aphroditè arose from its spray;
And it broke, as she gazed on its face the while,
Into its countless-dimpled smile.
" What a poky, stupid picture!" said she:
" I don't believe he *can* paint the sea!"

Then he painted a raging, tossing sea,
Storming, with fierce and sudden shock,
A towering, mighty fastness-rock;—
In its sides, above those leaping crests,
The thronging sea-birds built their nests.
" What a disagreeable daub!" said she:
" Why, it isn't anything like the sea!"

Then he painted a stretch of hot brown sand,
With a big hotel on either hand,
And a handsome pavilion for the band;—
Not a sign of water to be seen,
Except one faint little streak of green.
" What a perfectly exquisite picture!" said she:
" It's the very *image* of the sea!"

EVA L. OGDEN.

## THE PROUD MISS MACBRIDE.

### A LEGEND OF GOTHAM.

O, TERRIBLY proud was Miss MacBride,
The very personification of pride,
As she minced along in fashion's tide,
Adown Broadway—on the proper side—
    When the golden sun was setting;
There was pride in the head she carried so high,
Pride in her lip, and pride in her eye,
And a world of pride in the very sigh
    That her stately bosom was fretting!

O, terribly proud was Miss MacBride,
Proud of her beauty, and proud of her pride,
And proud of fifty matters beside—
    That wouldn't have borne dissection;
Proud of her wit, and proud of her walk,
Proud of her teeth, and proud of her talk,
Proud of " knowing cheese from chalk,"
    On a very slight inspection!

Proud abroad, and proud at home,
Proud wherever she chanced to come—
When she was glad, and when she was glum;
    Proud as the head of a Saracen
Over the door of a tippling-shop!—
Proud as a duchess, proud as a fop,
" Proud as a boy with a brand-new top,"
    Proud beyond comparison!

It seems a singular thing to say,
But her very senses led her astray
    Respecting all humility;
In sooth, her dull auricular drum
Could find in *humble* only a " hum,"
And heard no sound of " gentle " come,
    In talking about gentility.

What *lowly* meant she didn't know,
For she always avoided " everything low,"
    With care the most punctilious;
And, queerer still, the audible sound
Of " super-silly " she never had found
    In the adjective supercilious!

The meaning of *meek* she never knew,
But imagined the phrase had something to do
With " Moses," a peddling German Jew,
Who, like all hawkers, the country through,
    Was " a person of no position; "
And it seemed to her exceedingly plain,
If the word was really known to pertain
To a vulgar German, it wasn't germane
    To a lady of high condition!

Even her graces—not her grace—
For that was in the " vocative case "—
Chilled with the touch of her icy face,
    Sat very stiffly upon her!
She never confessed a favor aloud,
Like one of the simple, common crowd—
But coldly smiled, and faintly bowed,
As who should say, " You do me proud,
    And do yourself an honor! "

And yet the pride of Miss MacBride,
Although it had fifty hobbies to ride,
   Had really no foundation;
But, like the fabrics that gossips devise—
Those single stories that often arise
And grow till they reach a four-story size—
   Was merely a fancy creation!


Her birth, indeed, was uncommonly high—
For Miss MacBride first opened her eye
Through a skylight dim, on the light of the sky;
   But pride is a curious passion—
And in talking about her wealth and worth,
She always forgot to mention her birth
   To people of rank and fashion!


Of all the notable things on earth,
The queerest one is pride of birth
   Among our " fierce democracie "!
A bridge across a hundred years,
Without a prop to save it from sneers,—
Not even a couple of rotten *peers*,—
A thing for laughter, fleers, and jeers,
   Is American aristocracy!


English and Irish, French and Spanish,
German, Italian, Dutch and Danish,
Crossing their veins until they vanish
   In one conglomeration!
So subtle a tangle of blood, indeed,
No Heraldry Harvey will ever succeed
   In finding the circulation.

Depend upon it, my snobbish friend,
Your family thread you can't ascend,
Without good reason to apprehend
You may find it waxed, at the farther end,
    By some plebeian vocation!
Or, worse than that, your boasted line
May end in a loop of *stronger* twine,
    That plagued some worthy relation!

But Miss MacBride had something beside
Her lofty birth to nourish her pride—
For rich was the old paternal MacBride,
    According to public rumor;
And he lived " up town," in a splendid square,
And kept his daughter on dainty fare,
And gave her gems that were rich and rare,
And the finest rings and things to wear,
    And feathers enough to plume her.

A thriving tailor begged her hand,
But she gave " the fellow " to understand,
    By a violent manual action,
She perfectly scorned the best of his clan,
And reckoned the ninth of any man
    An exceedingly vulgar fraction!

Another, whose sign was a golden boot,
Was mortified with a bootless suit,
    In a way that was quite appalling;
For, though a regular *sutor* by trade,
He wasn't a suitor to suit the maid,
Who cut him off with a saw—and bade
    " The cobbler keep to his calling!"

A rich tobacconist comes and sues,
And, thinking the lady would scarce refuse
A man of his wealth, and liberal views,
Began, at once, with " If you *choose*—
        And could you really love him—"
But the lady spoiled his speech in a huff,
With an answer rough and ready enough,
To let him know she was up to snuff,
        And altogether above him!


A young attorney, of winning grace,
Was scarce allowed to " open his face,"
Ere Miss MacBride had closed his case
        With true judicial celerity;
For the lawyer was poor, and " seedy " to boot,
And to say the lady discarded his *suit*,
        Is merely a double verity!


The last of those who came to court,
Was a lively beau, of the dapper sort,
" Without any visible means of support,"
        A crime by no means flagrant
In one who wears an elegant coat,
But the very point on which they vote
        A ragged fellow " a vagrant!"


Now dapper Jim his courtship plied
(I wish the fact could be denied)
With an eye to the purse of the old MacBride,
        And really " nothing shorter!"
For he said to himself, in his greedy lust,
" Whenever he dies—as die he must—
And yields to Heaven his vital trust,

He 's very sure to ' come down with his dust,'
    In behalf of his only daughter."


And the very magnificent Miss MacBride,
Half in love, and half in pride,
    Quite graciously relented;
And, tossing her head, and turning her back,
No token of proper pride to lack—
To be a bride, without the " Mac,"
    With much disdain, consented!


Old John MacBride, one fatal day,
Became the unresisting prey
    Of fortune's undertakers;
And staking all on a single die,
His foundered bark went high and dry
    Among the brokers and breakers!


But, alas, for the haughty Miss MacBride,
'T was such a shock to her precious pride!
She couldn't recover, although she tried
    Her jaded spirits to rally;
'T was a dreadful change in human affairs,
From a place " up town " to a nook " up stairs,"
    From an avenue down to an alley!


'T was little condolence she had, God wot,
From her " troops of friends," who hadn't forgot
    The airs she used to borrow!
They had civil phrases enough, but yet
'T was plain to see that their " deepest regret "
    Was a different thing from sorrow!

And one of those chaps who make a **pun,**
As if it were quite legitimate fun
To be blazing away at every one
With a regular, double-loaded gun—
    Remarked that moral transgression
Always brings retributive stings
To candle-makers as well as kings;
For " making light of *cereous* things "
    Was a very *wick*-ed profession!

And vulgar people—the saucy churls—
Inquired about " the price of pearls,"
    And mocked at her situation:
" She wasn't ruined—they ventured to hope—
Because she was poor, she needn't mope;
Few people were better off for *soap,*
    And that was a consolation! "

And to make her cup of woe run over,
Her elegant, ardent plighted lover
    Was the very first to forsake her;
" He quite regretted the step, 't was true—
The lady had pride enough ' for two,'
But that alone would never do
    To quiet the butcher and baker! "

And now the unhappy Miss MacBride—
The merest ghost of her early pride—
    Bewails her lonely position;
Cramped in the very narrowest niche,
Above the poor, and below the rich—
    Was ever a worse condition!

MORAL.

Because you flourish in worldly affairs,
Don't be haughty, and put on airs,
    With insolent pride of station!
Don't be proud, and turn up your nose
At poorer people in plainer clothes,
But learn, for the sake of your mind's repose,
That wealth 's a bubble that comes—and goes!
And that all proud flesh, wherever it grows,
    Is subject to irritation!

                JOHN GODFREY SAXE.

---

## ON AN OLD MUFF.

TIME has a magic wand!
What is this meets my hand,
Moth-eaten, mouldy, and
    Covered with fluff,
Faded and stiff and scant?
Can it be? no, it can't,—
Yes,—I declare 't is Aunt
    Prudence's Muff!

Years ago—twenty-three!
Old Uncle Barnaby
Gave it to Aunty P.,
    Laughing and teasing,—
" Pru. of the breezy curls,
Whisper these solemn churls,
*What holds a pretty girl's*
    *Hand without squeezing?* "

Uncle was then a lad,
Gay, but, I grieve to add,
Gone to what 's called " the bad,"—
    Smoking,—and worse!
Sleek sable then was this
Muff, lined with *pinkiness*,—
Bloom to which beauty is
    Seldom averse.

I see in retrospect
Aunt, in her best bedecked,
Gliding, with mien erect,
    Gravely to meeting:
Psalm-book, and kerchief new,
Peeped from the Muff of Pru.,
Young men—and pious, too—
    Giving her greeting.

Pure was the life she led
Then: from her Muff, 't is said,
Tracts she distributed;—
    Scapegraces many,
Seeing the grace they lacked,
Followed her; one attacked
Prudence, and got his tract,
    Oftener than any!

Love has a potent spell!
Soon this bold ne'er-do-well,
Aunt's sweet susceptible
    Heart undermining,
Slipped, so the scandal runs,
Notes in the pretty nun's

Muff,—triple-cornered ones,—
　　Pink as its lining!

Worse, even, soon the jade
Fled (to oblige her blade!)
Whilst her friends thought that they 'd
　　Locked her up tightly:
After such shocking games,
Aunt is of wedded dames
Gayest,—and now her name 's
　　Mrs. Golightly.

In female conduct flaw
Sadder I never saw,
Still I 've faith in the law
　　Of compensation.
Once uncle went astray,—
Smoked, joked, and swore away;
Sworn by, he 's now, by a
　　Large congregation!

Changed is the child of sin;
Now he 's (he once was thin)
Grave, with a double chin,—
　　Blest be his fat form!
Changed is the garb he wore:
Preacher was never more
Prized than is uncle for
　　Pulpit or platform.

If all 's as best befits
Mortals of slender wits,
Then beg this Muff, and its
　　Fair owner pardon;

*All's for the best,*—indeed,
Such is my simple creed ;
Still I must go and weed
    Hard in my garden.

FREDERICK LOCKER-LAMPSON

---

## HOW PADDY GOT "UNDER GOVERN-MENT."

A PLACE under Government
    Was all that Paddy wanted.
He married soon a scolding wife,
    And thus his wish was granted.

ANONYMOUS.

# II.

## MISCELLANEOUS.

------

### SAINT ANTHONY'S SERMON TO THE FISHES.

Saint Anthony at church
Was left in the lurch,
So he went to the ditches
And preached to the fishes;
They wriggled their tails,
In the sun glanced their scales.

The carps, with their spawn,
Are all hither drawn;
Have opened their jaws,
Eager for each clause.
No sermon beside
Had the carps so edified.

Sharp-snouted pikes,
Who keep fighting like tikes,
Now swam up harmonious
To hear Saint Antonius.
No sermon beside
Had the pikes so edified.

And that very odd fish,
Who loves fast-days, the cod-fish,—
The stock-fish, I mean,—
At the sermon was seen.
    No sermon beside
    Had the cods so edified.

Good eels and sturgeon,
Which aldermen gorge on,
Went out of their way
To hear preaching that day.
    No sermon beside
    Had the eels so edified.

Crabs and turtles also,
Who always move slow,
Made haste from the bottom,
As if the Devil had got 'em.
    No sermon beside
    Had the crabs so edified.

Fish great and fish small,
Lords, lackeys, and all,
Each looked at the preacher
Like a reasonable creature:
    At God's word,
    They Anthony heard.

The sermon now ended,
Each turned and descended;
The pikes went on stealing,
The eels went on eeling:
    Much delighted were they,
    But preferred the old way.

The crabs are backsliders,
The stock-fish thick-siders,
The carps are sharp-set;
All the sermon forget:
    Much delighted were they,
    But preferred the old way.

ANONYMOUS.

------

## KING JOHN AND THE ABBOT OF CANTERBURY.

### FROM "PERCY'S RELIQUES."

An ancient story I 'll tell you anon
Of a notable prince that was called King John;
And he ruled England with main and with might,
For he did great wrong, and maintained little
    right.

And I 'll tell you a story, a story so merry,
Concerning the Abbot of Canterbury;
How for his house-keeping and high renowne,
They rode poste for him to fair London towne.

An hundred men the king did heare say,
The abbot kept in his house every day;
And fifty golde chaynes without any doubt,
In velvet coates waited the abbot about.

" How now, father abbot, I hear it of thee,
Thou keepest a farre better house than mee;
And for thy house-keeping and high renowne,
I feare thou work'st treason against my crowne."

16

"My liege," quo' the abbot, "I would it were
      knowne
I never spend nothing, but what is my owne;
And I trust your grace will doe me no deere,
For spending of my owne true-gotten geere."

"Yes, yes, father abbot, thy fault it is highe,
And now for the same thou needest must dye;
For except thou canst answer me questions three,
Thy head shall be smitten from thy bodie.

"And first," quo' the king, "when I'm in this
      stead,
With my crowne of golde so faire on my head,
Among all my liege-men so noble of birthe,
Thou must tell me to one penny what I am worthe.

"Secondly, tell me, without any doubt,
How soone I may ride the whole world about;
And at the third question thou must not shrink,
But tell me here truly what I do think."

"O these are hard questions for my shallow witt.
Nor I cannot answer your grace as yet:
But if you will give me but three weeks' space,
Ile do my endeavor to answer your grace."

"Now three weeks' space to thee will I give,
And that is the longest time thou hast to live;
For if thou dost not answer my questions three,
Thy lands and the livings are forfeit to mee."

Away rode the abbot all sad at that word,
And he rode to Cambridge, and Oxenford;

But never a doctor there was so wise,
That could with his learning an answer devise.

Then home rode the abbot of comfort so cold,
And he met his shepheard a-going to fold:
" How now, my lord abbot, you are welcome home;
What news do you bring us from good King
    John? "

" Sad news, sad news, shepheard, I must give,
That I have but three days more to live;
For if I do not answer him questions three,
My head will be smitten from my bodie.

" The first is to tell him, there in that stead,
With his crowne of golde so fair on his head,
Among all his liege-men so noble of birth,
To within one penny of what he is worth.

" The seconde, to tell him without any doubt,
How soone he may ride this whole world about;
And at the third question I must not shrinke,
But tell him there truly what he does thinke."

" Now cheare up, sire abbot, did you never hear
    yet,
That a fool he may learne a wise man witt?
Lend me horse, and serving-men, and your ap-
    parel,
And Ile ride to London to answere youre quarrel.

" Nay, frowne not, if it hath bin told unto me,
I am like your lordship, as ever may be;

And if you will but lend me your gowne,
There is none shall know us at fair London
    towne."

" Now horses and serving-men thou shalt have,
With sumptuous array most gallant and brave,
With crozier, and mitre, and rochet, and cope,
Fit to appear 'fore our fader the pope."

" Now welcome, sire abbot," the king he did say,
" 'T is well thou 'rt come back to keepe thy day :
For and if thou canst answer my questions three,
Thy life and thy living both savèd shall be.

" And first, when thou seest me here in this stead,
With my crowne of golde so fair on my head,
Among all my liege-men so noble of birthe,
Tell me to one penny what I am worthe."

" For thirty pence our Saviour was sold
Among the false Jews, as I have bin told,
And twenty-nine is the worth of thee,
For I thinke thou art one penny worser than he."

The king he laughed, and swore by Saint Bittel,
" I did not think I had been worth so littel !
—Now secondly tell me, without any doubt,
How soone I may ride this whole world about."

" You must rise with the sun, and ride with the
    same
Until the next morning he riseth againe;
And then your grace need not make any doubt
But in twenty-four hours you 'll ride it about."

The king he laughed, and swore by Saint Jone,
" I did not think it could be gone so soone!
—Now from the third question thou must not
    shrinke,
But tell me here truly what I do thinke."

" Yea, that shall I do, and make your grace merry;
You thinke I 'm the Abbot of Canterbury;
But I 'm his poor shepheard, as plain you may
    see,
That am come to beg pardon for him and for me."

The king he laughed, and swore by the Masse,
" Ile make thee lord abbot this day in his place!"
" Now naye, my liege, be not in such speede,
For alacke I can neither write ne reade."

" Four nobles a week then I will give thee,
For this merry jest thou hast showne unto me;
And tell the old abbot when thou comest home,
Thou hast brought him a pardon from good King
    John."

ANONYMOUS.

------

## GLUGGITY GLUG.

FROM " THE MYRTLE AND THE VINE."

A JOLLY fat friar loved liquor good store,
    And he had drunk stoutly at supper;
He mounted his horse in the night at the door,
    And sat with his face to the crupper:

" Some rogue," quoth the friar, " quite dead to
    remorse,
  Some thief, whom a halter will throttle,
Some scoundrel has cut off the head of my horse,
  While I was engaged at the bottle,
      Which went gluggity, gluggity—glug—glug
      —glug."

The tail of the steed pointed south on the dale,
  'T was the friar's road home, straight and level;
But, when spurred, a horse follows his nose, not
    his tail,
  So he scampered due north, like a devil:
" This new mode of docking," the friar then said,
  " I perceive doesn't make a horse trot ill;
And 't is cheap,—for he never can eat off his head
  While I am engaged at the bottle,
      Which goes gluggity, gluggity—glug—glug
      —glug."

The steed made a stop,—in a pond he had got,
  He was rather for drinking than grazing;
Quoth the friar, " 'T is strange headless horses
    should trot,
  But to drink with their tails is amazing!"
Turning round to see whence this phenomenon
    rose,
  In the pond fell this son of a pottle;
Quoth he, " The head 's found, for I 'm under his
    nose,—
  I wish I were over a bottle,
      Which goes gluggity, gluggity—glug—glug
      —glug!"

          GEORGE COLMAN THE YOUNGER.

# I AM A FRIAR OF ORDERS GRAY.

### FROM THE OPERA OF "ROBIN HOOD."

I AM a friar of orders gray,
And down in the valleys I take my way;
I pull not blackberry, haw, or hip,—
Good store of venison fills my scrip;
My long bead-roll I merrily chant;
Where'er I walk no money I want;
And why I 'm so plump the reason I tell,—
Who leads a good life is sure to live well.
    What baron or squire,
    Or knight of the shire,
    Lives half so well as a holy friar?

After supper of heaven I dream,
But that is a pullet and clouted cream;
Myself, by denial, I mortify—
With a dainty bit of a warden-pie;
I 'm clothed in sackcloth for my sin,—
With old sack wine I 'm lined within;
A chirping cup is my matin song,
And the vesper's bell is my bowl, ding dong.
    What baron or squire,
    Or knight of the shire,
    Lives half so well as a holy friar?

              JOHN O'KEEFFE.

## GOOD ALE.

I CANNOT eat but little meat,—
  My stomach is not good;
But, sure, I think that I can drink
  With him that wears a hood.
Though I go bare, take ye no care;
  I nothing am a-cold,—
I stuff my skin so full within
  Of jolly good ale and old.
    *Back and side go bare, go bare;*
      *Both foot and hand go cold;*
    *But, belly, God send thee good ale enough,*
      *Whether it be new or old!*


I love no roast but a nut-brown toast,
  And a crab laid in the fire;
A little bread shall do me stead,—
  Much bread I not desire.
No frost, nor snow, nor wind, I trow,
  Can hurt me if I wold,—
I am so wrapt, and thorowly lapt
  Of jolly good ale and old.
    *Back and side,* etc.


And Tyb, my wife, that as her life
  Loveth well good ale to seek,
Full oft drinks she, till you may see
  The tears run down her cheek;
Then doth she trowl to me the bowl,
  Even as a malt-worm should;

And saith, " Sweetheart, I took my part
  Of this jolly good ale and old."
    *Back and side,* etc.

Now let them drink till they nod and wink,
  Even as good fellows should do;
They shall not miss to have the bliss
  Good ale doth bring men to;
And all poor souls that have scoured bowls,
  Or have them lustily trowled,
God save the lives of them and their wives,
  Whether they be young or old!
    *Back and side go bare, go bare;*
      *Both foot and hand go cold;*
    *But, belly, God send thee good ale enough,*
      *Whether it be new or old!*
                JOHN STILL.

---

## THE PILGRIMS AND THE PEAS.

A BRACE of sinners, for no good,
  Were ordered to the Virgin Mary's shrine,
Who at Loretto dwelt, in wax, stone, wood,
  And in a fair white wig looked wondrous fine.
Fifty long miles had those sad rogues to travel,
With something in their shoes much worse than
      gravel;
In short, their toes so gentle to amuse,
The priest had ordered peas into their shoes:
A nostrum famous in old popish times
For purifying souls that stunk of crimes:
    A sort of apostolic salt,
    Which popish parsons for its powers exalt,

For keeping souls of sinners sweet,
Just as our kitchen salt keeps meat.

The knaves set off on the same day,
Peas in their shoes, to go and pray;
    But very different was their speed, I wot:
One of the sinners galloped on,
Swift as a bullet from a gun;
    The other limped, as if he had been shot.
One saw the Virgin soon, Peccavi cried,
    Had his soul whitewashed all so clever;
Then home again he nimbly hied,
    Made fit with saints above to live forever.

In coming back, however, let me say,
He met his brother rogue about half-way,—
Hobbling, with outstretched arms and bended
        knees,
Cursing the souls and bodies of the peas;
His eyes in tears, his cheeks and brow in sweat,
Deep sympathizing with his groaning feet.

" How now," the light-toed, whitewashed pilgrim
        broke,
    " You lazy lubber! "
" Ods curse it! " cried the other, " 't is no joke;
My feet, once hard as any rock,
    Are now as soft as blubber.

" Excuse me, Virgin Mary, that I swear,
As for Loretto, I shall not get there;
No, to the devil my sinful soul must go,
For damme if I ha'n't lost every toe.
But, brother sinner, pray explain

How 't is that you are not in pain.
What power hath worked a wonder for your
    toes,
Whilst I just like a snail am crawling,
Now swearing, now on saints devoutly bawling,
    Whilst not a rascal comes to ease my woes?

" How is 't that you can like a greyhound go,
    Merry as if that naught had happened, burn
        ye!"
"Why," cried the other, grinning, "you must
        know,
That just before I ventured on my journey,
    To walk a little more at ease,
    I took the liberty to *boil my peas.*"

DR. JOHN WOLCOTT (Peter Pindar).

---

## THE VICAR OF BRAY.*

In good King Charles's golden days,
    When loyalty no harm meant,
A zealous high-churchman was I,
    And so I got preferment.

* " The Vicar of Bray in Berkshire, England, was
Simon Alleyn, or Allen, who held his place from 1540 to
1588. He was a Papist under the reign of Henry the
Eighth, and a Protestant under Edward the Sixth. He was
a Papist again under Mary, and once more became a Protestant in the reign of Elizabeth. When this scandal to
the gown was reproached for his versatility of religious
creeds, and taxed for being a turn-coat and an inconstant
changeling, as Fuller expresses it, he replied : ' Not so
neither ; for if I changed my religion, I am sure I kept
true to my principle, which is to live and die the Vicar of
Bray.' "—DISRAELI.

To teach my flock I never missed:
  Kings were by God appointed,
And lost are those that dare resist
  Or touch the Lord's anointed.
    *And this is law that I 'll maintain*
      *Until my dying day, sir,*
    *That whatsoever king shall reign,*
      *Still I 'll be the Vicar of Bray, sir.*

When royal James possessed the crown,
  And popery came in fashion,
The penal laws I hooted down,
  And read the Declaration;
The Church of Rome I found would fit
  Full well my constitution;
And I had been a Jesuit
  But for the Revolution.
    *And this is law,* etc.

When William was our king declared,
  To ease the nation's grievance;
With this new wind about I steered,
  And swore to him allegiance;
Old principles I did revoke,
  Set conscience at a distance;
Passive obedience was a joke,
  A jest was non-resistance.
    *And this is law,* etc.

When royal Anne became our queen,
  The Church of England's glory,
Another face of things was seen,
  And I became a Tory;

Occasional conformists base,
  I blamed their moderation;
And thought the Church in danger was,
  By such prevarication.
    *And this is law,* etc.


When George in pudding-time came o'er,
  And moderate men looked big, sir,
My principles I changed once more,
  And so became a Whig, sir;
And thus preferment I procured
  From our new faith's-defender,
And almost every day adjured
  The Pope and the Pretender.
    *And this is law,* etc.


The illustrious house of Hanover,
  And Protestant succession,
To these I do allegiance swear—
  While they can keep possession:
For in my faith and loyalty
  I nevermore will falter,
And George my lawful king shall be—
  Until the times do alter.
    *And this is law that I 'll maintain*
    *Until my dying day, sir,*
    *That whatsoever king shall reign,*
    *Still I 'll be the Vicar of Bray, sir.*

ANONYMOUS.

## HUDIBRAS' SWORD AND DAGGER.

FROM " HUDIBRAS," PART I.

His puissant sword unto his side
Near his undaunted heart was tied,
With basket hilt that would hold broth,
And serve for fight and dinner both.
In it he melted lead for bullets
To shoot at foes, and sometimes pullets,
To whom he bore so fell a grutch
He ne'er gave quarter to any such.
The trenchant blade, Toledo trusty,
For want of fighting was grown rusty,
And ate into itself, for lack
Of somebody to hew and hack.
The peaceful scabbard, where it dwelt,
The rancor of its edge had felt;
For of the lower end two handful
It had devoured, it was so manful;
And so much scorned to lurk in case,
As if it durst not show its face.

.　　.　　.　　.　　.　　.

This sword a dagger had, his page,
That was but little for his age,
And therefore waited on him so
As dwarfs unto knight-errants do.
It was a serviceable dudgeon,
Either for fighting or for drudging.
When it had stabbed or broke a head,
It would scrape trenchers or chip bread,
Toast cheese or bacon, though it were

To bait a mouse-trap 't would not care;
'T would make clean shoes, and in the earth
Set leeks and onions, and so forth:
It had been 'prentice to a brewer,
Where this and more it did endure;
But left the trade, as many more
Have lately done on the same score.

DR. SAMUEL BUTLER.

---

## THE FINE OLD ENGLISH GENTLEMAN.*

I 'll sing you a good old song,
  Made by a good old pate,
Of a fine old English gentleman
  Who had an old estate,
And who kept up his old mansion
  At a bountiful old rate;
With a good old porter to relieve
  The old poor at his gate,
Like a fine old English gentleman
  All of the olden time.

His hall so old was hung around
  With pikes and guns and bows,
And swords, and good old bucklers,
  That had stood some tough old blows;
'T was there " his worship " held his state
  In doublet and trunk hose,
And quaffed his cup of good old sack,
  To warm his good old nose,
      Like a fine, etc.

* Modelled upon an old black-letter song, called " The
Old and Young Courtier."

When winter's cold brought frost and snow,
  He opened house to all;
And though threescore and ten his years,
  He featly led the ball;
Nor was the houseless wanderer
  E'er driven from his hall;
For while he feasted all the great,
  He ne'er forgot the small;
      Like a fine, etc.

But time, though old, is strong in flight,
  And years rolled swiftly by;
And Autumn's falling leaves proclaimed
  This good old man must die!
He laid him down right tranquilly,
  Gave up life's latest sigh;
And mournful stillness reigned around,
  And tears bedewed each eye,
      For this good, etc.

Now surely this is better far
  Than all the new parade
Of theatres and fancy balls,
  "At home" and masquerade:
And much more economical,
  For all his bills were paid.
Then leave your new vagaries quite,
  And take up the old trade
Of a fine old English gentleman,
  All of the olden time.

                  ANONYMOUS.

## TOBY TOSSPOT.

Alas! what pity 't is that regularity,
   Like Isaac Shove's, is such a rarity!
But there are swilling wights in London town,
   Termed jolly dogs, choice spirits, alias swine,
Who pour, in midnight revel, bumpers down,
   Making their throats a thoroughfare for wine.

These spendthrifts, who life's pleasures thus run
      on,
   Dozing with headaches till the afternoon,
Lose half men's regular estate of sun,
   By borrowing too largely of the moon.

One of this kidney—Toby Tosspot hight—
Was coming from the Bedford late at night;
   And being *Bacchi plenus,* full of wine,
      Although he had a tolerable notion
      Of aiming at progressive motion,
   'T wasn't direct,—'t was serpentine.
He worked with sinuosities, along,
Like Monsieur Corkscrew, worming through a
      cork,
Not straight, like Corkscrew's proxy, stiff Don
      Prong,—a fork.

At length, with near four bottles in his pate,
He saw the moon shining on Shove's brass plate,
When reading, " Please to ring the bell,"
   And being civil beyond measure,
   17

"Ring it!" says Toby,—"very well;
  I'll ring it with a deal of pleasure."
Toby, the kindest soul in all the town,
Gave it a jerk that almost jerked it down.

He waited full two minutes,—no one came;
  He waited full two minutes more;—and then
Says Toby, "If he's deaf, I'm not to blame;
  I'll pull it for the gentleman again."

But the first peal woke Isaac in a fright,
  Who, quick as lightning, popping up his head,
  Sat on his head's antipodes, in bed,
Pale as a parsnip,—bolt upright.

At length he wisely to himself doth say, calming
    his fears,—
"Tush! 't is some fool has rung and run away;"
When peal the second rattled in his ears.

Shove jumped into the middle of the floor;
  And, trembling at each breath of air that
    stirred,
He groped down stairs, and opened the street
    door,
  While Toby was performing peal the third.

Isaac eyed Toby, fearfully askant,
  And saw he was a strapper, stout and tall;
Then put this question, "Pray, sir, what d'ye
    want?"
  Says Toby, "I want nothing sir, at all."

"Want nothing! Sir, you 've pulled my bell, I
　　vow,
　As if you 'd jerk it off the wire."
Quoth Toby, gravely making him a bow,
　" I pulled it, sir, at your desire."

"At mine?"　" Yes, yours; I hope I 've done
　　it well.
　High time for bed, sir; I was hastening to it;
But if you write up, ' Please to ring the bell,'
　Common politeness makes me stop and do it."

GEORGE COLMAN THE YOUNGER.

---

## THE MILKMAID.

A milkmaid, who poised a full pail on her head,
Thus mused on her prospects in life, it is said:
" Let me see,—I should think that this milk will
　　procure
One hundred good eggs, or fourscore, to be sure.

" Well then,—stop a bit,—it must not be for-
　　gotten,
Some of these may be broken, and some may be
　　rotten;
But if twenty for accident should be detached,
It will leave me just sixty sound eggs to be
　　hatched.

" Well, sixty sound eggs.—no, sound chickens, I
　　mean :
Of these some may die,—we 'll suppose seventeen,
Seventeen! not so many—say ten at the most,
Which will leave fifty chickens to boil or to roast.

" But then there's their barley: how much will
    they need?
Why, they take but one grain at a time when they
    feed,—
So that's a mere trifle; now then, let us see,
At a fair market price how much money there'll
    be.

" Six    shillings    a    pair—five—four—three-and-
    six.
To prevent all mistakes, that low price I will fix;
Now what will that make? fifty chickens, I said,—
Fifty times three-and-sixpence—*I 'll ask Brother
    Ned.*

" O, but stop,—three-and-sixpence a *pair* I must
    sell 'em ;
Well, a pair is a couple,—now then let us tell
    'em ;
A couple in fifty will go (my poor brain !)
Why, just a score times and five pair will remain.

" Twenty-five pair of fowls—now how tiresome
    it is
That I can't reckon up so much money as this!
Well, there's no use in trying, so let's give a
    guess,—
I 'll say twenty pounds, *and it can't be no less.*

" Twenty pounds, I am certain, will buy me a cow,
Thirty geese and two turkeys,—eight pigs and a
    sow;

Now if these turn out well, at the end of a year,
I shall fill both my pockets with guineas, 't is
    clear."

Forgetting her burden, when this she had said,
The maid superciliously tossed up her head;
When, alas for her prospects! her milk-pail de-
    scended,
And so all her schemes for the future were ended.

This moral, I think, may be safely attached,—
" Reckon not on your chickens before they are
    hatched."

JEFFREYS TAYLOR.

## MORNING MEDITATIONS.

LET Taylor preach, upon a morning breezy,
How well to rise while nights and larks are
    flying,—
For my part, getting up seems not so easy
      By half as *lying*.

What if the lark does carol in the sky,
Soaring beyond the sight to find him out,—
Wherefore am I to rise at such a fly?
      I 'm not a trout.

Talk not to me of bees and such-like hums,
The smell of sweet herbs at the morning prime,—
Only lie long enough, and bed becomes
      A bed of *time*.

To me Dan Phœbus and his car are naught,
His steeds that paw impatiently about,—
Let them enjoy, say I, as horses ought,
        The first turn-out!

Right beautiful the dewy meads appear
Besprinkled by the rosy-fingered girl;
What then,—if I prefer my pillow-beer
        To early pearl?

My stomach is not ruled by other men's,
And, grumbling for a reason, quaintly begs
Wherefore should master rise before the hens
        Have laid their eggs?

Why from a comfortable pillow start
To see faint flushes in the east awaken?
A fig, say I, for any streaky part,
        Excepting bacon.

An early riser Mr. Gray has drawn,
Who used to haste the dewy grass among,
" To meet the sun upon the upland lawn,"—
        Well,—he died young.

With charwomen such early hours agree,
And sweeps that earn betimes their bit and sup;
But I 'm no climbing boy, and need not be
        All up,—all up!

So here I lie, my morning calls deferring,
Till something nearer to the stroke of noon;—
A man that 's fond precociously of *stirring*
        Must be a spoon.

                                        THOMAS HOOD.

# ELEGY ON THE DEATH OF A MAD DOG.

Good people all, of every sort,
  Give ear unto my song;
And if you find it wondrous short,
  It cannot hold you long.

In Islington there was a man
  Of whom the world might say,
That still a godly race he ran—
  Whene'er he went to pray.

A kind and gentle heart he had,
  To comfort friends and foes:
The naked every day he clad—
  When he put on his clothes.

And in that town a dog was found,
  As many dogs there be,
Both mongrel, puppy, whelp, and hound,
  And curs of low degree.

This dog and man at first were friends;
  But when a pique began,
The dog to gain his private ends,
  Went mad, and bit the man.

Around from all the neighboring streets
  The wondering neighbors ran,
And swore the dog had lost his wits,
  To bite so good a man!

The wound it seemed both sore and sad
   To every Christian eye:
And while they swore the dog was mad,
   They swore the man would die.

But soon a wonder came to light,
   That showed the rogues they lied:—
The man recovered of the bite,
   The dog it was that died!

                  OLIVER GOLDSMITH.

## OLD GRIMES.

OLD GRIMES is dead, that good old man,—
   We ne'er shall see him more;
He used to wear a long black coat,
   All buttoned down before.

His heart was open as the day,
   His feelings all were true;
His hair was some inclined to gray,—
   He wore it in a queue.

Whene'er he heard the voice of pain,
   His breast with pity burned;
The large round head upon his cane
   From ivory was turned.

Kind words he ever had for all;
   He knew no base design;
His eyes were dark and rather small,
   His nose was aquiline.

He lived at peace with all mankind,
  In friendship he was true;
His coat had pocket-holes behind,
  His pantaloons were blue.

Unharmed, the sin which earth pollutes
  He passed securely o 'er,—
And never wore a pair of boots
  For thirty years or more.

But good Old Grimes is now at rest,
  Nor fears misfortune's frown;
He wore a double-breasted vest,—
  The stripes ran up and down.

He modest merit sought to find,
  And pay it its desert;
He had no malice in his mind,
  No ruffles on his shirt.

His neighbors he did not abuse,—
  Was sociable and gay;
He wore large buckles on his shoes,
  And changed them every day.

His knowledge, hid from public gaze,
  He did not bring to view,
Nor make a noise, town-meeting days,
  As many people do.

His worldly goods he never threw
  In trust to fortune's chances,
But lived (as all his brothers do)
  In easy circumstances.

Thus undisturbed by anxious cares
His peaceful moments ran;
And everybody said he was
A fine old gentleman.

ALBERT G. GREENE.

## ELEGY ON MADAM BLAIZE.

Good people all, with one accord,
Lament for Madam Blaize;
Who never wanted a good word—
From those who spoke her praise.

The needy seldom passed her door,
And always found her kind;
She freely lent to all the poor—
Who left a pledge behind.

She strove the neighborhood to please,
With manner wondrous winning;
She never followed wicked ways—
Unless when she was sinning.

At church, in silk and satins new,
With hoop of monstrous size,
She never slumbered in her pew—
But when she shut her eyes.

Her love was sought, I do aver,
By twenty beaux, or more;
The king himself has followed her—
When she has walked before.

But now her wealth and finery fled,
　　Her hangers-on cut short all,
Her doctors found, when she was dead—
　　Her last disorder mortal.

Let us lament, in sorrow sore;
　　For Kent Street well may say,
That, had she lived a twelvemonth more—
　　She had not died to-day.

　　　　　　　　　　　OLIVER GOLDSMITH.

---

## THE GRAVE–YARD.

### FROM " A FABLE FOR CRITICS."

LET us glance for a moment, 't is well worth the
　　pains,
And note what an average grave-yard contains;
There lie levellers levelled, duns done up them-
　　selves,
There are booksellers finally laid on their shelves,
Horizontally there lie upright politicians,
Dose-a-dose with their patients sleep faultless
　　physicians,
There are slave-drivers quietly whipt under-
　　ground,
There bookbinders, done up in boards, are fast
　　bound,
There card-players wait till the last trump be
　　played,
There all the choice spirits get finally laid,
There the babe that 's unborn is supplied with a
　　berth,

There men without legs get their six feet of earth,
There lawyers repose, each wrapt up in his case,
There seekers of office are sure of a place,
There defendant and plaintiff get equally cast,
There shoemakers quietly stick to the last,
There brokers at length become silent as stocks,
There stage-drivers sleep without quitting their
  box,
And so forth and so forth and so forth and so on,
With this kind of stuff one might endlessly go on;
To come to the point, I may safely assert you
Will find in each yard every cardinal virtue;
(And at this just conclusion will surely arrive,
That the goodness of earth is more dead than
  alive).

JAMES RUSSELL LOWELL.

## FAITHLESS NELLY GRAY.

### A PATHETIC BALLAD.

BEN BATTLE was a soldier bold,
  And used to war's alarms;
But a cannon-ball took off his legs,
  So he laid down his arms.

Now as they bore him off the field,
  Said he, " Let others shoot;
For here I leave my second leg,
  And the Forty-second Foot."

The army-surgeons made him limbs:
  Said he, " They 're only pegs;

But there 's as wooden members quite
    As represent my legs."


Now Ben he loved a pretty maid,—
    Her name was Nelly Gray;
So he went to pay her his devours,
    When he devoured his pay.


But when he called on Nelly Gray,
    She made him quite a scoff;
And when she saw his wooden legs,
    Began to take them off.


" O Nelly Gray! O Nelly Gray!
    Is this your love so warm?
The love that loves a scarlet coat
    Should be more uniform."


Said she, " I loved a soldier once,
    For he was blithe and brave;
But I will never have a man
    With both legs in the grave.


" Before you had those timber toes
    Your love I did allow;
But then, you know, you stand upon
    Another footing now."


" O Nelly Gray! O Nelly Gray!
    For all your jeering speeches,
At duty's call I left my legs
    In Badajos's breaches."

"Why, then," said she, "you 've lost the feet
    Of legs in war's alarms,
And now you cannot wear your shoes
    Upon your feats of arms!"

"O false and fickle Nelly Gray!
    I know why you refuse:
Though I 've no feet, some other man
    Is standing in my shoes.

"I wish I ne'er had seen your face;
    But, now a long farewell!
For you will be my death;—alas!
    You will not be my Nell!"

Now when he went from Nelly Gray
    His heart so heavy got,
And life was such a burden grown,
    It made him take a knot.

So round his melancholy neck
    A rope he did intwine,
And, for his second time in life,
    Enlisted in the Line.

One end he tied around a beam,
    And then removed his pegs;
And as his legs were off,—of course
    He soon was off his legs.

And there he hung till he was dead
    As any nail in town;
For, though distress had cut him up,
    It could not cut him down.

A dozen men sat on his corpse,
　To find out why he died,—
And they buried Ben in four cross-roads,
　With a stake in his inside.

THOMAS HOOD.

---

## FAITHLESS SALLY BROWN.

YOUNG BEN he was a nice young man,
　A carpenter by trade;
And he fell in love with Sally Brown,
　That was a lady's maid.

But as they fetched a walk one day,
　They met a press-gang crew;
And Sally she did faint away,
　Whilst Ben he was brought to.

The boatswain swore with wicked words
　Enough to shock a saint,
That, though she did seem in a fit,
　'T was nothing but a feint.

" Come, girl," said he, " hold up your head,
　He 'll be as good as me;
For when your swain is in our boat
　A boatswain he will be."

So when they 'd made their game of her,
　And taken off her elf,
She roused, and found she only was
　A coming to herself.

" And is he gone, and is he gone? "
  She cried and wept outright;
" Then I will to the water-side,
  And see him out of sight."

A waterman came up to her;
  " Now, young woman," said he,
" If you weep on so, you will make
  Eye-water in the sea."

" Alas! they 've taken my beau, Ben,
  To sail with old Benbow; "
And her woe began to run afresh,
  As if she 'd said, Gee woe!

Says he, " They 've only taken him
  To the tender-ship, you see."
" The tender-ship," cried Sally Brown,—
  " What a hard-ship that must be! "

" O, would I were a mermaid now,
  For then I 'd follow him!
But O, I 'm not a fish-woman,
  And so I cannot swim.

" Alas! I was not born beneath
  The Virgin and the Scales,
So I must curse my cruel stars,
  And walk about in Wales."

Now Ben had sailed to many a place
  That 's underneath the world;
But in two years the ship came home,
  And all her sails were furled.

But when he called on Sally Brown,
    To see how she got on,
He found she 'd got another Ben,
    Whose Christian-name was John.

" O Sally Brown! O Sally Brown!
    How could you serve me so?
I 've met with many a breeze before,
    But never such a blow! "

Then, reading on his 'bacco box,
    He heaved a heavy sigh,
And then began to eye his pipe,
    And then to pipe his eye.

And then he tried to sing, " All 's Well! "
    But could not, though he tried;
His head was turned,—and so he chewed
    His pigtail till he died.

His death, which happened in his berth,
    At forty-odd befell;
They went and told the sexton, and
    The sexton tolled the bell.

THOMAS HOOD.

## ORATOR PUFF.

MR. ORATOR PUFF had two tones in his voice,
    The one squeaking *thus,* and the other down *so;*
In each sentence he uttered he gave you your
        choice,
18

For one half was B alt, and the rest G below.
   O! O! Orator Puff,
   One voice for an orator's surely enough.


But he still talked away, spite of coughs and of
    frowns,
So distracting all ears with his ups and his
    downs,
That a wag once, on hearing the orator say,
   " My voice is for war!" asked, "Which of
    them, pray?"
   O! O! Orator Puff, etc.


Reeling homeward one evening, top-heavy with
    gin,
And rehearsing his speech on the weight of the
    crown,
He tripped near a saw-pit, and tumbled right in,
   " Sinking fund" the last words as his noddle
    came down.
   O! O! Orator Puff, etc.


" Good Lord!" he exclaimed, in his he-and-she
    tones,
   " HELP ME OUT! *Help me out!* I have broken
    my bones!"
" Help you out?" said a Paddy who passed,
   " what a bother!
Why, there's two of you there—can't you help
    one another?"
   O! O! Orator Puff,
   One voice for an orator's surely enough.

                   THOMAS MOORE.

## THE GOUTY MERCHANT AND THE STRANGER.

In Broad Street building (on a winter night),
Snug by his parlor-fire, a gouty wight
Sat all alone, with one hand rubbing
His feet rolled up in fleecy hose:
With t' other he 'd beneath his nose
The Public Ledger, in whose columns grubbing,
  He noted all the sales of hops,
  Ships, shops, and slops;
Gum, galls, and groceries; ginger, gin,
Tar, tallow, turmeric, turpentine, and tin;
When lo! a decent personage in black
Entered and most politely said,—
  "Your footman, sir, has gone his nightly track
  To the King's Head,
And left your door ajar; which I
Observed in passing by,
  And thought it neighborly to give you notice."
  "Ten thousand thanks; how very few get,
In time of danger,
Such kind attention from a stranger!
Assuredly, that fellow's throat is
Doomed to a final drop at Newgate:
He knows, too, (the unconscionable elf!)
That there 's no soul at home except myself."
  "Indeed," replied the stranger (looking grave),
  "Then he 's a double knave;
He knows that rogues and thieves by scores
Nightly beset unguarded doors:

And see, how easily might one
    Of these domestic foes,
    Even beneath your very nose,
Perform his knavish tricks;
Enter your room, as I have done,
Blow out your candles—thus—and thus—
Pocket your silver candlesticks,
    And—walk off—thus "—
So said, so done; he made no more remark
    Nor waited for replies,
    But marched off with his prize,
Leaving the gouty merchant in the dark.

HORACE SMITH.

## THE DIVERTING HISTORY OF JOHN GILPIN.

SHOWING HOW HE WENT FARTHER THAN
HE INTENDED, AND CAME SAFE
HOME AGAIN.

JOHN GILPIN was a citizen
    Of credit and renown,
A trainband captain eke was he
    Of famous London town.

John Gilpin's spouse said to her dear—
    " Though wedded we have been
These twice ten tedious years, yet we
    No holiday have seen.

" To-morrow is our wedding-day,
    And we will then repair

Unto the Bell at Edmonton
   All in a chaise and pair.

" My sister and my sister's child,
   Myself and children three,
Will fill the chaise; so you must ride
   On horseback after we."

He soon replied, " I do admire
   Of womankind but one,
And you are she, my dearest dear:
   Therefore it shall be done.

" I am a linendraper bold,
   As all the world doth know,
And my good friend the calender
   Will lend his horse to go."

Quoth Mrs. Gilpin, " That's well said;
   And for that wine is dear,
We will be furnished with our own,
   Which is both bright and clear."

John Gilpin kissed his loving wife;
   O'erjoyed was he to find,
That, though on pleasure she was bent,
   She had a frugal mind.

The morning came, the chaise was brought,
   But yet was not allowed
To drive up to the door, lest all
   Should say that she was proud.

So three doors off the chaise was stayed,
    Where they did all get in;
Six precious souls, and all agog
    To dash through thick and thin.

Smack went the whip, round went the wheels,
    Were never folks so glad;
The stones did rattle underneath,
    As if Cheapside were mad.

John Gilpin at his horse's side
    Seized fast the flowing mane,
And up he got in haste to ride,
    But soon came down again;

For saddle-tree scarce reached had he,
    His journey to begin,
When, turning round his head, he saw
    Three customers come in.

So down he came; for loss of time,
    Although it grieved him sore,
Yet loss of pence, full well he knew,
    Would trouble him much more.

'T was long before the customers
    Were suited to their mind,
When Betty screaming came down stairs,
    " The wine is left behind!"

" Good lack!" quoth he, " yet bring it me,
    My leathern belt likewise,
In which I bear my trusty sword
    When I do exercise."

Now Mistress Gilpin (careful soul!)
　Had two stone bottles found,
To hold the liquor that she loved,
　And keep it safe and sound.

Each bottle had a curling ear,
　Through which the belt he drew,
And hung a bottle on each side,
　To make his balance true.

Then over all, that he might be
　Equipped from top to toe,
His long red cloak, well brushed and neat,
　He manfully did throw.

Now see him mounted once again
　Upon his nimble steed,
Full slowly pacing o'er the stones,
　With caution and good heed.

But finding soon a smoother road
　Beneath his well-shod feet,
The snorting beast began to trot,
　Which galled him in his seat.

" So, fair and softly," John he cried,
　But John he cried in vain;
That trot became a gallop soon,
　In spite of curb and rein.

So stooping down, as needs he must
　Who cannot sit upright,

He grasped the mane with both his hands,
    And eke with all his might.

His horse, who never in that sort
    Had handled been before,
What thing upon his back had got
    Did wonder more and more.

Away went Gilpin, neck or naught;
    Away went hat and wig;
He little dreamt, when he set out,
    Of running such a rig.

The wind did blow, the cloak did fly,
    Like streamer long and gay,
Till, loop and button failing both,
    At last it flew away.

Then might all people well discern
    The bottles he had slung;
A bottle swinging at each side,
    As hath been said or sung.

The dogs did bark, the children screamed,
    Up flew the windows all;
And every soul cried out, " Well done!"
    As loud as he could bawl.

Away went Gilpin,—who but he?
    His fame soon spread around,
" He carries weight! he rides a race!
    'T is for a thousand pound!"

And still as fast as he drew near,
   'T was wonderful to view,
How in a trice the turnpike men
   Their gates wide open threw.

And now, as he went bowing down
   His reeking head full low,
The bottles twain behind his back
   Were shattered at a blow.

Down ran the wine into the road,
   Most piteous to be seen,
Which made his horse's flanks to smoke
   As they had basted been.

But still he seemed to carry weight,
   With leathern girdle braced;
For all might see the bottle necks
   Still dangling at his waist.

Thus all through merry Islington
   These gambols did he play,
Until he came unto the Wash
   Of Edmonton so gay;

And there he threw the wash about
   On both sides of the way,
Just like unto a trundling mop,
   Or a wild goose at play.

At Edmonton his loving wife
   From the balcony spied

Her tender husband, wondering much
　　To see how he did ride.


" Stop, stop, John Gilpin!—Here 's the house,"
　　They all at once did cry;
" The dinner waits, and we are tired."
　　Said Gilpin," So am I ! "


But yet his horse was not a whit
　　Inclined to tarry there;
For why?—his owner had a house
　　Full ten miles off, at Ware.


So like an arrow swift he flew,
　　Shot by an archer strong;
So did he fly—which brings me to
　　The middle of my song.


Away went Gilpin out of breath,
　　And sore against his will,
Till at his friend the calender's
　　His horse at last stood still.


The calender, amazed to see
　　His neighbor in such trim,
Laid down his pipe, flew to the gate,
　　And thus accosted him:


" What news? what news? your tidings tell;
　　Tell me you must and shall,—
Say why bareheaded you are come,
　　Or why you come at all? "

Now Gilpin had a pleasant wit,
    And loved a timely joke;
And thus unto the calender
    In merry guise he spoke:

" I came because your horse would come;
    And, if I well forebode,
My hat and wig will soon be here,
    They are upon the road."

The calender, right glad to find
    His friend in merry pin,
Returned him not a single word,
    But to the house went in;

Whence straight he came with hat and wig;
    A wig that flowed behind,
A hat not much the worse for wear,
    Each comely in its kind.

He held them up, and in his turn
    Thus showed his ready wit,
" My head is twice as big as yours,
    They therefore needs must fit.

" But let me scrape the dirt away
    That hangs upon your face;
And stop and eat, for well you may
    Be in a hungry case."

Said John, " It is my wedding-day,
    And all the world would stare,

If wife should dine at Edmonton,
   And I should dine at Ware."


So turning to his horse, he said,
   " I am in haste to dine;
'T was for your pleasure you came here,
   You shall go back for mine."


Ah, luckless speech, and bootless boast!
   For which he paid full dear;
For, while he spake, a braying ass
   Did sing most loud and clear;


Whereat his horse did snort, as he
   Had heard a lion roar,
And galloped off with all his might,
   As he had done before.


Away went Gilpin, and away
   Went Gilpin's hat and wig:
He lost them sooner than at first,
   For why?—they were too big.


Now Mistress Gilpin, when she saw
   Her husband posting down
Into the country far away,
   She pulled out half a crown;


And thus unto the youth she said,
   That drove them to the Bell,
" This shall be yours when you bring back
   My husband safe and well."

The youth did ride, and soon did meet
    John coming back amain;
Whom in a trice he tried to stop
    By catching at his rein;

But not performing what he meant,
    And gladly would have done,
The frightened steed he frightened more,
    And made him faster run.

Away went Gilpin, and away
    Went postboy at his heels,
The postboy's horse right glad to miss
    The lumbering of the wheels.

Six gentlemen upon the road,
    Thus seeing Gilpin fly,
With postboy scampering in the rear,
    They raised the hue and cry:—

" Stop thief! stop thief!—a highwayman!"
    Not one of them was mute;
And all and each that passed that way
    Did join in the pursuit.

And now the turnpike-gates again
    Flew open in short space;
The toll-man thinking, as before,
    That Gilpin rode a race.

And so he did, and won it too,
    For he got first to town;

Nor stopped till where he had got up
He did again get down.

Now let us sing, " Long live the king,
And Gilpin, long live he;
And when he next doth ride abroad,
May I be there to see!"

WILLIAM COWPER.

---

## EPIGRAMS BY S. T. COLERIDGE.

### COLOGNE.

In Köln, a town of monks and bones,
And pavements fanged with murderous stones,
And rags, and hags, and hideous wenches,—
I counted two-and-seventy stenches,
All well-defined and several stinks!
Ye nymphs that reign o'er sewers and sinks,
The river Rhine, it is well known,
Doth wash your city of Cologne;
But tell me, nymphs! what power divine
Shall henceforth wash the river Rhine?

---

Sly Beelzebub took all occasions
To try Job's constancy and patience.
He took his honor, took his health;
He took his children, took his wealth,
His servants, oxen, horses, cows—
But cunning Satan did *not* take his spouse.

But Heaven, that brings out good from evil,
And loves to disappoint the devil,

Had predetermined to restore
*Twofold* all he had before;
His servants, horses, oxen, cows—
Short-sighted devil, not to take his spouse!

---

HOARSE Mævius reads his hobbling verse
   To all, and at all times,
And finds them both divinely smooth,
   His voice as well as rhymes.

Yet folks say Mævius is no ass;
   But Mævius makes it clear
That he 's a monster of an ass,—
   An ass without an ear!

---

SWANS sing before they die,—'t were no bad thing
Did certain persons die before they sing.

---

## THE RAZOR-SELLER.

A FELLOW in a market-town,
Most musical, cried razors up and down,
   And offered twelve for eighteen pence;
Which certainly seemed wondrous cheap,
And, for the money, quite a heap,
   As every man would buy, with cash and sense.

A country bumpkin the great offer heard,—
Poor Hodge, who suffered by a broad black beard,
That seemed a shoe-brush stuck beneath his
      nose:
With cheerfulness the eighteen pence he paid,

And proudly to himself in whispers said,
  " This rascal stole the razors, I suppose.

" No matter if the fellow *be* a knave,
Provided that the razors *shave;*
  It certainly will be a monstrous prize."
So home the clown, with his good fortune, went,
Smiling in heart and soul content,
  And quickly soaped himself to ears and eyes.

Being well lathered from a dish or tub,
Hodge now began with grinning pain to grub,
  Just like a hedger cutting furze;
'T was a vile razor!—then the rest he tried,—
All were impostors. " Ah! " Hodge sighed,
  " I wish my eighteen pence within my purse."

In vain to chase his beard, and bring the graces,
  He cut, and dug, and winced, and stamped, and
      swore;
Brought  blood,  and  danced,  blasphemed,  and
      made wry faces,
  And cursed each razor's body o'er and o'er:

His muzzle formed of *opposition* stuff,
Firm as a Foxite, would not lose its ruff;
  So kept it,—laughing at the steel and suds.
Hodge, in a passion, stretched his angry jaws,
Vowing the direst vengeance with clenched claws,
  On the vile cheat that sold the goods.
" Razors! a mean, confounded dog,
  Not fit to scrape a hog! "

Hodge sought the fellow,—found him,—and be-
    gun:
" P'rhaps, Master Razor-rogue, to you 't is fun,
    That people flay themselves out of their lives.
You rascal; for an hour have I been grubbing,
Giving my crying whiskers here a scrubbing,
    With razors just like oyster-knives.
Sirrah! I tell you you 're a knave,
To cry up razors that can't shave!"


" Friend," quoth the razor-man, " I 'm not a
    knave;
    As for the razors you have bought,
    Upon my soul, I never thought
That they would *shave.*"
" Not think they 'd *shave!* " quoth Hodge, with
    wondering eyes,
    And voice not much unlike an Indian yell;
" What were they made for, then, you dog? "
    he cries.
    " *Made,*" quoth the fellow with a smile,—" *to
    sell.*"

DR. JOHN WOLCOTT (Peter Pindar).

------

## PAPER.

### A CONVERSATIONAL PLEASANTRY.

Some wit of old—such wits of old there were,
Whose hints showed meaning, whose allusions
    care—
By one brave stroke to mark all human kind,
Called clear, blank paper every infant mind:

19

Where still, as opening sense her dictates wrote,
Fair virtue put a seal, or vice a blot.

The thought was happy, pertinent, and true;
Methinks a genius might the plan pursue.
I (can you pardon my presumption?)—I,
No wit, no genius, yet for once will try.

Various the paper various wants produce,—
The wants of fashion, elegance, and use.
Men are as various; and, if right I scan,
Each sort of paper represents some man.

Pray note the fop, half powder and half lace;
Nice, as a bandbox were his dwelling-place;
He 's the *gilt-paper,* which apart you store,
And lock from vulgar hands in the 'scrutoire.

Mechanics, servants, farmers, and so forth
Are *copy-paper* of inferior worth;
Less prized, more useful, for your desk decreed;
Free to all pens, and prompt at every need.

The wretch whom avarice bids to pinch and spare,
Starve, cheat, and pilfer, to enrich an heir,
Is *coarse brown paper,* such as pedlers choose
To wrap up wares, which better men will use.

Take next the miser's contrast, who destroys
Health, fame, and fortune in a round of joys;
Will any paper match him?   Yes, throughout;
He 's a true *sinking-paper,* past all doubt.

The retail politician's anxious thought
Deems this side always right, and that stark
    naught;
He foams with censure; with applause he raves;
A dupe to rumors and a tool of knaves;
He 'll want no type, his weakness to proclaim,
While such a thing as *foolscap* has a name.

The hasty gentleman, whose blood runs high,
Who picks a quarrel, if you step awry,
Who can't a jest, a hint, or look endure,—
What is he?—what? *Touch-paper,* to be sure.

What are our poets, take them as they fall,
Good, bad, rich, poor, much read, not read at all?
They and their works in the same class you 'll
    find;
They are the mere *waste-paper* of mankind.

Observe the maiden, innocently sweet!
She 's fair, *white paper,* an unsullied sheet;
On which the happy man whom fate ordains
May write his name, and take her for his pains.

One instance more, and only one I 'll bring;
'T is the great man who scorns a little thing;
Whose thoughts, whose deeds, whose maxims, are
    his own,
Formed on the feelings of his heart alone,
True, genuine, *royal paper* is his breast;
Of all the kinds most precious, purest, best.

                BENJAMIN FRANKLIN.

## EPITAPH

FOR THE TOMBSTONE ERECTED OVER THE MARQUIS
OF ANGLESEA'S LEG, LOST AT WATERLOO.

Here rests, and let no saucy knave
    Presume to sneer and laugh,
To learn that moldering in the grave
    Is laid a British Calf.

For he who writes these lines is sure,
    That those who read the whole
Will find such laugh was premature,
    For here, too, lies a sole.

And here five little ones repose,
    Twin born with other five,
Unheeded by their brother toes,
    Who all are now alive.

A leg and foot to speak more plain,
    Rests here of one commanding;
Who though his wits he might retain,
    Lost half his understanding.

And when the guns, with thunder fraught,
    Poured bullets thick as hail,
Could only in this way be taught
    To give the foe leg-bail.

And now in England, just as gay
    As in the battle brave,

Goes to a rout, review, or play,
    With one foot in the grave.

Fortune in vain here showed her spite,
    For he will still be found,
Should England's sons engage in fight,
    Resolved to stand his ground.

But Fortune's pardon I must beg;
    She meant not to disarm,
For when she lopped the hero's leg,
    She did not seek his harm,

And but indulged a harmless whim;
    Since he could walk with one,
She saw two legs were lost on him,
    Who never meant to run.

GEORGE CANNING.

---

## RUDOLPH THE HEADSMAN.

### FROM "THIS IS IT."

RUDOLPH, professor of the headsman's trade,
Alike was famous for his arm and blade.
One day a prisoner Justice had to kill
Knelt at the block to test the artist's skill.
Bare-armed, swart-visaged, gaunt, and shaggy-
    browed,
Rudolph the headsman rose above the crowd.
His falchion lightened with a sudden gleam,
As the pike's armor flashes in the stream.
He sheathed his blade; he turned as if to go;

The victim knelt, still waiting for the blow.
"Why strikest not? Perform thy murderous
act,"
The prisoner said. (His voice was slightly
cracked.)
"Friend, I *have* struck," the artist straight re-
plied;
"Wait but one moment, and yourself decide."
He held his snuff-box,—"Now then, if you
please!"
The prisoner sniffed, and, with a crashing sneeze,
Off his head tumbled, bowled along the floor,
Bounced down the steps;—the prisoner said no
more.

OLIVER WENDELL HOLMES.

## SONG

OF ONE ELEVEN YEARS IN PRISON.

WHENE'ER with haggard eyes I view
This dungeon that I 'm rotting in,
I think of those companions true
Who studied with me at the U-
niversity of Gottingen,
niversity of Gottingen.

[*Weeps and pulls out a blue kerchief, with which
he wipes his eyes; gazing tenderly at it, he
proceeds:*]

Sweet kerchief, checked with heavenly blue,
Which once my love sat knotting in—

Alas, Matilda then was true!
At least I thought so at the U-
      niversity of Gottingen,
      niversity of Gottingen.

[*At the repetition of this line he clanks his chains
in cadence.*]

Barbs! barbs! alas! how swift you flew,
Her neat post-wagon trotting in!
Ye bore Matilda from my view;
  Folorn I languished at the U-
      niversity of Gottingen,
      niversity of Gottingen.

This faded form! this pallid hue!
This blood my veins is clotting in!
My years are many—they were few
  When first I entered at the U-
      niversity of Gottingen,
      niversity of Gottingen.

There first for thee my passion grew,
Sweet, sweet Matilda Pottingen!
Thou wert the daughter of my tu-
  tor, law-professor at the U-
      niversity of Gottingen,
      niversity of Gottingen.

Sun, moon, and thou, vain world, adieu,
That kings and priests are plotting in;
Here doomed to starve on water gru-
  el, never shall I see the U-
      niversity of Gottingen,
      niversity of Gottingen.

[*During the last stanza he dashes his head re-
peatedly against the walls of his prison, and
finally so hard as to produce a visible contusion.
He then throws himself on the floor in an
agony. The curtain drops, the music still con-
tinuing to play till it is wholly fallen.*]

GEORGE CANNING.

---

## LITTLE BILLEE.

THERE were three sailors of Bristol City
  Who took a boat and went to sea,
But first with beef and captain's biscuits
  And pickled pork they loaded she.

There was gorging Jack, and guzzling Jimmy,
  And the youngster he was little Billee;
Now when they'd got as far as the Equator,
  They'd nothing left but one split pea.

Says gorging Jack to guzzling Jimmy,
  "I am extremely hungaree."
To gorging Jack says guzzling Jimmy,
  "We've nothing left, us must eat we."

Says gorging Jack to guzzling Jimmy,
  "With one another we shouldn't agree!
There's little Bill, he's young and tender,
  We're old and tough, so let's eat he."

"O Billy! we're going to kill and eat you,
  So undo the button of your chemie."
When Bill received this information,
  He used his pocket-handkerchie.

" First let me say my catechism
  Which my poor mother taught to me."
" Make haste! make haste!" says guzzling Jimmy,
  While Jack pulled out his snickersnee.

Billy went up to the main-top-gallant mast,
  And down he fell on his bended knee,
He scarce had come to the Twelfth Command-
    ment
  When up he jumps—" There 's land I see!

" Jerusalem and Madagascar
  And North and South Amerikee,
There 's the British flag a-riding at anchor,
  With Admiral Napier, K. C. B."

So when they got aboard of the Admiral's,
  He hanged fat Jack and flogged Jimmee,
But as for little Bill he made him
  The Captain of a Seventy-three.

WILLIAM MAKEPEACE THACKERAY.

---

## CAPTAIN REECE.*

OF all the ships upon the blue,
No ship contained a better crew
Than that of worthy Captain Reece,
Commanding of The Mantelpiece.

* Containing the germs of Gilbert's two famous comic operas,—" H. M. S. Pinafore," with its amiable captain, cheerful crew, and the " sisters and the cousins and the aunts," and " The Pirates of Penzance, or the Slave of Duty."

He was adored by all his men,
For worthy Captain Reece, R. N.,
Did all that lay within him to
Promote the comfort of his crew.

If ever they were dull or sad,
Their captain danced to them like mad,
Or told, to make the time pass by,
Droll legends of his infancy.

A feather-bed had every man,
Warm slippers and hot-water can,
Brown windsor from the captain's store,
A valet, too, to every four.

Did they with thirst in summer burn,
Lo, seltzogenes at every turn,
And on all very sultry days
Cream ices handed round on trays.

Then currant wine and ginger pops
Stood handily on all the " tops:"
And, also, with amusement rife,
A " Zoetrope, or Wheel of Life."

New volumes came across the sea
From Mister Mudie's libraree;
The Times and Saturday Review
Beguiled the leisure of the crew.

Kind-hearted Captain Reece, R. N.,
Was quite devoted to his men;
In point of fact, good Captain Reece
Beatified The Mantelpiece.

One summer eve, at half past ten,
He said (addressing all his men),
" Come, tell me, please, what I can do,
To please and gratify my crew.

" By any reasonable plan
I 'll make you happy if I can;
My own convenience count as *nil;*
It is my duty, and I will."

Then up and answered William Lee
(The kind captain's coxswain he,
A nervous, shy, low-spoken man) ;
He cleared his throat and thus began:

" You have a daughter, Captain Reece,
Ten female cousins and a niece,
A ma, if what I 'm told is true,
Six sisters, and an aunt or two.

" Now, somehow, sir, it seems to me,
More friendly-like we all should be,
If you united of 'em to
Unmarried members of the crew.

" If you 'd ameliorate our life,
Let each select from them a wife;
And as for nervous me, old pal,
Give me your own enchanting gal ! "

Good Captain Reece, that worthy man,
Debated on his coxswain's plan:
" I quite agree," he said, " O Bill;
It is my duty, and I will.

" My daughter, that enchanting gurl,
Has just been promised to an earl,
And all my other familee
To peers of various degree.

" But what are dukes and viscounts to
The happiness of all my crew?
The word I gave you I 'll fulfil;
It is my duty, and I will.

" As you desire it shall befall,
I 'll settle thousands on you all,
And I shall be, despite my hoard,
The only bachelor on board."

The boatswain of The Mantelpiece,
He blushed and spoke to Captain Reece:
" I beg your honor's leave," he said,
" If you would wish to go and wed,

" I have a widowed mother who
Would be the very thing for you—
She long has loved you from afar,
She washes for you, Captain R."

The captain saw the dame that day—
Addressed her in his playful way—
" And did it want a wedding-ring?
It was a tempting ickle sing!

" Well, well, the chaplain I will seek,
We 'll all be married this day week
At yonder church upon the hill;
It is my duty, and I will! "

The sisters, cousins, aunts, and niece,
And widowed ma of Captain Reece,
Attended there as they were bid;
It was their duty, and they did.

WILLIAM SCHWENCK GILBERT.

---

## THE YARN OF THE "NANCY BELL."

### FROM "THE BAB BALLADS."

'T WAS on the shores that round our coast
　　From Deal to Ramsgate span,
That I found alone, on a piece of stone,
　　An elderly naval man.

His hair was weedy, his beard was long,
　　And weedy and long was he;
And I heard this wight on the shore recite,
　　In a singular minor key:—

" O, I am a cook and a captain bold,
　　And the mate of the Nancy brig,
And a bo'sun tight, and a midshipmite,
　　And the crew of the captain's gig."

And he shook his fist and he tore his hair,
　　Till I really felt afraid,
For I couldn't help thinking the man had been
　　　　drinking,
　　And so I simply said:—

" O elderly man, it 's little I know
　　Of the duties of men of the sea,

And I 'll eat my hand if I understand
    How you can possibly be

" At once a cook and a captain bold,
    And the mate of the Nancy brig,
And a bo'sun tight, and a midshipmite,
    And the crew of the captain's gig!"

Then he gave a hitch to his trousers, which
    Is a trick all seamen larn,
And having got rid of a thumping quid
    He spun this painful yarn:—

" 'T was in the good ship Nancy Bell
    That we sailed to the Indian sea,
And there on a reef we come to grief,
    Which has often occurred to me.

" And pretty nigh all o' the crew was drowned
    (There was seventy-seven o' soul);
And only ten of the Nancy's men
    Said ' Here ' to the muster-roll.

" There was me, and the cook, and the captain
        bold,
    And the mate of the Nancy brig,
And the bo'sun tight, and a midshipmite,
    And the crew of the captain's gig.

" For a month we 'd neither wittles nor drink,
    Till a-hungry we did feel,
So we drawed a lot, and accordin', shot
    The captain for our meal.

" The next lot fell to the Nancy's mate,
     And a delicate dish he made;
Then our appetite with the midshipmite
     We seven survivors stayed.

And then we murdered the bo'sun tight,
     And he much resembled pig;
Then we wittled free, did the cook and me,
     On the crew of the captain's gig.

" Then only the cook and me was left,
     And the delicate question, ' Which
Of us two goes to the kettle? ' arose,
     And we argued it out as sich.

" For I loved that cook as a brother, I did,
     And the cook he worshipped me;
But we 'd both be blowed if we 'd either be stowed
     In the other chap's hold, you see.

" ' I 'll be eat if you dines off me,' says Tom.
     ' Yes, that,' says I, ' you 'll be.
I 'm boiled if I die, my friend,' quoth I;
     And ' Exactly so,' quoth he.

" Says he: ' Dear James, to murder me
     Were a foolish thing to do,
For don't you see that you can't cook me,
     While I can—and will—cook you!'

" So he boils the water, and takes the salt
     And the pepper in portions true

(Which he never forgot), and some chopped sha-
lot,
 And some sage and parsley too.

" ' Come here,' says he, with a proper pride,
 Which his smiling features tell;
' 'T will soothing be if I let you see
 How extremely nice you 'll smell.'

" And he stirred it round, and round, and round,
 And he sniffed at the foaming froth;
When I ups with his heels, and smothers his
 squeals
 In the scum of the boiling broth.

" And I eat that cook in a week or less,
 And as I eating be
The last of his chops, why I almost drops,
 For a wessel in sight I see.

 .  .  .  .  .

" And I never larf, and I never smile,
 And I never lark nor play;
But I sit and croak, and a single joke
 I have—which is to say:

" O, I am a cook and a captain bold
 And the mate of the Nancy brig,
And a bo'sun tight, and a midshipmite,
 And the crew of the captain's gig!"

     WILLIAM SCHWENCK GILBERT.

# THE ART OF BOOK-KEEPING.

How hard, when those who do not wish
  To lend, thus lose, their books,
Are snared by anglers—folks that fish
  With literary hooks—
Who call and take some favorite tome,
  But never read it through;
They thus complete their set at home
  By making one at you.

I, of my " Spenser " quite bereft,
  Last winter sore was shaken;
Of " Lamb " I 've but a quarter left,
  Nor could I save my " Bacon ";
And then I saw my " Crabbe " at last,
  Like Hamlet, backward go,
And, as the tide was ebbing fast,
  Of course I lost my " Rowe."

My " Mallet " served to knock me down,
  Which makes me thus a talker,
And once, when I was out of town,
  My " Johnson " proved a " Walker."
While studying o'er the fire one day
  My " Hobbes " amidst the smoke,
They bore my " Colman " clean away,
  And carried off my " Coke."

They picked my " Locke," to me far more
  Than Bramah's patent worth,
20

And now my losses I deplore,
　　Without a " Home " on earth.
If once a book you let them lift,
　　Another they conceal,
For though I caught them stealing " Swift,"
　　As swiftly went my " Steele."


" Hope " is not now upon my shelf,
　　Where late he stood elated,
But, what is strange, my " Pope " himself
　　Is excommunicated.
My little " Suckling " in the grave
　　Is sunk to swell the ravage,
And what was Crusoe's fate to save,
　　'T was mine to lose—a " Savage."


Even " Glover's " works I cannot put
　　My frozen hands upon,
Though ever since I lost my " Foote "
　　My " Bunyan " has been gone.
My " Hoyle " with " Cotton " went oppressed,
　　My " Taylor," too, must fail,
To save my " Goldsmith " from arrest,
　　In vain I offered " Bayle."


I " Prior " sought, but could not see
　　The " Hood " so late in front,
And when I turned to hunt for " Lee,"
　　O, where was my " Leigh Hunt "?
I tried to laugh, old Care to tickle,
　　Yet could not " Tickell " touch,
And then, alack! I missed my " Mickle,"
　　And surely mickle's much.

'T is quite enough my griefs to feed,
    My sorrows to excuse,
To think I cannot read my " Reid,"
    Nor even use my " Hughes."
My classics would not quiet lie,—
    A thing so fondly hoped;
Like Dr. Primrose, I may cry,
    My " Livy " has eloped.

My life is ebbing fast away;
    I suffer from these shocks;
And though I fixed a lock on " Gray,"
    There 's gray upon my locks.
I 'm far from " Young," am growing pale,
    I see my " Butler " fly,
And when they ask about my ail,
    'T is " Burton " I reply.

They still have made me slight returns,
    And thus my griefs divide;
For O, they cured me of my " Burns,"
    And eased my " Akenside."
But all I think I shall not say,
    Nor let my anger burn,
For, as they never found me " Gay,"
    They have not left me " Sterne."

THOMAS HOOD.

---

## ADDRESS TO THE TOOTHACHE.

My curse upon thy venomed stang,
That shoots my tortured gums alang;
An' through my lugs gies mony a twang,
    Wi' gnawing vengeance!

Tearing my nerves wi' bitter pang,
   Like racking engines.

When fevers burn, or ague freezes,
Rheumatics gnaw, or cholic squeezes;
Our neighbor's sympathy may ease us,
   Wi' pitying moan;
But thee,—thou hell o' a' diseases,
   Aye mocks our groan.

Adown my beard the slavers trickle;
I throw the wee stools o'er the mickle,
As round the fire the giglets keckle
   To see me loup;
While, raving mad, I wish a heckle
   Were in their doup.

O' a' the numerous human dools,
Ill har'sts, daft bargains, cutty-stools,
Or worthy friends raked i' the mools,
   Sad sight to see!
The tricks o' knaves or fash o' fools,
   Thou bear'st the gree.

Where'er that place be priests ca' hell,
Whence a' the tones o' mis'ry yell,
And rankèd plagues their numbers tell,
   In dreadfu' raw,
Thou, Toothache, surely bear'st the bell,
   Among them a';

O thou grim mischief-making chiel,
And surely mickle 's much.

Till daft mankind aft dance a reel
    In gore a shoe-thick!—
Gie a' the faes o' Scotland's weal
    A fowmond's Toothache!

ROBERT BURNS.

---

## TO THE TERRESTRIAL GLOBE.

### BY A MISERABLE WRETCH.

ROLL on, thou ball, roll on!
Through pathless realms of space
        Roll on!
What though I 'm in a sorry case?
What though I cannot meet my bills?
What though I suffer toothache's ills?
What though I swallow countless pills?
    Never *you* mind!
        Roll on!

Roll on, thou ball, roll on!
Through seas of inky air
        Roll on!
It 's true I 've got no shirts to wear,
It 's true my butcher's bill is due,
It 's true my prospects all look blue,—
But don't let that unsettle you!
    Never *you* mind!
        Roll on!
            [*It rolls on.*

WILLIAM SCHWENCK GILBERT.

## THE NOSE AND THE EYES.

BETWEEN Nose and Eyes a strange contest arose;
The spectacles set them, unhappily, wrong;
The point in dispute was, as all the world knows,
　　To whom the said spectacles ought to belong.

So Tongue was the lawyer, and argued the cause,
　　With a great deal of skill, and a wig full of
　　　　learning,
While chief baron Ear sat to balance the laws,—
　　So famed for his talent in nicely discerning.

" In behalf of the Nose, it will quickly appear
　　(And your lordship," he said, " will undoubt-
　　　　edly find)
That the Nose has the spectacles always to wear,
　　Which amounts to possession, time out of
　　　　mind."

Then, holding the spectacles up to the court,
　　" Your lordship observes, they are made with
　　　　a straddle,
As wide as the ridge of the Nose is; in short,
　　Designed to sit close to it, just like a saddle.

" Again, would your lordship a moment suppose
　　('T is a case that has happened, and may hap-
　　　　pen again)
That the visage or countenance had *not* a Nose,
　　Pray, who *would,* or who *could,* wear spectacles
　　　　then?

"On the whole, it appears, and my argument
    shows,
With a reasoning the court will never condemn,
That the spectacles, plainly, were made for the
    Nose,
    And the Nose was, as plainly, intended for
    them."

Then shifting his side (as a lawyer knows how),
    He pleaded again in behalf of the Eyes:
But what were his arguments, few people know,
    For the court did not think them equally wise.

So his lordship decreed, with a grave, solemn
    tone,
    Decisive and clear, without one *if* or *but,*
That whenever the Nose put his spectacles on,
    By daylight or candlelight,—Eyes should be
    *shut.*

WILLIAM COWPER.

## THE VOWELS: AN ENIGMA.

WE are little airy creatures,
All of different voice and features;
One of us in glass is set,
One of us you'll find in jet,
T'other you may see in tin,
And the fourth a box within;
If the fifth you should pursue,
It can never fly from you.

JONATHAN SWIFT.

## ALNWICK CASTLE.

HOME of the Percys' high-born race,
   Home of their beautiful and brave,
Alike their birth and burial place,
   Their cradle and their grave!
Still sternly o'er the castle gate
Their house's Lion stands in state,
   As in his proud departed hours;
And warriors frown in stone on high,
And feudal banners " flout the sky "
   Above his princely towers.

A gentle hill its side inclines,
   Lovely in England's fadeless green,
To meet the quiet stream which winds
   Through this romantic scene
As silently and sweetly still
As when, at evening, on that hill,
   While summer's wind blew soft and low,
Seated by gallant Hotspur's side,
His Katherine was a happy bride,
   A thousand years ago.

I wandered through the lofty halls
   Trod by the Percys of old fame,
And traced upon the chapel walls
   Each high, heroic name,
From him who once his standard set
Where now, o'er mosque and minaret,
   Glitter the Sultan's crescent moons,

To him who, when a younger son,
Fought for King George at Lexington,
    A major of dragoons.

That last half-stanza,—it has dashed
    From my warm lips the sparkling cup;
The light that o'er my eyebeam flashed,
    The power that bore my spirit up
Above this bank-note world, is gone;
And Alnwick's but a market town,
And this, alas! its market day,
And beasts and borderers throng the way;
Oxen and bleating lambs in lots,
Northumbrian boors and plaided Scots,
    Men in the coal and cattle line;
From Teviot's bard and hero land,
From royal Berwick's beach of sand,
    From Wooller, Morpeth, Hexham, and
    Newcastle-upon-Tyne.

These are not the romantic times
So beautiful in Spenser's rhymes,
    So dazzling to the dreaming boy;
Ours are the days of fact, not fable,
Of knights, but not of the round table,
    Of Bailie Jarvie, not Rob Roy;
'T is what "Our President," Monroe,
    Has called "the era of good feeling;"
The Highlander, the bitterest foe
To modern laws, has felt their blow,
Consented to be taxed, and vote,
And put on pantaloons and coat,
    And leave off cattle-stealing:

Lord Stafford mines for coal and salt,
The Duke of Norfolk deals in malt,
    The Douglas in red herrings;
And noble name and cultured land,
Palace, and park, and vassal band,
Are powerless to the notes of hand
    Of Rothschilds or the Barings.


The age of bargaining, said Burke,
Has come : to-day the turbaned Turk
(Sleep, Richard of the lion heart!
Sleep on, nor from your cerements start)
    Is England's friend and fast ally;
The Moslem tramples on the Greek,
    And on the Cross and altar-stone,
    And Christendom looks tamely on,
And hears the Christian maiden shriek,
    And sees the Christian father die;
And not a sabre-blow is given
For Greece and fame, for faith and heaven,
    By Europe's craven chivalry.


You'll ask if yet the Percy lives
    In the armed pomp of feudal state.
The present representatives
    Of Hotspur and his " gentle Kate,"
Are some half-dozen serving-men
In the drab coat of William Penn;
    A chambermaid, whose lip and eye,
And cheek, and brown hair, bright and
            curling,
    Spoke nature's aristocracy;

And one, half groom, half seneschal,
Who bowed me through court, bower, and hall,
From donjon keep to turret wall,
  For ten-and-six-pence sterling.

FITZ-GREENE HALLECK.

---

## THE LATEST DECALOGUE.

Thou shalt have one God only: who
Would be at the expense of two?
No graven images may be
Worshipped, save in the currency.
Swear not at all; since for thy curse
Thine enemy is none the worse.
At church on Sunday to attend
Will serve to keep the world thy friend:
Honor thy parents; that is, all
From whom advancement may befall.
Thou shalt not kill; but need'st not strive
Officiously to keep alive.
Adultery it is not fit
Or safe (for woman) to commit.
Thou shalt not steal: an empty feat,
When 't is as lucrative to cheat.
Bear not false witness: let the lie
Have time on its own wings to fly.
Thou shalt not covet; but tradition
Approves all forms of competition.

ARTHUR HUGH CLOUGH.

## THE NEW CHURCH ORGAN.

THEY 'VE got a bran new organ, Sue,
 For all their fuss and search;
They 've done just as they said they 'd do,
 And fetched it into church.
They 're bound the critter shall be seen,
 And on the preacher's right,
They 've hoisted up their new machine
 In everybody's sight.
They 've got a chorister and choir,
 Ag'in *my* voice and vote;
For it was never *my* desire
 To praise the Lord by note!

I 've been a sister good an' true,
 For five an' thirty year;
I 've done what seemed my part to do,
 An' prayed my duty clear;
I 've sung the hymns both slow and quick,
 Just as the preacher read;
And twice, when Deacon Tubbs was sick,
 I took the fork an' led!
An' now, their bold, new-fangled ways
 Is comin' all about;
And I, right in my latter days,
 Am fairly crowded out!

To-day, the preacher, good old dear,
 With tears all in his eyes,
Read—" I can read my title clear
 To mansions in the skies."—
I al'ays liked that blessèd hymn—
 I s'pose I al'ays will;

It somehow gratifies *my* whim,
   In good old Ortonville;
But when that choir got up to sing,
   I couldn't catch a word;
They sung the most dog-gonedest thing
   A body ever heard!

Some worldly chaps was standin' near,
   An' when I see them grin,
I bid farewell to every fear,
   And boldly waded in.
I thought I'd chase the tune along,
   An' tried with all my might;
But though my voice is good an' strong,
   I couldn't steer it right.
When they was high, then I was low,
   An' also contra'wise;
And I too fast, or they too slow,
   To " mansions in the skies."

An' after every verse, you know,
   They played a little tune;
I didn't understand, an' so
   I started in too soon.
I pitched it purty middlin' high,
   And fetched a lusty tone,
But O, alas! I found that I
   Was singin' there alone!
They laughed a little, I am told;
   But I had done my best;
And not a wave of trouble rolled
   Across my peaceful breast.

And Sister Brown,—I could but look,—
   She sits right front of me;

She never was no singin' book,
　An' never went to be;
But then she al'ays tried to do
　The best she could, she said;
She understood the time, right through,
　An' kep' it with her head;
But when she tried this mornin', O,
　I had to laugh, or cough!
It kep' her head a bobbin' so,
　It e'en a'most come off!

An' Deacon Tubbs,—he all broke down,
　As one might well suppose;
He took one look at Sister Brown,
　And meekly scratched his nose.
He looked his hymn-book through and through,
　And laid it on the seat,
And then a pensive sigh he drew,
　And looked completely beat.
An' when they took another bout,
　He didn't even rise;
But drawed his red bandanner out,
　An' wiped his weepin' eyes.

I 've been a sister, good an' true,
　For five an' thirty year;
I 've done what seemed my part to do,
　An' prayed my duty clear;
But death will stop my voice, I know,
　For he is on my track;
And some day, I 'll to meetin' go,
　And nevermore come back.
And when the folks get up to sing—
　Whene'er that time shall be—

I do not want no *patent* thing
A squealin' over me!

WILL CARLETON.

---

## TONIS AD RESTO MARE.

AIR: " *O Mary, heave a sigh for me.*"

O MARE æva si forme;
  Forme ure tonitru;
Iambicum as amandum,
  Olet Hymen promptu;
Mihi is vetas an ne se,
  As humano erebi;
Olet mecum marito te,
  Or *eta beta pi.*

Alas, plano more meretrix,
  Mi ardor vel uno;
Inferiam ure artis base,
  Tolerat me urebo.
Ah me ve ara silicet,
  Vi laudu vimin thus?
Hiatus as arandum sex—
  Illuc Ionicus.

Heu sed heu vix en imago,
  My missis mare sta;
O cantu redit in mihi
  Hibernas arida?
A veri vafer heri si,
  Mihi resolves indu:
Totius olet Hymen cum—
  Accepta tonitru.

JONATHAN SWIFT.

## THE IRISHMAN AND THE LADY.

THERE was a lady lived at Leith,
    A lady very stylish, man;
And yet, in spite of all her teeth,
    She fell in love with an Irishman—
        A nasty, ugly Irishman,
        A wild, tremendous Irishman,
A tearing, swearing, thumping, bumping, ranting,
        roaring Irishman.

His face was no ways beautiful,
    For with small-pox 't was scarred across;
And the shoulders of the ugly dog
    Were almost double a yard across.
        Oh, the lump of an Irishman,
        The whiskey-devouring Irishman,
The great he-rogue with his wonderful brogue—
        the fighting, rioting Irishman.

One of his eyes was bottle-green,
    And the other eye was out, my dear;
And the calves of his wicked-looking legs
    Were more than two feet about, my dear.
        Oh, the great big Irishman,
        The rattling, battling Irishman—
The stamping, ramping, swaggering, staggering,
        leathering swash of an Irishman.

He took so much of Lundy-foot
    That he used to snort and snuffle—O!

And in shape and size the fellow's neck
  Was as bad as the neck of a buffalo.
    Oh, the horrible Irishman,
    The thundering, blundering Irishman—
The slashing, dashing, smashing, lashing, thrash-
      ing, hashing Irishman.

His name was a terrible name, indeed,
  Being Timothy Thady Mulligan;
And whenever he emptied his tumbler of punch
  He'd not rest till he filled it full again.
    The boozing, bruising Irishman,
    The 'toxicated Irishman—
The whiskey, frisky, rummy, gummy, brandy, no
      dandy Irishman.

This was the lad the lady loved,
  Like all the girls of quality;
And he broke the skulls of the men of Leith,
  Just by the way of jollity.
    Oh, the leathering Irishman,
    The barbarous, savage Irishman—
The hearts of the maids, and the gentlemen's
      heads, were bothered I'm sure by this
      Irishman.

WILLIAM MAGINN.

------

## THE RECRUIT.

Sez Corporal Madden to Private McFadden:
    "Bedad, yer a bad 'un!
    Now turn out yer toes!
    Yer belt is unhookit,

21

Yer cap is on crookit,
Ye may not be dhrunk,
But, be jabers, ye look it!
    Wan—two!
    Wan—two!
Ye monkey-faced divil, I'll jolly ye through!
    Wan—two!—
    Time! Mark!
Ye march like the aigle in Cintheral Parrk!"


Sez Corporal Madden to Private McFadden:
    " A saint it ud sadden
    To dhrill such a mug!
    Eyes front!—ye baboon, ye!—
    Chin up!—ye gossoon, ye!
    Ye 've jaws like a goat—
    Halt! ye leather-lipped loon, ye!
        Wan—two!
        Wan—two!
Ye whiskered orang-outang, I'll fix you!
        Wan—two!—
        Time! Mark!
Ye 've eyes like a bat!—can ye see in the dark?"


Sez Corporal Madden to Private McFadden:
    " Yer figger wants padd'n'—
    Sure, man, ye 've no shape!
    Behind ye yer shoulders
    Stick out like two bowlders;
    Yer shins is as thin
    As a pair of pen-holders!
        Wan—two!
        Wan—two!

Yer belly belongs on yer back, ye Jew!
    Wan—two!—
      Time!  Mark!
I 'm dhry as a dog—I can't shpake but I bark!' "

Sez Corporal Madden to Private McFadden:
    " Me heart it ud gladden
    To blacken yer eye.
    Ye 're gettin' too bold, ye
    Compel me to scold ye,—
    'T is halt! that I say,—
    Will ye heed what I told ye?
      Wan—two!
      Wan—two!
Be jabers, I 'm dhryer than Brian Boru!
    Wan—two!—
      Time!  Mark!
What 's wur-ruk for chickens is sport for the
    lark!' "

Sez Corporal Madden to Private McFadden:
    " I 'll not stay a gadd'n
    Wid dagoes like you!
    I 'll travel no farther,
    I 'm dyin' for—wather;—
    Come on, if ye like,—
    Can ye loan me a quather?
      Ya-as, you,
      What,—two?
And ye 'll pay the potheen?  Ye 're a daisy!
    Whurroo!
      You'll do!
      Whist!  Mark!
The Rigiment's flatthered to own ye, me spark!' "
ROBERT WILLIAM CHAMBERS.

## RITTER HUGO.

Der noble Ritter Hugo
  Von Schwillensanfenstein
Rode out mit shpeer und helmet,
  Und he coom to de panks of de Rhine.

Und oop dere rose a meermaid,
  Vot hadn't got nodings on,
Und she say, " O, Ritter Hugo,
  Vare you goes mit yourself alone? "

Und he says, " I ride in de creen-wood,
  Mit helmet and mit shpeer,
Till I cooms into ein Gasthaus,
  Und dere I drinks some peer."

Und den outshpoke de maiden,
  Vot hadn't got nodings on,
" I ton't dink mooch of beebles
  Dat goes mit demselfs alone.

You 'd petter come down in de wasser,
  Vare dere's heaps of dings to see,
Und hafe a shplendid dinner,
  Und trafel along mit me.

" Dare you sees de fish a schwimmin,
  Und you catches dem efery one."
So sang dis wasser maiden,
  Vot hadn't got nodings on.

" Dare is drunks all full mit money,
  In ships dat vent down of old;
Und you helpsh yourself, by dunder!
  To shimmerin crowns of gold.

" Shoost look at dese shpoons und vatches!
  Shoost look at dese diamond rings!
Come down und fill your bockets,
  Und I'll kiss you like eferydings!

"Vot you vantsh mit your schnapps und your
    lager?
  Coom down into der Rhine!
Dere ish pottles der Kaiser Charlemagne,
  Vonce filled mit gold-red vine!"

*Dat* fetched him,—he shtood all shpell-pound,
  She pulled his coat-tails down,
She drawed him under de wasser,
  Dis maid mit nodings on.

CHARLES GODFREY LELAND.

------

## HANS BREITMANN'S PARTY.

HANS BREITMANN gife a barty,
  Dey had biano-blayin;
I felled in lofe mit a Merican frau,
  Her name was Madilda Yane.
She had haar as prown ash a pretzel,
  Her eyes vas himmel-plue,
Und ven dey looket indo mine,
  Dey shplit mine heart in two.

Hans Breitmann gife a barty,
  I vent dere you 'll pe pound.
I valtzet mit Madilda Yane
  Und vent shpinnen round und round.
De pootiest Frauelein in de house,
  She vayed 'pout dwo hoondred pound,
Und efery dime she gife a shoomp
  She make de vindows sound.

Hans Breitmann gife a barty;
  I dells you it cost him dear.
Dey rolled in more as sefen kecks
  Of foost-rate Lager Beer.
Und venefer dey knocks de shpicket in
  De Deutschers gifes a cheer.
I dinks dat so vine a barty
  Nefer coom to a het dis year.

Hans Breitmann gife a barty;
  Dere all vas Souse und Brouse.
Ven de sooper comed in, de gompany
  Did make demselfs to house;
Dey ate das Brot und Gensy broost,
  De Bratwurst und Braten vine,
Und vash der Abendessen down
  Mit four parrels of Neckarwein.

Hans Breitmann gife a barty;
  We all cot troonk ash bigs.
I poot mine mout to a parrel of bier,
  Und emptied it oop mit a schwigs.
Und denn I gissed Madilda Yane
  Und she shlog me on de kop,

Und de gompany fited mit daple-lecks
  Dill de coonshtable made oos shtop.

Hans Breitmann gife a barty—
  Where ish dat barty now?
Where ish de lofely golden cloud
  Dat float on de moundain's prow?
Where ish de himmelstrahlende Stern—
  De shtar of de shpirit's light?
All goned afay mit de Lager Beer—
  Afay in de Ewigkeit!

CHARLES GODFREY LELAND.

## LEEDLE YAWCOB STRAUSS.

I HAF von funny leedle poy,
  Vot gomes schust to mine knee;
Der queerest chap, der createst rogue,
  As efer you dit see.
He runs und schumps und schmashes dings
  In all barts off der house;
But vot off dot? he vas mine son,
  Mine leedle Yawcob Strauss.

He get der measles und der mumbs,
  Und efferyding dot's oudt;
He sbills mine glass off lager-bier,
  Poots snoof indo mine kraut;
He fills mine pipe mit Limberg cheese—
  Dot vas der roughest chouse;
I'd take dot from no oder poy
  But little Yawcob Strauss.

He dakes der milk-ban for a dhrum
  Und cuts mine cane in two

To make der schticks to beat it mit—
  Mine cracious! dot vas drue.
I dinks mine hed vas schplit abart,
  He kicks oup sooch a touse;
But neffer mind—der poys vas few
  Like dot young Yawcob Strauss.

He ask me questions sooch as dose:
  Who baints mine nose so red?
Who vas it cuts dot schmoodth blace oudt
  Vrom der hair upon mine hed?
Und vhere der plaze goes vrom der lamp
  Vene'er der glim I douse;
How gan I all dose dings eggsblain
  To dot schmall Yawcob Strauss?

I somedimes dink I shall go vild
  Mit sooch a grazy poy,
Und vish vonce more I gould haf rest,
  Und beaceful dimes enshoy;
But ven he vas ashleep in ped,
  So guiet as a mouse,
I brays der Lord, " Dake anydings,
  But leaf dot Yawcob Strauss."

                    CHARLES FOLLEN ADAMS.

## DOT LONG-HANDLED DIPPER.

Der boet may sing off " Der Oldt Oaken Bookit,"
  Und in schveetest langvitch its virtues may tell;
Und how, ven a poy, he mit eggsdasy dook it,
  Vhen dripping mit coolness it rose vrom der
    vell.

I don'd take some schtock in dot manner off trink-
    ing!
It vas too mooch like horses und cattle, I dink.
Dhere vas more sadisfactions, in my vay of dink-
    ing,
    Mit dot long-handled dipper dot hangs by der
        sink.

" How schveet from der green mossy brim to re-
    ceive it "—
    Dot vould soundt pooty goot—eef it only vas
        drue—
Der vater schbills ofer, you petter pelieve it!
    Und runs down your schleeve and schlops into
        your shoe.
Dhen down on your nose comes dot oldt iron
    handle,
    Und makes your eyes vater so gvick as a vink.
I dells you dot bookit don'd hold a candle
    To dot long-handled dipper dot hangs py der
        sink.

How nice it musd been in der rough vinter ved-
    dher,
    Vhen it settles righdt down to a cold, freezing
        rain,
To haf dot rope coom oup so light as a feddher,
    Und findt dot der bookit vas proke off der chain.
Dhen down in der vell mit a pole you go fishing,
    Vhile indo your back cooms an oldt-fashioned
        kink;
I pet you mine life all der time you vas vishing
    For dot long-handled dipper dot hangs by der
        sink.

How handy it vas schust to turn on der faucet,
  Vhere der vater flows down vrom der schpring
    on der hill!
I schust vas der schap dot vill alvays indorse
    it,
  Oxsbecially nighds vhen der veddher vas chill.
Vhen Pfeiffer's oldt vell mit der schnow vas all
    cofered,
  Und he vades droo der schnow drift to get
    him a trink,
I schlips vrom der hearth vhere der schiltren
    vas hofered,
  To dot long-handled dipper dot hangs by der
    sink.


  Dhen gife oup der bookits und pails to der
    horses;
    Off mikerobes und tadpoles schust gif dhem
      dheir fill!
Gife me dot pure vater dot all der time courses
    Droo dhose pipes dot run down vrom der
      schpring on der hill.
Und eef der goot dings of dis vorld I gets rich
    in,
    Und frendts all aroundt me dheir glasses
      schall clink,
I  schtill vill rememper dot oldt coundtry
    kitchen,
    Und dot long-handled dipper dot hangs by der
      sink.

                    CHARLES FOLLEN ADAMS.

## THE JACKDAW OF RHEIMS.

The Jackdaw sat on the Cardinal's chair!
Bishop and abbot and prior were there;
    Many a monk, and many a friar,
    Many a knight, and many a squire,
With a great many more of lesser degree,—
In sooth, a goodly company;
And they served the Lord Primate on bended
      knee.
    Never, I ween,
    Was a prouder seen,
Read of in books, or dreamt of in dreams,
Than the Cardinal Lord Archbishop of Rheims!
    In and out,
    Through the motley rout,
That little Jackdaw kept hopping about:
    Here and there,
    Like a dog in a fair,
    Over comfits and cates,
    And dishes and plates,
Cowl and cope, and rochet and pall,
Mitre and crosier, he hopped upon all.
    With a saucy air,
    He perched on the chair
Where, in state, the great Lord Cardinal sat,
In the great Lord Cardinal's great red hat;
    And he peered in the face
    Of his Lordship's Grace,
With a satisfied look, as if he would say,
" We two are the greatest folks here to-day!"

And the priests, with awe,
As such freaks they saw,
Said, " The Devil must be in that Little Jack-
      daw!"
The feast was over, the board was cleared,
The flawns and the custards had all disappeared,
And six little Singing-boys,—dear little souls
In nice clean faces, and nice white stoles,—
      Came, in order due,
      Two by two,
Marching that grand refectory through!
A nice little boy held a golden ewer,
Embossed and filled with water, as pure
As any that flows between Rheims and Namur.
Which a nice little boy stood ready to catch
In a fine golden hand-basin made to match.
Two nice little boys, rather more grown,
Carried lavender-water and eau-de-Cologne;
And a nice little boy had a nice cake of soap,
Worthy of washing the hands of the Pope!
      One little boy more
      A napkin bore,
Of the best white diaper, fringed with pink,
And a cardinal's hat marked in " permanent
      ink."


The great Lord Cardinal turns at the sight
Of these nice little boys dressed all in white;
      From his finger he draws
      His costly turquoise:
And, not thinking at all about little Jackdaws,
      Deposits it straight
      By the side of his plate,

While the nice little boys on his Eminence wait:
Till, when nobody 's dreaming of any such thing,
That little Jackdaw hops off with the ring!

.        .      .    .       .        .

There 's a cry and a shout,
And a deuce of a rout,
And nobody seems to know what they 're about.
But the monks have their pockets all turned in-
side out;
The friars are kneeling,
And hunting and feeling
The carpet, the floor, and the walls, and the ceil-
ing.
The Cardinal drew
Off each plum-colored shoe,
And left his red stockings exposed to the view;
He peeps, and he feels
In the toes and the heels.
They turn up the dishes,—they turn up the
plates,—
They take up the poker and poke out the grates,
—They turn up the rugs,
They examine the mugs;
But, no!—no such thing,—
They can't find THE RING!
And the Abbot declared that "when nobody
twigged it,
Some rascal or other had popped in and prigged
it!"

The Cardinal rose with a dignified look,
He called for his candle, his bell, and his book!
In holy anger and pious grief

He solemnly cursed that rascally thief!
He cursed him at board, he cursed him in bed;
From the sole of his foot to the crown of his
    head;
He cursed him in sleeping, that every night
He should dream of the Devil, and wake in a
    fright.
He cursed him in eating, he cursed him in drink-
    ing,
He cursed him in coughing, in sneezing, in
    winking;
He cursed him in sitting, in standing, in lying;
He cursed him in walking, in riding, in flying;
He cursed him living, he cursed him dying!—
Never was heard such a terrible curse!
      But what gave rise
      To no little surprise,
Nobody seemed one penny the worse!


      The day was gone,
      The night came on,
The monks and the friars they searched till dawn;
      When the sacristan saw,
      On crumpled claw,
Come limping a poor little lame Jackdaw!
      No longer gay,
      As on yesterday;
His feathers all seemed to be turned the wrong
    way;—
His pinions drooped,—he could hardly stand,—
His head was as bald as the palm of your hand;
      His eye so dim,
      So wasted each limb,

That, heedless of grammar, they all cried,
      " THAT 's HIM !—
That 's the scamp that has done this scandalous
      thing,
That 's the thief that has got my Lord Cardinal's
      Ring ! "
      The poor little Jackdaw,
      When the monks he saw,
Feebly gave vent to the ghost of a caw ;
And turned his bald head as much as to say,
" Pray be so good as to walk this way ! "
      Slower and slower
      He limped on before,
Till they came to the back of the belfry-door,
      Where the first thing they saw,
      Midst the sticks and the straw,
Was the RING, in the nest of that little Jackdaw !

Then the great Lord Cardinal called for his book,
And off that terrible curse he took :
      The mute expression
      Served in lieu of confession,
And, being thus coupled with full restitution,
The Jackdaw got plenary absolution !
      —When those words were heard,
      That poor little bird
Was so changed in a moment, 't was really ab-
      surd :
      He grew sleek and fat ;
      In addition to that,
A fresh crop of feathers came thick as a mat !
      His tail waggled more
      Even than before ;

But no longer it wagged with an impudent air,
No longer he perched on the Cardinal's chair:
    He hopped now about
    With a gait devout;
At Matins, at Vespers, he never was out;
And, so far from any more pilfering deeds,
He always seemed telling the Confessor's beads.
If any one lied, or if any one swore,
Or slumbered in prayer-time and happened to
    snore,
    That good Jackdaw
    Would give a great " Caw! "
As much as to say, " Don't do so any more! "
While many remarked, as his manners they saw,
That they " never had known such a pious Jack-
    daw! "
    He long lived the pride
    Of that country side,
And at last in the odor of sanctity died;
    When, as words were too faint
    His merits to paint,
The Conclave determined to make him a Saint.
And on newly made Saints and Popes, as you
    know,
It is the custom of Rome new names to bestow,
So they canonized him by the name of Jem Crow!

RICHARD HARRIS BARHAM.<br>(Thomas Ingoldsby, Esq.)

## AMERICA.

FROM "A FABLE FOR CRITICS."

THERE are truths you Americans need to be told,
And it never 'll refute them to swagger and scold;
John Bull, looking o'er the Atlantic, in choler,
At your aptness for trade, says you worship the
    dollar;
But to scorn i-dollar-try 's what very few do,
And John goes to that church as often as you do.
No matter what John says, don't try to outcrow
    him,
'T is enough to go quietly on and outgrow him;
Like most fathers, Bull hates to see Number One
Displacing himself in the mind of his son,
And detests the same faults in himself he 'd neg-
    lected
When he sees them again in his child's glass re-
    flected;
To love one another you 're too like by half,
If he is a bull, you 're a pretty stout calf,
And tear your own pasture for naught but to
    show
What a nice pair of horns you 're beginning to
    grow.

There are one or two things I should just like to
    hint,
For you don't often get the truth told you in
    print;
22

The most of you (this is what strikes all be-
    holders)
Have a mental and physical stoop in the
    shoulders;
Though you ought to be free as the winds and the
    waves,
You 've the gait and the manner of runaway
    slaves;
Though you brag of your New World, you don't
    half believe in it;
And as much of the Old as is possible weave in it;
Your goddess of freedom, a tight, buxom girl,
With lips like a cherry and teeth like a pearl,
With eyes bold as Herë 's, and hair floating free,
And full of the sun as the spray of the sea,
Who can sing at a husking or romp at a shearing,
Who can trip through the forests alone without
    fearing,
Who can drive home the cows with a song through
    the grass,
Keeps glancing aside into Europe's cracked glass,
Hides her red hands in gloves, pinches up her
    lithe waist,
And makes herself wretched with transmarine
    taste;
She loses her fresh country charm when she takes
Any mirror except her own rivers and lakes.

                        JAMES RUSSELL LOWELL.

## WHAT MR. ROBINSON THINKS.*

FROM "THE BIGLOW PAPERS," NO. III.

GUVENER B. is a sensible man;
　He stays to his home an' looks arter his folks;
He draws his furrer ez straight ez he can,
　An' into nobody's tater-patch pokes;—
　　　　　But John P.
　　　　　Robinson he
　　Sez he wunt vote for Guvener B.


My! ain't it terrible? Wut shall we du?
　We can't never choose him o' course,—thet 's
　　　　　flat;
Guess we shall hev to come round, (don't you?)
　An' go in fer thunder an' guns, an' all that;
　　　　　Fer John P.
　　　　　Robinson he
　　Sez he wunt vote for Guvener B.


Gineral C. is a dreffle smart man:
　He 's ben on all sides thet give places or pelf;
But consistency still wuz a part of his plan,—
　He 's ben true to *one* party,—an' thet is him-
　　　　　self;—
　　　　　So John P.
　　　　　Robinson he
　　Sez he shall vote for Gineral C.

* Written at the time of the Mexican war, which was
strongly opposed by the Anti-slavery party as being un-
necessary and wrong.

Gineral C, has gone in fer the war;
  He don't vally principle more 'n an old cud;
Wut did God make us raytional creeturs fer,
    But glory an' gunpowder, plunder an' blood?
        So John P.
        Robinson he
    Sez he shall vote for Gineral C.


We were gittin' on nicely up here to our village,
  With good old idees o' wut 's right an' wut ain't,
We kind o' thought Christ went agin war an'
        pillage,
  An' thet eppylets worn't the best mark of a
        saint;
        But John P.
        Robinson he
    Sez this kind o' thing 's an exploded idee.


The side of our country must ollers be took,
  An' President Polk, you know, *he* is our coun-
        try;
An' the angel thet writes all our sins in a book
  Puts the *debit* to him, an' to us the *per contry;*
        An' John P.
        Robinson he
    Sez this is his view o' the thing to a T.


Parson Wilbur he calls all these argimunts lies;
  Sez they 're nothin' on airth but jest *fee, faw,*
        *fum:*
And thet all this big talk of our destinies
  Is half ov it ign'ance, an' t' other half rum;

But John P.
Robinson he
Sez it ain't no sech thing; an', of course, so
must we.

Parson Wilbur sez *he* never heerd in his life
That th' Apostles rigged out in their swaller-
tail coats,
An' marched round in front of a drum an' a fife,
To git some on 'em office, an' some on 'em votes;
But John P.
Robinson he
Sez they didn't know everythin' down in Judee.

Wal, it's a marcy we've gut folks to tell us
The rights an' the wrongs o' these matters, I
vow,—
God sends country lawyers, an' other wise fellers,
To drive the world's team wen it gits in a
slough;
Fer John P.
Robinson he
Sez the world'll go right, ef he hollers out
Gee!

JAMES RUSSELL LOWELL.

## SWELL'S SOLILOQUY.

I DON'T appwove this hawid waw;
Those dweadful bannahs hawt my eyes;
And guns and dwums are such a baw,—
Why don't the pawties compwamise?

Of cawce, the twoilet has its chawms;
But why must all the vulgah cwowd

Pawsist in spawting unifawms,
　In cullahs so extwemely loud?

And then the ladies, pwecious deahs!—
　I mawk the change on ev'wy bwow;
Bai Jove! I weally have my feahs
　They wathah like the hawid wow!

To heah the chawming cweatures talk,
　Like patwons of the bloody wing,
Of waw and all its dawty wawk,—
　It doesn't seem a pwappah thing!

I called at Mrs. Gweene's last night,
　To see her niece, Miss Mawy Hertz,
And found her making—cwushing sight!—
　The weddest kind of flannel shirts!

Of cawce, I wose, and sought the daw,
　With fawyah flashing from my eyes!
I can't appwove this hawid waw;—
　Why don't the pawties compwamise?

ANONYMOUS.

## THE COMPLIMENT.

ARRAYED in snow-white pants and vest,
　And other rainment fair to view,
　I stood before my sweetheart Sue—
The charming creature I love best.
" Tell me and does my costume suit ? "
　I asked that apple of my eye—
　And then the charmer made reply,
" Oh, yes, you *do* look awful cute! "

Although I frequently had heard
  My sweetheart vent her pleasure so,
  I must confess I did not know
The meaning of that favorite word.

But presently at window side
  We stood and watched the passing throng,
  And soon a donkey passed along
With ears like wings extended wide.
And gazing at the doleful brute
  My sweetheart gave a merry cry—
  I quote her language with a sigh—
"O Charlie, ain't he awful cute?"

EUGENE FIELD.

## THE NANTUCKET SKIPPER.

MANY a long, long year ago,
  Nantucket skippers had a plan
Of finding out, though "lying low,"
  How near New York their schooners ran.

They greased the lead before it fell,
  And then by sounding through the night,
Knowing the soil that stuck so well,
  They always guessed their reckoning right.

A skipper gray, whose eyes were dim,
  Could tell, by tasting, just the spot,
And so below he'd "douse the glim,"—
  After, of course, his "something hot."

Snug in his berth at eight o'clock,
  This ancient skipper might be found;

No matter how his craft would rock,
    He slept,—for skippers' naps are sound.

The watch on deck would now and then
    Run down and wake him, with the lead;
He 'd up, and taste, and tell the men
    How many miles they went ahead.

One night 't was Jotham Marden's watch,
    A curious wag,—the pedler's son;
And so he mused, (the wanton wretch!)
    " To-night I 'll have a grain of fun.

" We 're all a set of stupid fools,
    To think the skipper knows, by tasting,
What ground he 's on; Nantucket schools
    Don't teach such stuff, with all their basting!"

And so he took the well-greased lead,
    And rubbed it o'er a box of earth
That stood on deck,—a parsnip-bed,—
    And then he sought the skipper's berth.

" Where are we now, sir?   Please to taste."
    The skipper yawned, put out his tongue,
Opened his eyes in wondrous haste,
    And then upon the floor he sprung!

The skipper stormed, and tore his hair,
    Hauled on his boots, and roared to Marden,
" Nantucket's sunk, and here we are
    Right over old Marm Hackett's garden!"

                            JAMES THOMAS FIELDS.

## THE ONE-HOSS SHAY;

OR, THE DEACON'S MASTERPIECE.

A LOGICAL STORY.

HAVE you heard of the wonderful one-hoss shay,
That was built in such a logical way
It ran a hundred years to a day,
And then of a sudden, it—ah, but stay,
I 'll tell you what happened without delay,
Scaring the parson into fits,
Frightening people out of their wits,—
Have you ever heard of that, I say?

Seventeen hundred and fifty-five.
*Georgius Secundus* was then alive,—
Snuffy old drone from the German hive.
That was the year when Lisbon-town
Saw the earth open and gulp her down,
And Braddock's army was done so brown,
Left without a scalp to its crown.
It was on the terrible Earthquake-day
That the deacon finished the one-hoss shay.

Now in the building of chaises, I tell you what,
There is always *somewhere* a weakest spot,—
In hub, tire, felloe, in spring or thill,
In panel, or crossbar, or floor, or sill,
In screw, bolt, thoroughbrace,—lurking still,
Find it somewhere you must and will,—
Above or below, or within or without,—
And that 's the reason, beyond a doubt,
A chaise *breaks down*, but doesn't wear *out*.

But the Deacon swore (as Deacons do,
With an " I dew vum," or an " I tell *yeou*,")
He would build one shay to beat the taown
'n' the keounty 'n' all the kentry raoun';
It should be so built that it *couldn't* break
        daown;
—" Fur," said the Deacon, " 't 's mighty plain
Thut the weakes' place mus' stan' the strain;
'n' the way t' fix it, uz I maintain,
      Is only jest
T' make that place uz strong uz the rest."

So the Deacon inquired of the village folk
Where he could find the strongest oak,
That couldn't be split nor bent nor broke,—
That was for spokes and floor and sills;
He sent for lancewood to make the thills;
The crossbars were ash, from the straightest trees;
The panels of whitewood, that cuts like cheese,
But lasts like iron for things like these;
The hubs of logs from the " Settler's ellum,"—
Last of its timber,—they couldn't sell 'em,
Never an axe had seen their chips,
And the wedges flew from between their lips,
Their blunt ends frizzled like celery-tips;
Step and prop-iron, bolt and screw,
Spring, tire, axle, and linchpin too,
Steel of the finest, bright and blue;
Thoroughbrace bison-skin, thick and wide;
Boot, top, dasher, from tough old hide
Found in the pit when the tanner died.
That was the way he " put her through."
" There!" said the Deacon, " naow she 'll dew!"

Do! I tell you, I rather guess
She was a wonder, and nothing less!
Colts grew horses, beards turned gray,
Deacon and deaconess dropped away,
Children and grandchildren,—where were they?
But there stood the stout old one-hoss shay
As fresh as on Lisbon-earthquake-day!

Eighteen hundred;—it came and found
The Deacon's masterpiece strong and sound.
Eighteen hundred increased by ten;—
"Hahnsum kerridge" they called it then.
Eighteen hundred and twenty came;—
Running as usual; much the same.
Thirty and forty at last arrive,
And then came fifty, and fifty-five.

Little of all we value here
Wakes on the morn of its hundredth year
Without both feeling and looking queer.
In fact, there's nothing that keeps its youth,
So far as I know, but a tree and truth.
(This is a moral that runs at large;
Take it.—You're welcome.— No extra charge.)

First of November,—the Earthquake-day.—
There are traces of age in the one-hoss shay,
A general flavor of mild decay,
But nothing local as one may say.
There couldn't be,—for the Deacon's art
Had made it so like in every part
That there wasn't a chance for one to start,
For the wheels were just as strong as the thills,
And the floor was just as strong as the sills,
And the panels just as strong as the floor,

And the whippletree neither less nor more,
And the back-crossbar as strong as the fore,
And spring and axle and hub *encore.*
And yet, *as a whole,* it is past a doubt
In another hour it will be *worn out!*

First of November, 'Fifty-five!
This morning the parson takes a drive.
Now, small boys, get out of the way!
Here comes the wonderful one-hoss shay,
Drawn by a rat-tailed, ewe-necked bay.
" Huddup ! " said the parson.—Off went they.
The parson was working his Sunday's text,—
Had got to *fifthly,* and stopped perplexed
At what the—Moses—was coming next.
All at once the horse stood still,
Close by the meetin'-house on the hill.
—First a shiver and then a thrill,
Then something decidedly like a spill,—
And the parson was sitting upon a rock,
At half past nine by the meetin'-house clock,—
Just the hour of the Earthquake shock!
—What do you think the parson found,
When he got up and stared around?
The poor old chaise in a heap or mound,
As if it had been to the mill and ground!
You see, of course, if you 're not a dunce,
How it went to pieces all at once,—
All at once, and nothing first,—
Just as bubbles do when they burst.

End of the wonderful one-hoss shay.
Logic is logic. That 's all I say.

OLIVER WENDELL HOLMES.

## GRIGGSBY'S STATION.

Pap's got his patent right, and rich as all creation;
    But where 's the peace and comfort that we all
had before?
Le's go a-visitin' back to Griggsby's Station—
    Back where we ust to be so happy and so pore!

The likes of us a-livin' here! It 's just a mortal
pity
    To see us in this great big house, with cyarpets
on the stairs,
And the pump right in the kitchen! And the
city! city! city!—
    And nothin' but the city all around us ever'-
wheres!

Climb clean above the roof and look from the
steeple,
    And never see a robin, nor a beech or ellum
tree!
And right here in ear-shot of at least a thousan'
people,
    And none that neighbors with us, or we want to
go and see!

Le's go a-visitin' back to Griggsby's Station—
    Back where the latch-string 's a-hangin' from
the door,

And ever' neighbor 'round the place is dear as a
    relation—
Back where we ust to be so happy and so pore!

I want to see the Wiggenses, the whole kit and
    bilin'
A-drivin' up from Shallor Ford to stay the Sun-
    day through;
And I want to see 'em hitchin' at their son-in-
    law's and pilin'
Out there at 'Lizy Ellen's like they ust to do!

I want to see the piece-quilts the Jones girls is
    makin';
And I want to pester Laury 'bout their freckled
    hired hand,
And joke her 'bout the widower she come purt'
    nigh a-takin',
Till her pap got his pension 'lowed in time to
    save his land.

Le's go a-visitin' back to Griggsby's station—
    Back where they's nothin' aggervatin' any-
    more;
Shet away safe in the woods around the old loca-
    tion—
    Back where we ust to be so happy and so pore!

I want to see Marindy and he'p her with her
    sewin',
    And hear her talk so lovin' of her man that's
    dead and gone,

And stand up with Emanuel to show me how he 's
    growin',
    And smile as I have saw her 'fore she put her
        mournin' on.

And I want to see the Samples, on the old lower
    eighty—
    Where John our oldest boy, he was tuk and
        buried—for
His own sake and Katy's—and I want to cry
    with Katy
    As she reads all his letters over, writ from The
        War.

What 's all this grand life and high situation,
    And nary pink nor hollyhawk bloomin' at the
        door?—
Le's go a-visitin' back to Griggsby's Station—
    Back where we ust to be so happy and so pore!
                  JAMES WHITCOMB RILEY.

---

## HE 'D HAD NO SHOW.

    JOE BEALL 'ud set upon a keg
    Down to the groc'ry store, an' throw
One leg right over t'other leg
    An' swear he 'd never had no show,
      " O, no," said Joe,
      " Hain't hed no show,"
Then shift his quid to t'other jaw,
An' chaw, an' chaw, an' chaw, an' chaw.

He said he got no start in life,
   Didn't get no money from his dad,
The washin' took in by his wife
      Earned all the funds he ever had.
         " O, no," said Joe,
         " Hain't hed no show,"
An' then he 'd look up at the clock
An' talk, an' talk, an' talk, an' talk.

" I 've waited twenty year—let 's see—
   Yes, twenty-four, an' never struck,
Altho, I 've sot roun' patiently,
      The fust tarnation streak er luck.
         O, no," said Joe,
         " Hain't hed no show,"
Then stuck like mucilage to the spot,
An' sot, an' sot, an' sot, an' sot.

" I 've come down regerlar every day
   For twenty years to Piper's store.
I 've sot here in a patient way,
      Say, hain't I, Piper? "   Piper swore.
         " I tell ye, Joe,
         Yer hain't no show ;
Yer too dern patient "—ther hull raft
Jest laffed, an' laffed, an' laffed, an' laffed.

                              SAM WALTER FOSS.

---

## THE MYSTIFIED QUAKER IN NEW YORK.

RESPECTED WIFE: By these few lines my where-
   abouts thee 'll learn:
Moreover, I impart to thee my serious concern.

The language of this people is a riddle unto me;
For words with them are figments of a reckless
    mockery.
For instance, as I left the cars, a youth with
    smutty face
Said, "Shine?" "Nay I'll not shine," I said,
    "except with inward grace."
"What's inward grace?" said this young Turk;
"A liquid or a paste? Hi, daddy, how does the
    old thing work?"
I then said to a jehu, whose breath suggested gin,
"Friend, can thee take me to a reputable inn?"
But this man's gross irrelevance I shall not soon
    forget;
Instead of simply Yea or Nay, he gruffly said,
    "You bet!"
"Nay, nay, I will not bet," I said, "for that would
    be a sin.
Why dost not answer plainly? can thee take me
    to an inn?
Thy vehicle is doubtless made to carry folks about
    in;
Why then prevaricate?" Said he, "Aha! well
    now, you're shoutin'!"
"I did not shout," I said, "my friend; surely my
    speech is mild:
But thine (I grieve to say it) with falsehood is
    defiled.
Thee ought to be admonished to rid thy heart of
    guile."
"Look here, my lovely moke," said he, "you sling
    on too much style."
23

" I 've had these plain drab garments twenty years
    or more," said I;
" And when thee says I ' sling on style ' thee tells
    a wilful lie."
With that he pranced about as tho' a bee were in
    his bonnet,
And with hostile demonstrations inquired if I was
    " on it."
" On what? Till thee explain, I cannot tell," I
    said;
But he swore that something was " too thin,"
    moreover it was " played."
But all his antics were surpassed in wild ab-
    surdity
By threats, profanely emphasized, to " put a
    head " on me.
" No son of Belial," I said, " that miracle can do."
With that he fell upon me with blows and curses
    too;
But failed to work that miracle, if such was his
    design;
Instead of putting on a head, he strove to smite
    off mine.
Thee knows that I profess the peaceful precepts
    of our sect,
But this man's acts worked on me to a curious
    effect;
And when he knocked my broad-brim off, and
    said, " How 's that for high! "
It roused the Adam in me, and I smote him hip
    and thigh.
This was a signal for the crowd, for calumny
    broke loose;

They said I'd " snatched him bald-headed," and
   likewise " cooked his goose."
But yet I do affirm, that I had not pulled his
   hair;
Nor had I cooked his poultry, for he had no
   poultry there.
They called me " bully boy," though I have seen
   full three-score year;
And they said that I was " lightning when I got
   upon my ear."
And when I asked if lightning climbed its ear,
   and dressed in drab,
" You know how 't is yourself," said one insolent
   young blab.
So I left them in disgust: plain-spoken men like
   me
With such perverters of our tongue can have no
   unity.

ANONYMOUS.

---

## TO THE " SEXTANT."

O SEXTANT of the meetin house, wich sweeps
And dusts, or is supposed to! and makes fires,
And lites the gass, and sumtimes leaves a screw
   loose,
in wich case it smells orful, worse than lamp ile;
And wrings the Bel and toles it when men dyes,
   to the grief of survivin pardners, and sweeps
   paths
And for the servusses gets $100 per annum,
Wich them that thinks deer, let 'em try it;
Gettin up before starlite in all wethers and

Kindlin fires when the wether is as cold
As zero, and like as not green wood for kindlin,
i wouldn't be hired to do it for no sum.
But O Sextant! there are 1 kermoddity
Wich 's more than gold, wich doant cost nothin,
Worth more than anything except the sole of man!
i mean pewer *Are*, Sextant, i mean pewer are!
O it is plenty out of doors, so plenty it doant no
What on airth to dew with itself, but flys about
Scatterin leaves and bloin off men's hatts!
in short, it 's jest as " fre as are " out dores,
But O Sextant, in our church its scarce as buty,
Scarce as bank bills, when agints begs for misch-
    uns,
Wich some say is purty offten (taint nothin to
    me, wat I give aint nothin to nobody) but
    O Sextant
U shet 500 men, wimmin, and children,
Speshally the latter, up in a tite place,
And every 1 on em brethes in and out, and out
    and in,
Say 50 times a minnit, or 1 million and a half
    breths an our.
Now how long will a church ful of are last at that
    rate,
I ask you—say 15 minits—and then wats to be
    did?
Why then they must brethe it all over agin,
And then agin, and so on till each has took it
    down
At least 10 times, and let it up agin, and wats
    more
The same individoal don't have the priviledge

of brethin his own are, and no ones else,
Each one must take whatever comes to him.
O Sextant, doant you no our lungs is bellusses,
To blo the fier of life, and keep it from goin out;
and how can bellusses blo without wind
And aint wind *are?* i put it to your conschens.
Are is the same to us as milk to babies,
Or water is to fish, or pendlums to clox,
Or roots and airbs unto an injun doctor,
Or little pills unto an omepath,
Or boys to gurls. Are is for us to brethe,
What signifies who preaches if i cant brethe?
Wats Pol? Wats Pollus to sinners who are ded?
Ded for want of breth, why Sextant, when we dy
Its only coz we can't brethe no more, thats all.
And now O Sextant, let me beg of you
To let a little are into our church.
(Pewer are is sertain proper for the pews)
And do it weak days, and Sundays tew,
It aint much trouble, only make a hole
And the are will come of itself;
(It luvs to come in where it can git warm)
And O how it will rouze the people up,
And sperrit up the preacher, and stop garps,
And yawns and figgits, as effectooal
As wind on the dry boans the Profit tells of.

ARABELLA M. WILLSON.

## JIM  BLUDSO  OF  THE  PRAIRIE  BELLE.

PIKE  COUNTY  BALLADS.

WALL, no! I can't tell whar he lives,
    Becase he don't live, you see;
Leastways, he 's got out of the habit
    Of livin' like you and me.
Whar have you been for the last three year
    That you haven't heard folks tell
How Jimmy Bludso passed in his checks
    The night of the Prairie Belle?

He weren't no saint,—them engineers
    Is all pretty much alike,—
One wife in Natchez-under-the-Hill
    And another one here, in Pike;
A keerless man in his talk was Jim,
    And an awkward hand in a row,
But he never flunked, and he never lied,—
    I reckon he never knowed how.

And this was all the religion he had,—
    To treat his engine well;
Never be passed on the river;
    To mind the pilot's bell;
And if ever the Prairie Belle took fire,—
    A thousand times he swore
He 'd hold her nozzle agin the bank
    Till the last soul got ashore.

All boats has their day on the Mississip,
    And her day come at last,—

The Movastar was a better boat,
  But the Belle she *wouldn't* be passed.
And so she come tearin' along that night—
  The oldest craft on the line—
With a nigger squat on her safety-valve,
  And her furnace crammed, rosin and pine.

The fire bust out as she clared the bar,
  And burnt a hole in the night,
And quick as a flash she turned, and made
  For that willer-bank on the right.
There was runnin' and cursin', but Jim yelled out,
  Over all the infernal roar,
" I 'll hold her nozzle agin the bank
  Till the last galoot 's ashore."

Through the hot, black breath of the burnin' boat
  Jim Bludso's voice was heard,
And they all had trust in his cussedness,
  And knowed he would keep his word.
And, sure 's you 're born, they all got off
  Afore the smokestacks fell,—
And Bludso's ghost went up alone
  In the smoke of the Prairie Belle.

He weren't no saint,—but at jedgment
  I 'd run my chance with Jim,
'Longside of some pious gentlemen
  That wouldn't shook hands with him.
He seen his duty, a dead-sure thing,—
  And went for it thar and then;
And Christ ain't a going to be too hard
  On a man that died for men.

                                    JOHN HAY.

## TO THE PLIOCENE SKULL.

### A GEOLOGICAL ADDRESS.

"A human skull has been found in California, in the pliocene formation. This skull is the remnant, not only of the earliest pioneer of this State, but the oldest known human being. . . . The skull was found in a shaft one hundred and fifty feet deep, two miles from Angel's, in Calaveras County, by a miner named James Matson, who gave it to Mr. Scribner, a merchant, and he gave it to Dr. Jones, who sent it to the State Geological Survey. . . . The published volume of the State Survey on the Geology of California states that man existed contemporaneously with the mastodon, but this fossil proves that he was here before the mastodon was known to exist."—*Daily Paper.*

"Speak, O man, less recent! Fragmentary fossil!
Primal pioneer of pliocene formation,
Hid in lowest drifts below the earliest stratum
       Of Volcanic tufa!

"Older than the beasts, the oldest Palæotherium;
Older than the trees, the oldest Cryptogamia;
Older than the hills, those infantile eruptions
       Of earth's epidermis!

"Eo—Mio—Plio—whatsoe'er the 'cene' was
That those vacant sockets filled with awe and
             wonder,—
Whether shores Devonian or Silurian beaches,—
       Tell us thy strange story!

"Or has the Professor slightly antedated
By some thousand years thy advent on this planet,

Giving thee an air that 's somewhat better fitted
    For cold-blooded creatures?

" Wert thou true spectator of that mighty forest,
When above thy head the stately Sigillaria
Reared its columned trunks in that remote and
        distant
    Carboniferous epoch?

" Tell us of that scene,—the dim and watery wood-
        land,
Songless, silent, hushed, with never bird or in-
        sect,
Veiled with spreading fronds and screened with
        tall club-mosses,
    Lycopodiacea—

" When beside thee walked the solemn Plesio-
        saurus,
And around thee crept the festive Ichthyosaurus,
While from time to time above thee flew and
        circled
    Cheerful Pterodactyls.

" Tell us of thy food,—those half-marine refec-
        tions,
Crinoids on the shell, and Brachipods *au natu-*
        *rel,*—
Cuttle-fish to which the *pieuvre* of Victor Hugo
    Seems a periwinkle.

" Speak, thou awful vestige of the earth's crea-
        tion,—
Solitary fragment of remains organic!

Tell the wondrous secrets of thy past existence,---
    Speak! thou oldest primate!"

Even as I gazed, a thrill of the maxilla
And a lateral movement of the condyloid process,
With post-pliocene sounds of healthy mastica-
        tion,
    Ground the teeth together;

And from that imperfect dental exhibition,
Stained with expressed juices of the weed Nico-
        tian,
Came these hollow accents, blent with softer
        murmurs
    Of expectoration:

"Which my name is Bowers, and my crust was
        busted
Falling down a shaft, in Calaveras County,
But I'd take it kindly if you'd send the pieces
    Home to old Missouri!"

                                        BRET HARTE.

---

## LITTLE BREECHES.

A  PIKE  COUNTY  VIEW  OF  SPECIAL  PROVIDENCE.

    I DON'T go much on religion,
        I never ain't had no show;
    But I've got a middlin' tight grip, sir,
        On the handful o' things I know.
    I don't pan out on the prophets
        And free-will, and that sort o' thing,—
    But believe in God and the angels,
        Ever sence one night last spring.

I come into town with some turnips,
　And my little Gabe come along,—
No four-year-old in the county
　Could beat him for pretty and strong,
Peart and chipper and sassy,
　Always ready to swear and fight,—
And I 'd learnt him ter chaw terbacker,
　Jest to keep his milk-teeth white.


The snow come down like a blanket
　As I passed by Taggart's store;
I went in for a jug of molasses
　And left the team at the door.
They scared at something and started,—
　I heard one little squall,
And hell-to-split over the prairie
　Went team, Little Breeches and all.


Hell-to-split over the prairie!
　I was almost froze with skeer;
But we rousted up some torches,
　And sarched for 'em far and near.
At last we struck hosses and wagon,
　Snowed under a soft white mound,
Upsot, dead beat,—but of little Gabe
　No hide nor hair was found.


And here all hope soured on me
　Of my fellow-critter's aid,—
I jest flopped down on my marrow-bones,
　Crotch-deep in the snow, and prayed.

.　　.　　.　　.　　.

By this, the torches was played out,
   And me and Isrul Parr
Went off for some wood to a sheepfold
   That he said was somewhar thar.

We found it at last, and a little shed
   Where they shut up the lambs at night.
We looked in, and seen them huddled thar,
   So warm and sleepy and white;
And THAR sot Little Breeches and chirped,
   As pert as ever you see,
" I want a chaw of terbacker,
   And that 's what 's the matter of me."

How did he git thar?  Angels.
   He could never have walked in that storm.
They just scooped down and toted him
   To whar it was safe and warm.
And I think that saving a little child,
   And bringing him to his own,
Is a derned sight better business
   Than loafing around the Throne.

JOHN HAY.

---

## JIM

Say there!  P'r'aps
   Some on you chaps
   Might know Jim Wild?
Well,—no offence:
Thar ain't no sense
   In gettin' riled!

Jim was my chum
  Up on the Bar:
That 's why I come
  Down from up thar,
Lookin' for Jim.
Thank ye, sir! *you*
Ain't of that crew,—
  Blest if you are!

Money?—Not much:
  That ain't my kind;
I an't no such.
Rum?—I don't mind,
  Seein' it 's you.

Well, this yer Jim,
Did you know him?—
Jess 'bout your size;
Same kind of eyes?—
Well, that is strange:
  Why, it 's two year
  Since he come here,
Sick, for a change.

Well, here 's to us;
    Eh?
The *deuce* you say!
    Dead?—
That little cuss?

What makes you star,—
You over thar?
Can't a man drop
's glass in yer shop

But you must rar'?
It wouldn't take
*Derned* much to break
You and your bar.

Dead!
Poor—little—Jim!
—Why, there was me,
Jones, and Bob Lee,
Harry and Ben,—
No-account men:
Then to take *him!*

Well, thar— Good-bye,—
No more, sir,—I—
Eh?
What 's that you say?—
Why, dern it!—sho!—
No? Yes! By Jo!
Sold!
Sold! Why you limb,
You ornery,
Derned old
Long-leggèd Jim!

BRET HARTE.

## BANTY TIM.

[Remarks of Sergeant Tilmon Joy to the White Man's
Committee of Spunky Point, Illinois.]

I RECKON I git your drift, gents—
You 'low the boy sha'n't stay;
This is a white man's country:
You 're Dimocrats, you say:

And whereas, and seein', and wherefore,
  The times bein' all out o' jint,
The nigger has got to mosey
  From the limits o' Spunky P'int!

Let 's reason the thing a minute;
  I 'm an old-fashioned Dimocrat, too,
Though I laid my politics out o' the way
  For to keep till the war was through.
But I come back here allowin'
  To vote as I used to do,
Though it gravels me like the devil to train
  Along o' sich fools as you.

Now dog my cats if I kin see
  In all the light of the day,
What you 've got to do with the question
  Ef Tim shall go or stay.
And furder than that I give notice,
  Ef one of you tetches the boy,
He kin check his trunks to a warmer clime
  Than he 'll find in Illanoy.

Why, blame your hearts, jist hear me!
  You know that ungodly day
When our left struck Vicksburg Heights, how
     ripped
  And torn and tattered we lay.
When the rest retreated, I stayed behind,
  Fur reasons sufficient to me,—
With a rib caved in, and a leg on a strike,
  I sprawled on that cursed glacee.

Lord! how the hot sun went for us,
  And broiled and blistered and burned!

How the rebel bullets whizzed round us
　When a cuss in his death-grip turned!
Till along toward dusk I seen a thing
　I couldn't believe for a spell:
That nigger—that Tim—was a-crawlin' to me
　Through that fire-proof, gilt-edged hell!

The rebels seen him as quick as me,
　And the bullets buzzed like bees;
But he jumped for me, and shouldered me,
　Though a shot brought him once to his knees;
But he staggered up, and packed me off,
　With a dozen stumbles and falls,
Till safe in our lines he drapped us both,
　His black hide riddled with balls.

So, my gentle gazelles, thar's my answer,
　And here stays Banty Tim:
He trumped Death's ace for me that day,
　And I'm not goin' back on him!
You may rezoloot till the cows come home,
　But ef one of you tetches the boy,
He'll wrastle his hash to-night in hell,
　Or my name's not Tilmon Joy!

JOHN HAY.

---

## DOW'S FLAT.

### 1856.

Dow's Flat. That's its name.
　And I reckon that you
Are a stranger? The same?
　Well, I thought it was true,

For thar isn't a man on the river as can't spot
        the place at first view.


        It was called after Dow,—
            Which the same was an ass;
        And as to the how
            Thet the thing kem to pass,—
Just tie up your hoss to that buckeye, and sit ye
        down here in the grass.


        You see this yer Dow
            Hed the worst kind of luck;
        He slipped up somehow
            On each thing thet he struck.
Why, ef he 'd straddled thet fence-rail the derned
        thing 'ed get up and buck.


        He mined on the bar
            Till he couldn't pay rates;
        He was smashed by a car
            When he tunnelled with Bates;
And right on top of his trouble kem his wife and
        five kids from the States.


        It was rough,—mighty rough;
            But the boys they stood by,
        And they brought him the stuff
            For a house, on the sly;
And the old woman,—well, she did washing, and
        took on when no one was nigh.


        But this yer luck of Dow's
            Was so powerful mean
    24

That the spring near his house
    Dried right up on the green;
And he sunk forty feet down for water, but nary
    a drop to be seen.

Then the bar petered out,
    And the boys wouldn't stay;
And the chills got about,
    And his wife fell away;
But Dow, in his well, kept a peggin' in his usual
    ridikilous way.

One day,—it was June,—
    And a year ago, jest,—
This Dow kem at noon
    To his work like the rest,
With a shovel and pick on his shoulder, and a
    derringer hid in his breast.

He goes to the well,
    And he stands on the brink,
And stops for a spell
    Jest to listen and think:
For the sun in his eyes, (jest like this, sir!) you
    see, kinder made the cuss blink.

His two ragged gals
    In the gulch were at play,
And a gownd that was Sal's
    Kinder flapped on a bay:
Not much for a man to be leavin', but his all,—
    as I've heer'd the folks say.

And—that's a peart hoss
    Thet you've got—ain't it now?

What might be her cost?
Eh? Oh!—Well then, Dow—
Let's see,—well, that forty-foot grave wasn't his,
sir, that day, anyhow.

For a blow of his pick
Sorter caved in the side,
And he looked and turned sick,
Then he trembled and cried.
For you see the dern cuss had struck—" Water?"
—beg your parding, young man, there
you lied!

It was *gold*,—in the quartz,
And it ran all alike;
And I reckon five oughts
Was the worth of that strike;
And that house with coopilow's his'n,—which
the same isn't bad for a Pike.

Thet's why it's Dow's Flat;
And the thing of it is
That he kinder got that
Through sheer contrairiness:
For 't was *water* the derned cuss was seekin', and
his luck made him certain to miss.

Thet's so. Thar's your way
To the left of yon tree;
But—a—look h'yur, say,
Won't you come up to tea?
No? Well, then the next time you're passin'; and
ask after Dow,—and thet's *me*.

BRET HARTE.

## THE SOCIETY UPON THE STANISLAUS.

I RESIDE at Table Mountain, and my name is
    Truthful James:
I am not up to small deceit or any sinful games;
    And I 'll tell in simple language what I know
      about the row
      That broke up our Society upon the Stanislow.

But first I would remark, that 't is not a proper
    plan
For any scientific gent to whale his fellow-man;
    And, if a member don't agree with his peculiar
      whim,
      To lay for that same member for to " put a
      head " on him.

Now, nothing could be finer, or more beautiful to
    see,
Than the first six months' proceedings of that
    same society;
    Till Brown of Calaveras brought a lot of fossil
      bones
      That he found within a tunnel near the tene-
      ment of Jones.

Then Brown he read a paper, and he reconstructed
    there,
From those same bones, an animal that was ex-
    tremely rare;
    And Jones then asked the Chair for a suspen-
      sion of the rules,

Till he could prove that those same bones was
   one of his lost mules.

Then Brown he smiled a bitter smile, and said he
   was at fault;
It seemed he had been trespassing on Jones's
   family vault;
   He was a most sarcastic man this quiet Mr.
   Brown,
   And on several occasions he had cleaned out
   the town.

Now I hold it is not decent for a scientific gent
To say another is an ass,—at least, to all intent;
   Nor should the individual who happens to be
   meant
   Reply by heaving rocks at him to any great ex-
   tent.

Then Abner Dean of Angel's raised a point of
   order, when
A chunk of old red sandstone took him in the
   abdomen;
   And he smiled a kind of sickly smile, and curled
   upon the floor,
   And the subsequent proceedings interested him
   no more.

For in less time than I write it, every member did
   engage
In a warfare with the remnants of a palæozoic
   age;

And the way they heaved those fossils in their
    anger was a sin,
Till the skull of an old mammoth caved the
    head of Thompson in.


And this is all I have to say of these improper
    games,
For I live at Table Mountain and my name is
    Truthful James,
    And I 've told in simple language what I know
        about the row
That broke up our Society upon the Stanislow.

BRET HARTE.

---

## PLAIN LANGUAGE FROM TRUTHFUL JAMES.

POPULARLY KNOWN AS "THE HEATHEN CHINEE."

WHICH I wish to remark—
    And my language is plain—
That for ways that are dark
    And for tricks that are vain,
The heathen Chinee is peculiar:
    Which the same I would rise to explain.


Ah Sin was his name;
    And I shall not deny
In regard to the same
    What that name might imply;
But his smile it was pensive and childlike,
    As I frequent remarked to Bill Nye.

It was August the third,
  And quite soft was the skies,
Which it might be inferred
  That Ah Sin was likewise;
Yet he played it that day upon William
  And me in a way I despise.

Which we had a small game,
  And Ah Sin took a hand:
It was euchre.  The same
  He did not understand,
But he smiled, as he sat by the table,
  With the smile that was childlike and bland.

Yet the cards they were stocked
  In a way that I grieve,
And my feelings were shocked
  At the state of Nye's sleeve,
Which was stuffed full of aces and bowers,
  And the same with intent to deceive.

But the hands that were played
  By that heathen Chinee,
And the points that he made,
  Were quite frightful to see,—
Till at last he put down a right bower,
  Which the same Nye had dealt unto me.

Then I looked up at Nye,
  And he gazed upon me;
And he rose with a sigh,
  And said, " Can this be?
We are ruined by Chinese cheap labor,"—
  And he went for that heathen Chinee.

In the scene that ensued
  I did not take a hand,
But the floor it was strewed,
  Like the leaves on the strand,
With the cards that Ah Sin had been hiding
  In the game " he did not understand."

In his sleeves, which were long,
  He had twenty-four jacks,—
Which was coming it strong,
  Yet I state but the facts.
And we found on his nails, which were taper,—
  What is frequent in tapers,—that 's wax.

Which is why I remark,
  And my language is plain,
That for ways that are dark,
  And for tricks that are vain,
The heathen Chinee is peculiar,—
  Which the same I am free to maintain.

BRET HARTE.

------

## A PLANTATION DITTY.

DE gray owl sing fum de chimbly top:
  " Who—who—is—you-oo?"
En I say: " Good Lawd, hit 's des po' me,
En I ain't quite ready fer de Jasper Sea;
I 'm po' en sinful, en you 'lowed I 'd be;
  Oh, wait, good Lawd, 'twell ter-morror!"

De gray owl sing fum de cypress tree:
  " Who—who—is—you-oo?"

En I say: " Good Lawd, ef you look you 'll see
Hit ain't nobody but des po' me,
En I like ter stay 'twell my time is free;
  Oh, wait, good Lawd, 'twell ter-morror ! "

FRANK LEBBY STANTON.

## DE FUST BANJO.

Go 'way, fiddle! folks is tired o' hearin' you
  a-squawkin'.
Keep silence fur yo' betters!—don't you hear de
  banjo talkin'?
About de 'possum's tail she 's gwine to lecter—
  ladies, listen!—
About de ha'r whut isn't dar, an' why de ha'r is
  missin':

" Dar's gwine to be a' oberflow," said Noah,
  lookin' solemn—
Fur Noah tuk the " Herald," an' he read de ribber
  column—
An' so he sot his hands to wuk a-cl'arin' timber-
  patches,
An' lowed he 's gwine to build a boat to beat the
  steamah Natchez.

Ol' Noah kep' a-nailin' an' a-chippin' an' a-sawin';
An' all de wicked neighbors kep' a-laughin' an'
  a-pshawin';
But Noah didn't min' 'em, knowin' whut wuz
  gwine to happen:
An' forty days an' forty nights de rain it kep'
  a-drappin'.

Now, Noah had done cotched a lot ob ebry sort o'
    beas'es—
Ob all de shows a-trabbelin', it beat 'em all to
    pieces!
He had a Morgan colt an' sebral head o' Jarsey
    cattle—
An' druv 'em 'board de Ark as soon 's he heered
    de thunder rattle.

Den sech anoder fall ob rain!—it come so awful
    hebby,
De ribber riz immejitly, an' busted troo de lebbee;
De people all wuz drowned out—'cep' Noah an'
    de critters,
An' men he 'd hired to work de boat—an' one to
    mix de bitters.

De Ark she kep' a-sailin' an' a-sailin' *an'* a-sailin';
De lion got his dander up, an' like to bruk de
    palin';
De sarpints hissed; de painters yelled; tell, whut
    wid all de fussin',
You c'u'dn't hardly heah de mate a-bossin' 'roun'
    an' cussin'.

Now Ham, de only nigger whut wuz runnin' on de
    packet,
Got lonesome in de barber-shop, an' c'u'dn't stan'
    de racket;
An' so, fur to amuse he-se'f, he steamed some wood
    an' bent it,
An' soon he had a banjo made—de fust dat wuz
    invented.

He wet de ledder, stretched it on; made bridge
    an' screws an' aprin;
An' fitted in a proper neck—'t wuz berry long
    an' tap'rin';
He tuk some tin an' twisted him a thimble fur to
    ring it;
An' den de mighty question riz: how wuz he gwine
    to string it?


De 'possum had as fine a tail as dis dat I 's
    a-singin';
De ha'rs so long an' thick an' strong,—des fit fur
    banjo-stringin';
Dat nigger shaved 'em off as short as washday-
    dinner graces;
An' sorted ob 'em by de size, f'om little E's to
    basses.


He strung her, tuned her, struck a jig,— 't wuz
    " Nebber min' de wedder,"—
She soun' like forty-lebben bands a-playin' all
    togedder;
Some went to pattin'; some to dancin': Noah
    called de figgers;
An' Ham he sot an' knocked de tune, de happiest
    ob niggers!


Now, sence dat time—it 's mighty strange—der 's
    not de slightes' showin'
Ob any ha'r at all upon de 'possum's tail a-grow-
    in';

An' curi's, too, dat nigger's ways: his people neb-
    ber los' 'em—
Fur whar you finds de nigger—dar's de banjo an'
    an' de 'possum!

IRWIN RUSSELL.

---

### PERILS OF THINKING.

A CENTIPEDE was happy quite,
    Until a frog in fun
Said, " Pray, which leg comes after which?"
This raised her mind to such a pitch,
She lay distracted in the ditch
    Considering how to run.

ANONYMOUS.

---

### NEBUCHADNEZZAR.

You, Nebuchadnezzah, whoa, sah!
Whar is you tryin' to go, sah?
I 'd hab you fur to know, sah,
    I 's a-holdin' ob de lines.
You better stop dat prancin',
You 's paw'ful fond ob dancin',
But I 'll bet my yeah's advancin'
    Dat I 'll cure you ob yo' shines.

Look heah, mule!  Better min' out;
Fus' t'ing you know you' ll fin' out
How quick I 'll wear dis line out
    On your ugly, stubbo'n back.
You needn't try to steal up;

An' lif' dat precious heel up;
You 's got to plough dis fiel' up,
You has, sah, fur a fac'.

Dar, *dat 's* de way to do it;
He 's comin' right down to it;
Jes watch him ploughin' troo it!
Dis nigger ain't no fool.
Some folks dey would 'a' beat him;
Now, dat would only heat him—
I know just how to treat him:
You mus' *reason* wid a mule.

He minds me like a nigger.
If he wuz only bigger
He 'd fotch a mighty figger,
He would, I *tell* you!  Yes, sah!
See how he keeps a-clickin'!
He 's as gentle as a chicken,
And nebber thinks o' kickin'—
*Whoa dar!  Nebuchadnezzah!*

Is this heah me, or not me?
Or is de debbil got me?
Wuz dat a cannon shot me?
Hab I laid heah more 'n a week?
Dat mule do kick amazin'!
De beast was sp'iled in raisin';
But now I spect he 's grazin'
On de oder side de creek.

                          IRWIN RUSSELL.

## A LIFE'S LOVE.

I LOVED him in my dawning years—
    Far years, divinely dim;
My blithest smiles, my saddest tears,
    Were evermore for him.
My dreaming when the day began,
    The latest thought I had,
Was still some little loving plan
    To make my darling glad.

They deemed he lacked the conquering wiles,
    That other children wear;
To me his face, in frowns or smiles,
    Was never aught but fair.
They said that self was all his goal,
    He knew no thought beyond;
To me, I know, no living soul
    Was half so true and fond.

In love's eclipse, in friendship's dearth,
    In grief and feud and bale,
My heart has learnt the sacred worth
    Of one that cannot fail;
And come what must, and come what may,
    Nor power, nor praise, nor pelf,
Shall lure my faith from thee to stray.
    My sweet, my own—*Myself.*

ANONYMOUS.

# DARWIN.

THERE was an ape in the days that were earlier;
Centuries passed, and his hair grew curlier;
Centuries more gave a thumb to his wrist,
Then he was a Man and a Positivist.

MORTIMER COLLINS.

---

## ODE FOR A SOCIAL MEETING.

WITH SLIGHT ALTERATIONS BY A TEETOTALLER.

COME! fill a fresh bumper,—for why should we
go
        logwood
While the ~~nectar~~ still reddens our cups as they
flow?
       decoction
Pour out the ~~rich juices~~ still bright with the sun,
          dye-stuff
Till o'er the brimmed crystal the ~~rubies~~ shall run.
     half-ripened apples
The ~~purple-globed clusters~~ their life-dews have
bled;
      taste           sugar of lead
How sweet is the ~~breath~~ of the ~~fragrance they
shed~~!
    rank-poisons          *wines!!!*
For summer's ~~last roses~~ lie hid in the ~~wines~~
          stable-boys smoking long-nines
That were garnered by ~~maidens who laughed
through the vines.~~

<u>scowl</u>      <u>howl</u>      <u>scoff</u>      <u>sneer</u>
Then a ~~smile,~~ and a ~~glass,~~ and a ~~toast,~~ and a ~~cheer,~~
strychnine and whiskey, and ratsbane and beer
For ~~all the good wine, and we've some of it here!~~
In cellar, in pantry, in attic, in hall,
Down, down with the tyrant that masters us all !
~~Long live the gay servant that laughs for us all!~~

OLIVER WENDELL HOLMES.

## HOLLOW HOSPITALITY.

FROM " SATIRES," BOOK III. SAT. 3.

THE courteous citizen bade me to his feast
With hollow words, and overly * request:
" Come, will ye dine with me this holiday? "
I yielded, though he hoped I would say nay:
For I had maidened it, as many use;
Loath for to grant, but loather to refuse.
" Alack, sir, I were loath—another day,—
I should but trouble you;—pardon me, if you
     may."
No pardon should I need; for, to depart
He gives me leave, and thanks too, in his heart.
Two words for money, Darbyshirian wise:
(That 's one too many) is a naughty guise.
Who looks for double biddings to a feast,
May dine at home for an importune guest.
I went, then saw, and found the great expense;
The face and fashions of our citizens.
Oh, Cleopatrical! what wanteth there
For curious cost, and wondrous choice of cheer?
Beef, that erst Hercules held for finest fare;

* Superficial.

Pork, for the fat Bœotian, or the hare
For Martial; fish for the Venetian;
Goose-liver for the licorous Roman;
Th' Athenian's goat; quail, Iolaus' cheer;
The hen for Esculape, and the Parthian deer;
Grapes for Arcesilas, figs for Pluto's mouth,
And chestnuts fair for Amarillis' tooth.
Hadst thou such cheer? wert thou ever there be-
    fore?
Never,—I thought so: nor come there no more.
Come there no more; for so meant all that cost:
Never hence take me for thy second host.
For whom he means to make an often guest,
One dish shall serve; and welcome make the rest.

DR. JOSEPH HALL.

## A RECIPE.

### ROASTED SUCKING-PIG.

*Air.*—" Scots wha hae."

Cooks who 'd roast a sucking-pig,
Purchase one not over big;
Coarse ones are not worth a fig;
    So a young one buy.
See that he is scalded well
(That is done by those who sell,
Therefore on that point to dwell
    Were absurdity).

Sage and bread, mix just enough,
Salt and pepper *quantum suff.,*
And the pig's interior stuff,
    With the whole combined.

25

To a fire that 's rather high,
Lay it till completely dry;
Then to every part apply
    Cloth, with butter lined.

Dredge with flour o'er and o'er,
Till the pig will hold no more;
Then do nothing else before
    'T is for serving fit.
Then scrape off the flour with care;
Then a buttered cloth prepare;
Rub it well; then cut—not tear—
    Off the head of it.

Then take out and mix the brains
With the gravy it contains;
While it on the spit remains,
    Cut the pig in two.
Chop the sage and chop the bread
Fine as very finest shred;
O'er it melted butter spread,—
    Stinginess won't do.

When it in the dish appears,
Garnish with the jaws and ears;
And when dinner-hour nears,
    Ready let it be.
Who can offer such a dish
May dispense with fowl and fish;
And if he a guest should wish,
    Let him send for me!

        PUNCH'S *Poetical Cookery Book.*

## A RECIPE FOR SALAD.

To make this condiment your poet begs
The pounded yellow of two hard boiled eggs;
Two boiled potatoes, passed through kitchen
    sieve,
Smoothness and softness to the salad give;
Let onion atoms lurk within the bowl,
And, half suspected, animate the whole;
Of mordant mustard add a single spoon,
Distrust the condiment that bites so soon;
But deem it not, thou man of herbs, a fault
To add a double quantity of salt;
Four times the spoon with oil from Lucca crown,
And twice with vinegar, procured from town;
And lastly, o'er the flavored compound toss
A magic *soupçon* of anchovy sauce.
O green and glorious! O herbaceous treat!
'T would tempt the dying anchorite to eat;
Back to the world he 'd turn his fleeting soul,
And plunge his fingers in the salad-bowl;
Serenely full, the epicure would say,
" Fate cannot harm me,—I have dined to-day."

SYDNEY SMITH.

## ODE TO TOBACCO.

THOU who, when fears attack,
Bid'st them avaunt, and Black
Care, at the horseman's back
    Perching, unseatest;
Sweet when the morn is gray;

Sweet, when they 've cleared away
Lunch; and at close of day
　　Possibly sweetest:

I have a liking old
For thee, though manifold
Stories, I know, are told,
　　Not to thy credit;
How one (or two at most)
Drops make a cat a ghost—
Useless, except to roast—
　　Doctors have said it:

How they who use fusees
All grow by slow degrees
Brainless as chimpanzees,
　　Meagre as lizards;
Go mad, and beat their wives;
Plunge (after shocking lives)
Razors and carving-knives
　　Into their gizzards.

Confound such knavish tricks!
Yet know I five or six
Smokers who freely mix
　　Still with their neighbors;
Jones—(who, I 'm glad to say,
Asked leave of Mrs. J.)—
Daily absorbs a clay
　　After his labors.

Cats may have had their goose
Cooked by tobacco-juice;

Still why deny its use
   Thoughtfully taken?
We 're not as tabbies are:
Smith, take a fresh cigar!
Jones, the tobacco-jar!
   Here 's to thee, Bacon!

CHARLES S. CALVERLEY.

## A FAREWELL TO TOBACCO.

MAY the Babylonish curse
Straight confound my stammering verse,
If I can a passage see
In this word-perplexity,
Or a fit expression find,
Or a language to my mind
(Still the phrase is wide or scant),
To take leave of thee, GREAT PLANT!
Or in any terms relate
Half my love, or half my hate;
For I hate, yet love, thee so,
That, whichever thing I show,
The plain truth will seem to be
A constrained hyperbole,
And the passion to proceed
More from a mistress than a weed.

   Sooty retainer to the vine!
Bacchus' black servant, negro fine!
Sorcerer! that mak'st us dote upon
Thy begrimed complexion,
And, for thy pernicious sake,

More and greater oaths to break
Than reclaimèd lovers take
'Gainst women! Thou thy siege dost lay
Much, too, in the female way,
While thou suck'st the laboring breath
Faster than kisses, or than death.

Thou in such a cloud dost bind us
That our worst foes cannot find us,
And ill fortune, that would thwart us,
Shoots at rovers, shooting at us;
While each man, through thy heightening steam,
Does like a smoking Etna seem;
And all about us does express
(Fancy and wit in richest dress)
A Sicilian fruitfulness.

Thou through such a mist dost show us
That our best friends do not know us,
And, for those allowèd features
Due to reasonable creatures,
Liken'st us to fell chimeras,
Monsters,—that who see us, fear us;
Worse than Cerberus or Geryon,
Or, who first loved a cloud, Ixion.

Bacchus we know, and we allow
His tipsy rites. But what art thou,
That but by reflex canst show
What his deity can do,—
As the false Egyptian spell
Aped the true Hebrew miracle?
Some few vapors thou mayst raise

The weak brain may serve to amaze;
But to the reins and nobler heart
Canst nor life nor heat impart.

Brother of Bacchus, later born!
The old world was sure forlorn,
Wanting thee, that aidest more
The god's victories than, before,
All his panthers, and the brawls
Of his piping Bacchanals.
These, as stale, we disallow,
Or judge of thee meant: only thou
His true Indian conquest art;
And, for ivy round his dart,
The reformèd god now weaves
A finer thyrsus of thy leaves.

Scent to match thy rich perfume
Chemic art did ne'er presume,
Through her quaint alembic strain,
None so sovereign to the brain.
Nature, that did in thee excel,
Framed again no second smell.
Roses, violets, but toys
For the smaller sort of boys,
Or for greener damsels meant;
Thou art the only manly scent.

Stinkingest of the stinking kind!
Filth of the mouth and fog of the mind!
Africa, that brags her foison,
Breeds no such prodigious poison!
Henbane, nightshade, both together,
Hemlock, aconite—

Nay rather,
Plant divine, of rarest virtue;
Blisters on the tongue would hurt you!
'T was but in a sort I blamed thee;
None e'er prospered who defamed thee;
Irony all, and feigned abuse,
Such as perplexèd lovers use
At a need, when, in despair
To paint forth their fairest fair,
Or in part but to express
That exceeding comeliness
Which their fancies doth so strike,
They borrow language of dislike;
And, instead of dearest Miss,
Jewel, honey, sweetheart, bliss,
And those forms of old admiring,
Call her cockatrice and siren,
Basilisk, and all that 's evil,
Witch, hyena, mermaid, devil,
Ethiop, wench, and blackamoor,
Monkey, ape, and twenty more;
Friendly trait'ress, loving foe,—
Not that she is truly so,
But no other way they know,
A contentment to express
Borders so upon excess
That they do not rightly wot
Whether it be from pain or not.

Or, as men, constrained to part
With what 's nearest to their heart,
While their sorrow 's at the height
Lose discrimination quite,

And their hasty wrath let fall,
To appease their frantic gall,
On the darling thing, whatever,
Whence they feel it death to sever,
Though it be, as they, perforce,
Guiltless of the sad divorce.

For I must (nor let it grieve thee,
Friendliest of plants, that I must) leave
    thee.
Would do anything but die,
And but seek to extend my days
Long enough to sing thy praise.
But, as she who once hath been
A king's consort is a queen
Ever after, nor will bate
Any tittle of her state
Though a widow, or divorced,
So I, from thy converse forced,
The old name and style retain,
A right Katherine of Spain;
And a seat, too, 'mongst the joys
Of the blest Tobacco Boys;
Where, though I, by sour physician,
Am debarred the full fruition
Of thy favors, I may catch
Some collateral sweets, and snatch
Sidelong odors, that give life
Like glances from a neighbor's wife;
And still live in the by-places
And the suburbs of thy graces;
And in thy borders take delight,
An unconquered Canaanite.

CHARLES LAMB.

## TOO GREAT A SACRIFICE.

THE maid, as by the papers doth appear,
Whom fifty thousand dollars made so dear,
To test Lothario's passion, simply said:
" Forego the weed before we go to wed.
For smoke take flame; I 'll be that flame's bright
    fanner:
To have your Anna, give up your Havana."
But he, when thus she brought him to the scratch,
Lit his cigar and threw away his match.

ANONYMOUS.

---

## FROM "LOVE SONNETS OF A HOOD-LUM."

### PROLOGUE.

WOULDN'T it jar you, wouldn't it make you sore
To see the poet, when the goods play out,
Crawl off of poor old Pegasus and tout
His skate to two-step sonnets off galore?
Then, when the plug, a dead one, can no more
Shake rag-time than a biscuit, right about
The poem-butcher turns with gleeful shout
And sends a batch of sonnets to the store.

The sonnet is a very easy mark,
A James P. Dandy as a carry-all
For brain-fag wrecks who want to keep it dark
Just why their crop of thinks is running small.
On the low down, dear Mame, my looty loo,
That 's why I 've cooked this batch of rhymes for
    you.

### EPILOGUE.

To just one girl I 've turned my sad bazoo,
Stringing my pipe-dream off as it occurred,
And as I 've tipped the straight talk every word,
If you don't like it you know what to do.
Perhaps you think I 've handed out to you
An idle jest, a touch-me-not, absurd
As any sky-blue-pink canary bird,
Billed for a record season at the Zoo.

If that 's your guess you 'll have to guess again,
For thus I fizzled in a burst of glory,
And this rhythmatic side-show doth contain
The sum and substance of my hard-luck story,
Showing how Vanity is still on deck
And Humble Virtue gets it in the neck.

WALLACE IRWIN.

---

## A SADDENED TRAMP.

" Now unto yonder wood-pile go,
    Where toil till I return;
And feel how proud a thing it is
    A livelihood to earn."
A saddened look came o'er the tramp;
    He seemed like one bereft.
He stowed away the victuals cold,
    He—saw the wood, and left.

ANONYMOUS.

# III.

## PARODIES: IMITATIONS.

---

### THE MODERN HOUSE THAT JACK BUILT.

BEHOLD the mansion reared by dædal Jack.

See the malt, stored in many a plethoric sack,
In the proud cirque of Ivan's bivouac.

Mark how the rat's felonious fangs invade
The golden stores in John's pavilion laid.

Anon, with velvet foot and Tarquin strides,
Subtle grimalkin to his quarry glides,—
Grimalkin grim, that slew the fierce rodent
Whose tooth insidious Johann's sackcloth rent.

Lo! now the deep-mouthed canine foe's assault,
That vexed the avenger of the stolen malt;
Stored in the hallowed precincts of the hall
That rose complete at Jack's creative call.

Here stalks the impetuous cow, with the crumpled
      horn,
Whereon the exacerbating hound was torn,

Who bayed the feline slaughter-beast, that slew
The rat predaceous, whose keen fangs ran through
The textile fibres that involved the grain
That lay in Hans' inviolate domain.

Here walks forlorn the damsel crowned with rue,
Lactiferous spoils from vaccine dugs who drew,
Of that corniculate beast whose tortuous horn
Tossed to the clouds, in fierce vindictive scorn,
The harrowing hound, whose braggart bark and
    stir
Arched the lithe spine and reared the indignant
    fur
Of puss, that with verminicidal claw
Struck the weird rat, in whose insatiate maw
Lay reeking malt, that erst in Ivan's courts we
    saw.

Robed in senescent garb, that seemed, in sooth,
Too long a prey to Chronos' iron tooth,
Behold the man whose amorous lips incline,
Full with young Eros' osculative sign,
To the lorn maiden, whose lac-albic hands
Drew albu-lactic wealth from lacteal glands
Of the immortal bovine, by whose horn,
Distort, to realm ethereal was borne
The beast catulean, vexer of that sly
Ulysses quadrupedal who made die
The old mordacious rat, that dared devour
Antecedaneous ale in John's domestic bower.

Lo! here, with hirsute honors doffed, succinct
Of saponaceous locks, the priest who linked
In Hymen's golden bands the torn unthrift,

Whose means exiguous stared from many a rift,
Even as he kissed the virgin all forlorn,
Who milked the cow with the implicated horn,
Who in fine wrath the canine torturer skied,
That dared to vex the insidious muricide,
Who let auroral effluence through the pelt
Of the sly rat that robbed the palace Jack had
    built.

The loud cantankerous Shanghai comes at last,
Whose shouts aroused the shorn ecclesiast,
Who sealed the vows of Hymen's sacrament
To him who, robed in garments indigent,
Exosculates the damsel lachrymose,
The emulgator of that hornèd brute moròse
That tossed the dog that worried the cat that
    kilt
The rat that ate the malt that lay in the house
    that Jack built.

ANONYMOUS.

---

## THE FRIEND OF HUMANITY AND
## THE KNIFE-GRINDER.*

### FRIEND OF HUMANITY.

NEEDY knife-grinder! whither are you going?
Rough is the road; your wheel is out of order.
Bleak blows the blast;—your hat has got a hole
        in 't;
        So have your breeches!

* A burlesque upon the humanitarian sentiments of
Southey in his younger days, as well as of the Sapphic
stanzas in which he sometimes embodied them.

Weary knife-grinder! little think the proud ones,
Who in their coaches roll along the turnpike-
Road, what hard work 't is crying all day,
        " Knives and
            Scissors to grind O ! "


Tell me, knife-grinder, how came you to grind
            knives?
Did some rich man tyrannically use you?
Was it the squire? or parson of the parish?
        Or the attorney?


Was it the squire for killing of his game? or
Covetous parson for his tithes distraining?
Or roguish lawyer made you lose your little
        All in a lawsuit?


(Have you not read the Rights of Man, by Tom
        Paine?)
Drops of compassion tremble on my eyelids,
Ready to fall as soon as you have told your
        Pitiful story.

### KNIFE-GRINDER.

Story! God bless you! I have none to tell, sir;
Only, last night, a-drinking at the Chequers,
This poor old hat and breeches, as you see, were
        Torn in a scuffle.


Constables came up for to take me into
Custody; they took me before the justice;
Justice Oldmixon put me into the parish
        Stocks for a vagrant.

I should be glad to drink your honor's health in
A pot of beer, if you will give me sixpence;
But for my part, I never love to meddle
    With politics, sir.

### FRIEND OF HUMANITY.

I give thee sixpence! I will see thee damned
        first,—
Wretch! whom no sense of wrongs can rouse to
        vengeance,—
Sordid, unfeeling, reprobate, degraded,
        Spiritless outcast!

(*Kicks the knife-grinder, overturns his wheel, and
    exit in a transport of republican enthusiasm
    and universal philanthropy.*)

                        GEORGE CANNING.

————

## DEBORAH LEE.*

'T is a dozen or so of years ago,
    Somewhere in the West countree,
That a nice girl lived, as ye Hoosiers know
    By the name of Deborah Lee;
Her sister was loved by Edgar Poe,
    But Deborah by me.

Now I was green, and she was green,
    As a summer's squash might be;
And we loved as warmly as other folks,—
    I and my Deborah Lee,—

* See Poe's " Annabel Lee," Volume III. p. 312.

With a love that the lasses of Hoosierdom
  Coveted her and me.


But somehow it happened a long time ago,
  In the aguish West countree,
That chill March morning gave the *shakes*
  To my beautiful Deborah Lee;
And the grim steam-doctor (drat him!) came,
  And bore her away from me,—
The doctor and death, old partners they,—
  In the aguish West countree.


The angels wanted her in heaven
  (But they never asked for me),
And that is the reason, I rather guess,
  In the aguish West countree,
That the cold March wind, and the doctor, and
    death,
  Took off my Deborah Lee—
  My beautiful Deborah Lee—
From the warm sunshine and the opening flowers,
  And bore her away from me.


Our love was as strong as a six-horse team,
  Or the love of folks older than we,
  Or possibly wiser than we;
But death, with the aid of doctor and steam,
  Was rather too many for me:
He closed the peepers and silenced the breath
  Of my sweetheart Deborah Lee,
And her form lies cold in the prairie mold,
  Silent and cold,—ah me!
  26

The foot of the hunter shall press her grave,
   And the prairie's sweet wild flowers
In their odorous beauty around it wave
   Through all the sunny hours,—
   The still, bright summer hours;
And the birds shall sing in the tufted grass
   And the nectar-laden bee,
With his dreamy hum, on his gauze wings pass,—
   She wakes no more to me;
   Ah, nevermore to me!
Though the wild birds sing and the wild flowers
     spring,
   She wakes no more to me.

Yet oft in the hush of the dim, still night,
   A vision of beauty I see
Gliding soft to my bedside,—a phantom of light,
   Dear, beautiful Deborah Lee,—
   My bride that was to be;
And I wake to mourn that the doctor, and death,
And the cold March wind, should stop the breath
   Of my darling Deborah Lee,—
   Adorable Deborah Lee,—
That angels should want her up in heaven
   Before they wanted me.
                 WILLIAM H. BURLEIGH.

---

## THE COCK AND THE BULL.*

You see this pebble-stone? It 's a thing I
   bought
Of a bit of a chit of a boy i' the mid o' the day—

* In imitation of Robert Browning—"The Ring and the
Book."

I like to dock the smaller parts-o'-speech,
As we curtail the already cur-tailed cur
(You catch the paronomasia, play o' words?)—
Did, rather, i' the pre-Landseerian days.
Well, to my muttons. I purchased the concern,
And clapt it i' my poke, and gave for same
By way, to-wit, of barter or exchange—
"Chop" was my snickering dandiprat's own
    term—
One shilling and fourpence, current coin o' the
    realm.
O-n-e one and f-o-u-r four
Pence, one and fourpence—you are with me,
    sir?—
What hour it skills not: ten or eleven o' the clock,
One day (and what a roaring day it was!)
In February, eighteen sixty-nine,
Alexandrina Victoria, Fidei
Hm—hm—how runs the jargon?—being on
    throne.

Such, sir, are all the facts, succinctly put,
The basis or substratum—what you will—
Of the impending eighty thousand lines.
"Not much in 'em either," quoth perhaps simple
    Hodge.
But there's a superstructure. Wait a bit.

Mark first the rationale of the thing:
Hear logic rival and levigate the deed.
That shilling—and for matter o' that, the pence—
I had o' course upo' me—wi' me, say—
(*Mecum*'s the Latin, make a note o' that)

When I popped pen i' stand, blew snout, scratched
    ear,
Sniffed—tch!—at snuff-box; tumbled up, he-heed,
Haw-hawed (not hee-hawed, that 's another guess
    thing:)
Then fumbled at, and stumbled out of, door,
I shoved the door ope wi' my omoplat;
And *in vestibulo*, i' the entrance-hall,
Donned galligaskins, antigropelos,
And so forth; and, complete with hat and gloves.
One on and one a-dangle i' my hand.
And ombrifuge, (Lord love you!) case o' rain,
I flopped forth, 's buddikins! on my own ten toes,
(I do assure you there be ten of them,)
And went clump-clumping up hill and down dale
To find myself o' the sudden i' front o' the boy.
Put case I hadn't 'em on me, could I ha' bought
This sort-o'-kind-o'-what-you-might-call toy,
This pebble-thing, o' the boy-thing? Q. E. D.
That 's proven without aid from mumping Pope,
Sleek porporate or bloated Cardinal,
(Isn't it, old Fatchaps? You 're in Euclid now.)
So, having the shilling—having i' fact a lot—
And pence and halfpence, ever so many o' them,
I purchased, as I think I said before,
The pebble (lapis, lapidis,—di,—dem,—de,—
What nouns 'crease short i' the genitive, Fat-
    chaps, eh?)
O' the boy, a bare-legged beggarly son of a gun,
For one and fourpence. Here we are again.
    Now Law steps in, big-wigged, voluminous-
    jawed;
Investigates and re-investigates.

Was the transaction illegal?  Law shakes head.
Perpend, sir, all the bearings of the case.

At first the coin was mine, the chattel his.
But now (by virtue of the said exchange
And barter) *vice versa* all the coin,
*Per juris operationem*, vests
I' the boy and his assigns till ding o' doom;
(*In sæcula sæculo-o-o-orum;*
I think I hear the Abbate mouth out that.)
To have and hold the same to him and them . . .
*Confer* some idiot on Conveyancing,
Whereas the pebble and every part thereof,
And all that appertaineth thereunto,
Or shall, will, may, might, can, could, would, or
      should,
(*Subandi cætera*—clap me to the close—
For what's the good of law in a case o' the kind?)
Is mine to all intents and purposes.
This settled, I resume the thread o' the tale.

Now for a touch o' the vendor's quality.
He says a gen'lman bought a pebble of him,
(This pebble i' sooth, sir, which I hold i' my
      hand)—
And paid for 't, *like* a gen'lman, on the nail.
" Did I o'ercharge him a ha'penny?  Devil a bit.
Fiddlestick's end!  Get out, you blazing ass!
Gabble o' the goose.  Don't bugaboo-baby *me!*
Go double or quits?  Yah! tittup! what's the
      odds? "
—There 's the transaction viewed, i' the vendor's
      light.

Next ask that dumpled hag, stood snuffling by,
With her three frowsy-browsy brats o' babes,
The scum o' the kennel, cream o' the filth-heap
    —Faugh?
Aie, aie, aie, aie! ὀτοτοτοτοτοῖ,
('Stead which we blurt out Hoighty-toighty
    now)—
And the baker and candlestick-maker, and Jack
    and Gill,
Bleared Goody this and queasy Gaffer that.
Ask the schoolmaster. Take schoolmaster first.

He saw a gentleman purchase of a lad
A stone, and pay for it *rite,* on the square,
And carry it off *per saltum,* jauntily,
*Propria quæ maribus,* gentleman's property now
(Agreeable to the law explained above),
*In proprium usum,* for his private ends.
The boy he chucked a brown i' the air, and bit
I' the face the shilling: heaved a thumping-stone
At a lean hen that ran cluck-clucking by,
(And hit her, dead as nail i' post o' door,)
Then *abiit*—what 's the Ciceronian phrase?—
*Excessit, evasit, erupit,*—off slogs boy;
Off in three flea-skips. *Hactenus,* so far,
So good, *tam bene. Bene, satis, male,*—
Where was I? who said what of one in a quag?
I did once hitch the syntax into verse:
*Verbum personale,* a verb personal,
*Concordat,*—ay, "agrees," old Fatchaps—*cum
Nominativo,* with its nominative,
*Genere,* i' point o' gender, *numero,*
O' number, *et persona,* and person. *Ut,*

Instance: *Sol ruit,* down flops sun, *ct,* and,
*Montes umbrantur,* snuffs out mountains. Pah!
Excuse me, sir, I think I 'm going mad.
You see the trick on 't though, and can yourself
Continue the discourse *ad libitum.*
It takes up about eighty thousand lines,
A thing imagination boggles at:
And might, odds-bobs, sir! in judicious hands,
Extend from here to Mesopotamy.

CHARLES STUART CALVERLEY.

## THE AULD WIFE.*

THE auld wife sat at her ivied door,
  (*Butter and eggs and a pound of cheese*)
A thing she had frequently done before;
  And her spectacles lay on her aproned knees.

The piper he piped on the hill-top high,
  (*Butter and eggs and a pound of cheese*)
Till the cow said " I die " and the goose asked
    " Why; "
  And the dog said nothing but searched for
    fleas.

The farmer he strode through the square farm-
    yard;
  (*Butter and eggs and a pound of cheese*)
His last brew of ale was a trifle hard,
  The connection of which with the plot one sees.

The farmer's daughter hath frank blue eyes,
  (*Butter and eggs and a pound of cheese*)

* Imitation of Rossetti.

She hears the rooks caw in the windy skies,
  As she sits at her lattice and shells her peas.

The farmer's daughter hath ripe red lips;
  (*Butter and eggs and a pound of cheese*)
If you try to approach her, away she skips
  Over tables and chairs with apparent ease.

The farmer's daughter hath soft brown hair;
  (*Butter and eggs and a pound of cheese*)
And I met with a ballad, I can't say where,
  Which wholly consists of lines like these.

She sat with her hands 'neath her dimpled cheeks,
  (*Butter and eggs and a pound of cheese*)
And spake not a word.  While a lady speaks
  There is hope, but she didn't even sneeze.

She sat with her hands 'neath her crimson cheeks
  (*Butter and eggs and a pound of cheese*)
She gave up mending her father's breeks,
  And let the cat roll in her best chemise.

She sat with her hands 'neath her crimson cheeks
  (*Butter and eggs and a pound of cheese*)
And gazed at the piper for thirteen weeks;
  Then she followed him out o'er the misty leas.

Her sheep followed her as their tails did them
  (*Butter and eggs and a pound of cheese*)
And this song is considered a perfect gem,
  And as to the meaning, it's what you please.

CHARLES STUART CALVERLEY.

## LOVERS, AND A REFLECTION.*

In moss-prankt dells which the sunbeams flatter
    (And heaven it knoweth what that may mean;
Meaning, however, is no great matter)
    Where woods are a-tremble, with rifts atween;

Through God's own heather we wonned together,
    I and my Willie (O love my love) :
I need hardly remark it was glorious weather,
    And flitterbats waved alow, above:

Boats were curtseying, rising, bowing
    (Boats in that climate are so polite),
And sands were a ribbon of green endowing,
    And O the sun-dazzle on bark and bight!

Through the rare red heather we danced together,
    (O love my Willie!) and smelt for flowers:
I must mention again it was glorious weather,
    Rhymes are so scarce in this world of ours:—

By rises that flushed with their purple favors,
    Through becks that brattled o'er grasses sheen,
We walked or waded, we two young shavers,
    Thanking our stars we were both so green.

We journeyed in parallels, I and Willie,
    In "fortunate parallels!" Butterflies,
Hid in weltering shadows of daffodilly
    Or marjoram, kept making peacock's eyes:

* See Jean Ingelow's "Divided," Volume III. p. 64.

Song-birds darted about, some inky
  As coal, some snowy (I ween) as curds;
Or rosy as pinks, or as roses pinky—
  They reck of no eerie To-come, those birds!

But they skim over bents which the mill-stream
    washes,
  Or hang in the lift 'neath a white cloud's hem;
They need no parasols, no galoshes;
  And good Mrs. Trimmer * she feedeth them.

Then we thrid God's cowslips (as erst his heather)
  That endowed the wan grass with their golden
    blooms;
And snapt—(it was perfectly charming weath-
    er)—
  Our fingers at Fate and her goddess glooms:

And Willie 'gan sing—(O, his notes were fluty;
  Wafts fluttered them out to the white-winged
    sea)—
Something made up of rhymes that have done
    much duty,
  Rhymes (better to put it) of " ancientry: "

Bowers of flowers encountered showers
  In William's carol (O love my Willie!)
When he bade sorrow borrow from blithe To-
    morrow
  I quite forget what—say a daffodilly:

* Mrs. Trimmer was the author of a famous little book
for children, "The History of the Robins." It has been
republished in America.

A nest in a hollow, " with buds to follow,"
  I think occurred next in his nimble strain;
And clay that was " kneaden " of course in Eden—
  A rhyme most novel, I do maintain :

Mists, bones, the singer himself, love-stories,
  And all least furlable things got " furled ;"
Not with any design to conceal their glories,
  But simply and solely to rhyme with " world."

O, if billows and pillows and hours and flowers,
  And all the brave rhymes of an elder day,
Could be furled together this genial weather,
  And carted, or carried on wafts away,
Nor ever again trotted out—ay me!
How much fewer volumes of verse there 'd be!

CHARLES STUART CALVERLEY.

## NEPHELIDIA.

FROM the depth of the dreamy decline of the dawn
    through a notable nimbus of nebulous noon-
    shine,
Pallid and pink as the palm of the flag-flower
    that flickers with fear of the flies as they float,
Are they looks of our lovers that lustrously lean
    from a marvel of mystic miraculous moon-
    shine,
These that we feel in the blood of our blushes
    that thicken and threaten with sobs from
    the throat?

Thicken and thrill as a theatre thronged at appeal
    of an actor's appalled agitation,
Fainter with fear of the fires of the future than
    pale with the promise of pride in the past;
Flushed with the famishing fulness of fever that
    reddens with radiance of rathe recreation,
Gaunt as the ghastliest of glimpses that gleam
    through the gloom of the gloaming when
    ghosts go aghast?
Nay, for the nick of the tick of the time is a trem-
    ulous touch on the temples of terror,
Strained as the sinews yet strenuous with strife
    of the dead who is dumb as the dust-heaps of
    death:
Surely no soul is it, sweet as the spasm of erotic
    emotional exquisite error,
Bathed in the balms of beatified bliss, beatific it-
    self by beatitude's breath.
Surely no spirit or sense of a soul that was soft to
    the spirit and soul of our senses
Sweetens the stress of suspiring suspicion that
    sobs in the semblance and sound of a sigh;
Only this oracle opens Olympian, in mystical
    moods and triangular tenses—
Life is the lust of a lamp for the light that is
    dark till the dawn of the day when we die.
Mild is the mirk and monotonous music of mem-
    ory, melodiously mute as it may be,
While the hope in the heart of a hero is bruised
    by the breach of men's rapiers resigned to the
    rod;
Made meek as a mother whose bosom-beats bound
    with the bliss-bringing bulk of a balm-breath-
    ing baby,

As they grope through the grave-yards of creeds,
    under skies growing green at a groan for the
    grimness of God.
Blank is the book of his bounty beholden of old
    and its binding is blacker than bluer:
Out of blue into black is the scheme of the skies,
    and their dews are the wine of the blood-shed
    of things;
Till the darkling desire of delight shall be free
    as a fawn that is freed from the fangs that
    pursue her,
Till the heart-beats of hell shall be hushed by
    a hymn from the hunt that has harried the
    kernel of kings.

        ALGERNON CHARLES SWINBURNE.

---

## THE ARAB.

On, on, my brown Arab, away, away!
Thou hast trotted o'er many a mile to-day,
And I trow right meagre hath been thy fare
Since they roused thee at dawn from thy straw-
    piled lair,
To tread with those echoless, unshod feet
Yon weltering flats in the noontide heat,
Where no palm-tree proffers a kindly shade,
And the eye never rests on a cool grass blade;
And lank is thy flank, and thy frequent cough,
O, it goes to my heart—but away, friend, off!

And yet, ah! what sculptor who saw thee stand,
As thou standest now, on thy native strand,
28

With the wild wind ruffling thine uncombed hair,
And thy nostril upturned to the odorous air,
Would not woo thee to pause, till his skill might
    trace
At leisure the lines of that eager face;
The collarless neck and the coal-black paws
And the bit grasped tight in the massive jaws;
The delicate curve of the legs, that seem
Too slight for their burden—and, O, the gleam
Of that eye, so sombre and yet so gay!
Still away, my lithe Arab, once more away!

Nay, tempt me not, Arab, again to stay;
Since I crave neither *Echo* nor *Fun* to-day.
For thy *hand* is not Echoless—there they are,
*Fun, Glowworm,* and *Echo,* and *Evening Star,*
And thou hintest withal that thou fain wouldst
    shine,
As I read them, these bulgy old boots of mine.
But I shrink from thee, Arab! Thou eatest eel-
    pie,
Thou evermore hast at least one black eye;
There is brass on thy brow, and thy swarthy hues
Are due not to nature, but handling shoes;
And the bit in thy mouth, I regret to see,
Is a bit of tobacco-pipe—Flee, child, flee!

CHARLES STUART CALVERLEY.

## THE MODERN HIAWATHA.

He killed the noble Mudjokivis.
Of the skin he made him mittens,
Made them with the fur side inside,

Made them with the skin side outside.
He, to get the warm side inside,
Put the inside skin side outside;
He, to get the cold side outside,
Put the warm side fur side inside.
That's why he put the fur side inside,
Why he put the skin side outside,
Why he turned them inside outside.

ANONYMOUS.

## POEMS

RECEIVED IN RESPONSE TO AN ADVERTISED
CALL FOR A NATIONAL ANTHEM.

### NATIONAL ANTHEM.

BY H. W. L——, OF CAMBRIDGE.

BACK in the years when Phlagstaff, the Dane, was
monarch
Over the sea-ribbed land of the fleet-footed
Norsemen,
Once there went forth young Ursa to gaze at the
heavens,—
Ursa, the noblest of all Vikings and horsemen.

Musing he sat in his stirrups and viewed the horizon,
Where the Aurora lapt stars in a north-polar
manner:
Wildly he started,—for there in the heavens before him
Fluttered and flew the original star-spangled
banner.

Two objections are in the way of the acceptance of this anthem by the committee : in the first place, it is not an anthem at all ; secondly, it is a gross plagiarism from an old Sclavonic war-song of the primeval ages.

Next we quote from a

## NATIONAL ANTHEM.

### BY THE HON. EDWARD E——, OF BOSTON.

PONDEROUS projectiles, hurled by heavy hands,
   Fell on our Liberty's poor infant head,
Ere she a stadium had well advanced
   On the great path that to her greatness led;
Her temple's propylon was shatter-ed;
   Yet, thanks to saving Grace and Washington,
Her incubus was from her bosom hurled;
   And, rising like a cloud-dispelling sun,
She took the oil with which her hair was curled
To grease the "hub" round which revolves the
   world.

This fine production is rather heavy for an "anthem," and contains too much of Boston to be considered strictly national. To set such an "anthem" to music would require a Wagner ; and even were it really accommodated to a tune, it could only be whistled by the populace.

We now come to a

## NATIONAL ANTHEM.

### BY JOHN GREENLEAF W——.

MY native land, thy Puritanic stock
Still finds its roots firm bound in Plymouth Rock;
And all thy sons unite in one grand wish,—
To keep the virtues of Preserv-ed Fish.

Preserv-ed Fish, the Deacon stern and true,
Told our New England what her sons should do;

And, should they swerve from loyalty and right,
Then the whole land were lost indeed in night.

The sectional bias of this "anthem" renders it unsuit-
able for use in that small margin of the world situated outside of New England. Hence the above must be rejected.
Here we have a very curious

### NATIONAL ANTHEM.

#### BY DR. OLIVER WENDELL H——.

A DIAGNOSIS of our history proves
Our native land a land its native loves:
Its birth a deed obstetric without peer,
Its growth a source of wonder far and near.

To love it more, behold how foreign shores
Sink into nothingness beside its stores.
Hyde Park at best—though counted ultra grand—
The "Boston Common" of Victoria's land—

The committee must not be blamed for rejecting the
above after reading thus far, for such an "anthem" could
only be sung by a college of surgeons or a Beacon Street
tea-party.
Turn we now to a

### NATIONAL ANTHEM.

#### BY WILLIAM CULLEN B——.

THE sun sinks softly to his evening post,
    The sun swells grandly to his morning crown;
Yet not a star our flag of heaven has lost,
    And not a sunset stripe with him goes down.

So thrones may fall; and from the dust of those
    New thrones may rise, to totter like the last;
But still our country's noble planet glows,
    While the eternal stars of Heaven are fast.
27

Upon finding that this does not go well to the air of
" Yankee Doodle," the committee feel justified in declin-
ing it ; it being furthermore prejudiced against it by a
suspicion that the poet has crowded an advertisement of a
paper which he edits into the first line.

Next we quote from a

### NATIONAL ANTHEM.

#### BY GENERAL GEORGE P. M——.

In the days that tried our fathers,
    Many years ago,
Our fair land achieved her freedom
    Blood-bought, you know.
Shall we not defend her ever,
    As we 'd defend
That fair maiden, kind and tender,
    Calling us friend?

Yes! Let all the echoes answer,
    From hill and vale ;
Yes! Let other nations hearing,
    Joy in the tale.
Our Columbia is a lady,
    High born and fair,
We have sworn allegiance to her,—
    Touch her who dare.

The tone of this "anthem" not being devotional enough
to suit the committee, it should be printed on an edition of
linen-cambric hankerchiefs for ladies especially.

Observe this

### NATIONAL ANTHEM.

#### BY N. P. W——.

One hue of our flag is taken
From the cheeks of my blushing pet,

And its stars beat time and sparkle
Like the studs on her chemisette.

Its blue is the ocean shadow
That hides in her dreamy eyes,
And it conquers all men, like her,
And still for a Union flies.

Several members of the committtee find that this " anthem" has too much of the Anacreon spice to suit them.
We next peruse a

## NATIONAL ANTHEM.

### BY THOMAS BAILEY A——.

THE little brown squirrel hops in the corn,
The cricket quaintly sings;
The emerald pigeon nods his head,
And the shad in the river springs;
The dainty sunflower hangs its head
On the shore of the summer sea;
And better far that I were dead,
If Maud did not love me.

I love the squirrel that hops in the corn,
And the cricket that quaintly sings;
And the emerald pigeon that nods his head,
And the shad that gayly springs.
I love the dainty sunflower, too,
And Maud with her snowy breast;
I love them all; but I love—I love—
I love my country best.

This is certainly very beautiful, and sounds somewhat
like Tennyson. Though it may be rejected by the com-

mittee, it can never lose its value as a piece of excellent reading for children. It is calculated to fill the youthful mind with patriotism and natural history, beside touching the youthful heart with an emotion palpitating for all.

ROBERT H. NEWELL (*Orpheus C. Kerr*).

## BELAGCHOLLY DAYS.

CHILLY Dovebber with its boadigg blast
   Dow cubs add strips the beddow add the lawd,
Eved October's suddy days are past—
      Add Subber 's gawd!

I kdow dot what it is to which I cligg
   That stirs to sogg add sorrow, yet I trust
That still I sigg, but as the liddets sigg—
      Because I bust.

Dear leaves that rustle sadly 'death by feet—
   By liggerigg feet—add fill by eyes with tears,
Ye bake be sad, add oh! it gars be greet
      That ye are sear!

The sud id sulled skies too early sigks;
   Do trees are greed but evergrees add ferds;
Gawd are the orioles add bobligks—
      Those Robert Burds!

Add dow, farewell to roses add to birds,
   To larded fields and tigkligg streablets eke;
Farewell to all articulated words
      I faid would speak.

Farewell, by cherished strolliggs od the sward,
  Greed glades add forest shades, farewell to you;
With sorrowigg heart I, wretched add forlord,
    Bid you—*achew!!!*

ANONYMOUS

## SNEEZING.

WHAT a moment, what a doubt!
All my nose is inside out,—
All my thrilling, tickling caustic,
Pyramid rhinocerostic,
  Wants to sneeze and cannot do it!
How it yearns me, thrills me, stings me,
How with rapturous torment wrings me!
  Now says, " Sneeze, you fool,—get through it."
Shee—shee—oh! 't is most del-ishi—
Ishi—ishi—most del-ishi!
(Hang it, I shall sneeze till spring!)
Snuff is a delicious thing.

LEIGH HUNT.

## TO MY NOSE.

KNOWS he that never took a pinch,
Nosey, the pleasure thence which flows?
Knows he the titillating joys
    Which my nose knows?
O nose, I am as proud of thee
As any mountain of its snows;
I gaze on thee, and feel that pride
    A Roman knows!

ALFRED A. FORRESTER (*Alfred Crowquill*).

## LAPSUS CALAMI.

TO R. K.

WILL there never come a season
Which shall rid us from the curse
Of a prose which knows no reason
And an unmelodious verse:
When the world shall cease to wonder
At the genius of an ass,
And a boy's eccentric blunder
Shall not bring success to pass:

When mankind shall be delivered
From the clash of magazines,
And the inkstand shall be shivered
Into countless smithereens:
When there stands a muzzled stripling,
Mute, beside a muzzled bore:
When the Rudyards cease from Kipling
And the Haggards ride no more?

JAMES KENNETH STEPHEN.

---

## A CONSERVATIVE.

THE garden beds I wandered by
    One bright and cheerful morn,
When I found a new-fledged butterfly,
    A-sitting on a thorn,
A black and crimson butterfly,
    All doleful and forlorn.

I thought that life could have no sting,
    To infant butterflies,
So I gazed on this unhappy thing
    With wonder and surprise,
While sadly with his waving wing
    He wiped his weeping eyes.

Said I, "What can the matter be?
    Why weepest thou so sore?
With garden fair and sunlight free
    And flowers in goodly store:"—
But he only turned away from me
    And burst into a roar.

Cried he, "My legs are thin and few
    Where once I had a swarm!
Soft fuzzy fur—a joy to view—
    Once kept my body warm,
Before these flapping wing-things grew,
    To hamper and deform!"

At that outrageous bug I shot
    The fury of mine eye;
Said I, in scorn all burning hot,
    In rage and anger high,
"You ignominious idiot!
    Those wings are made to fly!"

"I do not want to fly," said he,
    "I only want to squirm!"
And he drooped his wings dejectedly,
    But still his voice was firm:

" I do not want to be a fly!
I want to be a worm!"

O yesterday of unknown lack!
    To-day of unknown bliss!
I left my fool in red and black,
    The last I saw was this,—
The creature madly climbing back
    Into his chrysalis.

                CHARLOTTE PERKINS GILMAN.

## " FOREVER."

FOREVER! 'T is a single word!
    Our rude forefathers deemed it two;
Can you imagine so absurd
    A view?

Forever! What abysms of woe
    The word reveals, what frenzy, what
Despair! For ever (printed so)
    Did not.

It looks, ah me! how trite and tame;
    It fails to sadden or appall
Or solace—it is not the same
    At all.

O thou to whom it first occurred
    To solder the disjoined, and dower
Thy native language with a word
    Of power:

We bless thee! Whether far or near
   Thy dwelling, whether dark or fair
Thy kingly brow, is neither here
      Nor there.

But in men's hearts shall be thy throne,
   While the great pulse of England beats:
Thou coiner of a word unknown
      To Keats!

And nevermore must printer do
   As men did long ago; but run
" For " into " ever," bidding two
      Be one.

Forever! passion-fraught, it throws
   O'er the dim page a gloom, a glamour:
It 's sweet, it 's strange; and I suppose
      It 's grammar.

Forever! 'T is a single word!
   And yet our fathers deemed it two:
Nor am I confident they erred;—
      Are you?

           CHARLES STUART CALVERLEY.

# IV.

## INGENUITIES: ODDITIES.

---

### SIEGE OF BELGRADE.

An Austrian army, awfully arrayed,
Boldly by battery besieged Belgrade.
Cossack commanders cannonading come,
Dealing destruction's devastating doom.
Every endeavor engineers essay,
For fame, for fortune fighting,—furious fray!
Generals 'gainst generals grapple—gracious God!
How honors Heaven heroic hardihood!
Infuriate, indiscriminate in ill,
Kindred kill kinsmen, kinsmen kindred kill.
Labor low levels longest loftiest lines;
Men march mid mounds, mid moles, mid murderous mines;
Now noxious, noisy numbers nothing, naught
Of outward obstacles, opposing ought;
Poor patriots, partly purchased, partly pressed,
Quite quaking, quickly "Quarter! Quarter!"
    quest.
Reason returns, religious right redounds,
Suwarrow stops such sanguinary sounds.
Truce to thee, Turkey! Triumph to thy train,
Unwise, unjust, unmerciful Ukraine!

426

Vanish, vain victory! vanish, victory vain!
Why wish we warfare? Wherefore welcome were
Xerxes, Ximenes, Xanthus, Xavier?
Yield, yield, ye youths! ye yeomen, yield your
 yell!
Zeus's, Zarpater's, Zoroaster's zeal,
Attracting all, arms against acts appeal!

ANONYMOUS.

## MY LOVE.

I ONLY knew she came and went   *Lowell.*
 Like troutlets in a pool;    *Hood.*
She was a phantom of delight,  *Wordsworth.*
 And I was like a fool.    *Eastman.*


One kiss, dear maid, I said, and sighed, *Coleridge.*
 Out of those lips unshorn:   *Longfellow.*
She shook her ringlets round her head, *Stoddard.*
 And laughed in merry scorn.   *Tennyson.*


Ring out, wild bells, to the wild sky, *Tennyson.*
 You heard them, O my heart;  *Alice Carey.*
'T is twelve at night by the castle clock, *Coleridge.*
 Belovèd, we must part.    *Alice Carey.*


" Come back, come back! " she cried in grief,
*Campbell.*
 " My eyes are dim with tears, *Bayard Taylor.*
How shall I live through all the days? *Osgood.*
 All through a hundred years? " *T. S. Perry.*

428 HUMOROUS POEMS.

'T was in the prime of summer time      Hood.
    She blessed me with her hand;        Hoyt.
We strayed together, deeply blest,       Edwards.
    Into the dreaming land.               Cornwall.

The laughing bridal roses blow,          Patmore.
    To dress her dark-brown hair; Bayard Taylor.
My heart is breaking with my woe,        Tennyson.
    Most beautiful! most rare!            Read.

I clasped it on her sweet, cold hand,    Browning.
    The precious golden link!             Smith.
I calmed her fears, and she was calm, Coleridge
    "Drink, pretty creature, drink." Wordsworth.

And so I won my Genevieve,               Coleridge.
    And walked in Paradise;              Hervey.
The fairest thing that ever grew     Wordsworth.
    Atween me and the skies.             Osgood.

ANONYMOUS.

ODE TO THE HUMAN HEART.

BLIND Thamyris, and Blind Mæonides,      Milton.
Pursue the triumph and partake the gale! Pope.
Drop tears as fast as the Arabian trees,
                              Shakespeare.
    To point a moral or adorn a tale.   Johnson.

Full many a gem of purest ray serene,    Gray.
Thoughts that do often lie too deep for tears,
                              Tennyson.
Like angels' visits, few and far between, Campbell.
Deck the long vista of departed years.    ?

Man never is, but always to be blessed;  *Pope.*
The tenth transmitter of a foolish face, *Savage.*
Like Aaron's serpent, swallows up the rest, *Pope.*
And makes a sunshine in the shady place.
                                        *Spenser.*

For man the hermit sighed, till the woman smiled,
                                        *Campbell.*
To waft a feather or to drown a fly,   *Young.*
(In wit a man, simplicity a child,)     *Pope.*
With silent finger pointing to the sky.      *?*

But fools rush in where angels fear to tread, *Pope.*
Far out amid the melancholy main;   *Thomson.*
As when a vulture on Imaus bred,            *?*
Dies of a rose in aromatic pain.        *Pope.*

LAMAN BLANCHARD.

## METRICAL FEET.

TROCHEE trips from long to short;
From long to long in solemn sort
Slow Spondee stalks; strong foot! yet ill able
Ever to come up with dactyl trisyllable.
Iambics march from short to long;—
With a leap and a bound the swift Anapæsts
    throng;
One syllable long, with one short at each side,
Amphibrachys hastes with a stately stride;—
First and last being long, middle short, Amphi-
    macer
Strikes his thundering hoofs like a proud high-
    bred racer.

SAMUEL TAYLOR COLERIDGE.

## NOCTURNAL SKETCH.

EVEN is come; and from the dark Park, hark,
The signal of the setting sun—one gun!
And six is sounding from the chime, prime time
To go and see the Drury-Lane Dane slain,—
Or hear Othello's jealous doubt spout out,—
Or Macbeth raving at that shade-made blade,
Denying to his frantic clutch much touch;
Or else to see Ducrow with wide stride ride
Four horses as no other man can span;
Or in the small Olympic pit sit split
Laughing at Liston, while you quiz his phiz.

Anon Night comes, and with her wings brings
        things
Such as, with his poetic tongue, Young sung;
The gas upblazes with its bright white light,
And paralytic watchmen prowl, howl, growl
About the streets, and take up Pall-Mall Sal,
Who, hasting to her nightly jobs, robs fobs.

Now thieves to enter for your cash, smash, crash,
Past drowsy Charley, in a deep sleep, creep,
But, frightened by Policeman B. 3, flee,
And while they're going, whisper low, " No go! "

Now puss, when folks are in their beds, treads
        leads,
And sleepers, waking, grumble, " Drat that cat! "

Who in the gutter caterwauls, squalls, mauls
Some feline foe, and screams in shrill ill-will.

Now Bulls of Bashan, of a prize size, rise
In childish dreams, and with a roar gore poor
Georgy, or Charley, or Billy, willy-nilly;—
But Nursemaid in a nightmare rest, chest-pressed,
Dreameth of one of her old flames, James Games,
And that she hears—what faith is man's!—
    Ann's banns
And his, from Reverend Mr. Rice, twice, thrice;
White ribbons flourish, and a stout shout out,
That upward goes, shows Rose knows those bows'
    woes!

THOMAS HOOD.

## RAILROAD RHYME.

SINGING through the forests,
    Rattling over ridges;
Shooting under arches,
    Rumbling over bridges;
Whizzing through the mountains,
    Buzzing o'er the vale,—
Bless me! this is pleasant,
    Riding on the rail!

Men of different " stations "
    In the eye of fame,
Here are very quickly
    Coming to the same;
High and lowly people,
    Birds of every feather,

On a common level,
    Travelling together.

Gentleman in shorts,
    Looming very tall;
Gentleman at large
    Talking very small;
Gentleman in tights,
    With a loose-ish mien;
Gentleman in gray,
    Looking rather green;

Gentleman quite old,
    Asking for the news,
Gentleman in black,
    In a fit of blues;
Gentleman in claret,
    Sober as a vicar;
Gentleman in tweed,
    Dreadfully in liquor!

Stranger on the right
    Looking very sunny,
Obviously reading
    Something rather funny.
Now the smiles are thicker,—
    Wonder what they mean!
Faith, he's got the Knicker-
    Bocker Magazine!

Stranger on the left
    Closing up his peepers;

Now he snores amain,
    Like the Seven Sleepers;
At his feet a volume
    Gives the explanation,
How the man grew stupid
    From "Association"!

Ancient maiden lady
    Anxiously remarks,
That there must be peril
    'Mong so many sparks;
Roguish-looking fellow,
    Turning to the stranger,
Says it's his opinion
    *She* is out of danger!

Woman with her baby,
    Sitting *vis-à-vis;*
Baby keeps a-squalling,
    Woman looks at me;
Asks about the distance,
    Says it's tiresome talking,
Noises of the cars
    Are so very shocking!

Market-woman, careful
    Of the precious casket,
Knowing eggs are eggs,
    Tightly holds her basket;
Feeling that a smash,
    If it came, would surely
Send her eggs to pot,
    Rather prematurely.

28

Singing through the forests,
    Rattling over ridges;
Shooting under arches,
    Rumbling over bridges;
Whizzing through the mountains,
    Buzzing o'er the vale,—
Bless me! this is pleasant,
    Riding on the rail!

JOHN GODFREY SAXE.

## PHYSICS.

(THE UNCONSCIOUS POETIZING OF A PHI-
LOSOPHER.)

THERE is no force however great
    Can stretch a cord however fine
    Into a horizontal line
That shall be accurately straight.

WILLIAM WHEWELL.

## THE COLLEGIAN TO HIS BRIDE:

BEING A MATHEMATICAL MADRIGAL IN THE
SIMPLEST FORM.

CHARMER, on a given straight line,
And which we will call B C,
Meeting at a common point A,
Draw the lines A C, A B.
But, my sweetest, so arrange it
That they 're equal, all the three;
Then you 'll find that, in the sequel,
All their angles, too are equal.

Equal angles, so to term them,
Each one opposite its brother!
Equal joys and equal sorrows,
Equal hopes, 't were sin to smother,
Equal,—O, divine ecstatics,—
Based on Hutton's mathematics!

PUNCH.

## THE LAWYER'S INVOCATION TO SPRING.

WHEREAS, on certain boughs and sprays
Now divers birds are heard to sing,
And sundry flowers their heads upraise,
Hail to the coming on of spring!

The songs of those said birds arouse
The memory of our youthful hours,
As green as those said sprays and boughs,
As fresh and sweet as those said flowers.

The birds aforesaid,—happy pairs,—
Love, mid the aforesaid boughs, inshrines
In freehold nests; themselves, their heirs,
Administrators, and assigns.

O busiest term of Cupid's Court,
Where tender plaintiffs actions bring,—
Season of frolic and of sport,
Hail, as aforesaid, coming spring!

HENRY HOWARD BROWNELL.

## THE COSMIC EGG.

Upon a rock yet uncreate,
Amid a chaos inchoate,
An uncreated being sate;
Beneath him, rock,
Above him, cloud.
And the cloud was rock,
And the rock was cloud.
The rock then growing soft and warm,
The cloud began to take a form,
A form chaotic, vast, and vague,
Which issued in the cosmic egg.
Then the Being uncreate
On the egg did incubate,
And thus became the incubator;
And of the egg did allegate,
And thus became the alligator;
And the incubator was potentate,
But the alligator was potentator.

ANONYMOUS.

## THE HEN.

A famous hen 's my story's theme,
   Which ne'er was known to tire
Of laying eggs, but then she 'd scream
So loud o'er every egg, 't would seem
   The house must be on fire.
A turkey-cock, who ruled the walk,
   A wiser bird and older,

Could bear 't no more, so off did stalk
  Right to the hen, and told her:
" Madam, that scream, I apprehend,
  Adds nothing to the matter;
It surely helps the egg no whit;
Then lay your egg, and done with it!
I pray you, madam, as a friend,
  Cease that superfluous clatter!
You know not how 't goes through my head."
" Humph! very likely!" madam said,
Then proudly putting forth a leg,—
" Uneducated barnyard fowl!
You know, no more than any owl,
The noble privilege and praise
Of authorship in modern days—
  I 'll tell you why I do it:
First, you perceive, I lay the egg,
And then—review it."

From the German of MATTHAIAS CLAUDIUS.

## ODE—TO THE ROC.

O UNHATCHED Bird, so high preferred,
  As porter of the Pole,
Of beakless things, who have no wings,
  Exact no heavy toll.
If this my song its theme should wrong,
  The theme itself is sweet;
Let others rhyme the unborn time,
  I sing the Obsolete.

And first, I praise the nobler traits
  Of birds preceding Noah,

The giant clan, whose meat was Man,
    Dinornis, Apteryx, Moa.
These, by hints we get from prints
    Of feathers and of feet,
Excelled in wits the later tits,
    And so are obsolete.

I sing each race whom we displace
    In their primeval woods,
While Gospel Aid inspires Free-Trade
    To traffic with their goods.
With Norman Dukes the still Sioux
    In breeding might compete;
But where men talk the tomahawk
    Will soon grow obsolete.

I celebrate each perished State;
    Great cities ploughed to loam;
Chaldæan kings; the Bulls with wings;
    Dead Greece, and dying Rome.
The Druids' shrine may shelter swine,
    Or stack the farmer's peat;
'T is thus mean moths treat finest cloths,
    Mean men the obsolete.

Shall nought be said of theories dead?
    The Ptolemaic system?
Figure and phrase, that bent all ways
    Duns Scotus liked to twist 'em?
Averrhoes' thought? and what was taught,
    In Salamanca's seat?
Sihons and Ogs? and showers of frogs?
    Sea-serpents obsolete?

Pillion and pack have left their track;
  Dead is " the Tally-ho ; "
Steam rails cut down each festive crown
  Of the old world and slow;
Jack-in-the-Green no more is seen,
  Nor Maypole in the street;
No mummers play on Christmas-day;
  St. George is obsolete.

O fancy, why hast thou let die
  So many a frolic fashion?
Doublet and hose, and powdered beaux?
  Where are thy songs whose passion
Turned thought to fire in knight and squire,
  While hearts of ladies beat?
Where thy sweet style, ours, ours erewhile?
  All this is obsolete.

In Auvergne low potatoes grow
  Upon volcanoes old;
The moon, they say, had her young day,
  Though now her heart is cold;
Even so our earth, sorrow and mirth,
  Seasons of snow and heat,
Checked by her tides in silence glides
  To become obsolete.

The astrolabe of every babe
  Reads, in its fatal sky,
" Man's largest room is the low tomb—
  Ye all are born to die."
Therefore this theme, O Bird, I deem
  The noblest we may treat;

The final cause of Nature's laws
Is to grow obsolete.

WILLIAM JOHN COURTHOPE.

## MOTHERHOOD.

She laid it where the sunbeams fall
Unscanned upon the broken wall.
Without a tear, without a groan,
She laid it near a mighty stone,
Which some rude swain had haply cast
Thither in sport, long ages past,
And time with mosses had o'erlaid,
And fenced with many a tall grass-blade,
And all about bid roses bloom
And violets shed their soft perfume.
There, in its cool and quiet bed,
She set her burden down and fled:
Nor flung, all eager to escape,
One glance upon the perfect shape,
That lay, still warm and fresh and fair,
But motionless and soundless there.
No human eye had marked her pass
Across the linden-shadowed grass
Ere yet the minster clock chimed seven:
Only the innocent birds of heaven—
The magpie, and the rook whose nest
Swings as the elm-tree waves his crest—
And the lithe cricket, and the hoar
And huge-limbed hound that guards the door,
Looked on when, as a summer wind
That, passing, leaves no trace behind,

All unapparelled, barefoot all,
She ran to that old ruined wall,
To leave upon the chill dank earth
(For ah! she never knew its worth),
Mid hemlock rank, and fern and ling,
And dews of night, that precious thing!
And then it might have lain forlorn
From morn to eve, from eve to morn:
But, that, by some wild impulse led,
The mother, ere she turned and fled,
One moment stood erect and high;
Then poured into the silent sky
A cry so jubilant, so strange,
That Alice—as she strove to range
Her rebel ringlets at her glass—
Sprang up and gazed across the grass;
Shook back those curls so fair to see,
Clapped her soft hands in childish glee;
And shrieked—her sweet face all aglow,
   Her very limbs with rapture shaking—
" My hen has laid an egg, I know;
   And only hear the noise she 's making! "

     CHARLES STUART CALVERLEY.

---

## DISASTER.

'T was ever thus from childhood's hour
   My fondest hopes would not decay:
I never loved a tree or flower
   Which was the first to fade away!
The garden, where I used to delve
   Short-frocked, still yields me pinks in plenty;

The pear-tree that I climbed at twelve,
 I see still blossoming, at twenty.


I never nursed a dear gazelle.
 But I was given a paroquet—
How I did nurse him if unwell!
 He 's imbecile but lingers yet.
He 's green, with an enchanting tuft;
 He melts me with his small black eye:
He 'd look inimitable stuffed,
 And knows it—but he will not die!


I had a kitten—I was rich
 In pets—but all too soon my kitten
Became a full-sized cat, by which
 I 've more than once been scratched and bitten:
And when for sleep her limbs she curled
 One day beside her untouched plateful,
And glided calmly from the world,
 I freely own that I was grateful.


And then I bought a dog—a queen!
 Ah, Tiny, dear departing pug!
She lives, but she is past sixteen,
 And scarce can crawl across the rug.
I loved her beautiful and kind;
 Delighted in her pert bow-wow:
But now she snaps if you don't mind;
 'T were lunacy to love her now.


I used to think, should e'er mishap
 Betide my crumple-visaged Ti,

In shape of prowling thief, or trap,
   Or coarse bull-terrier—I should die.
But ah! disasters have their use;
   And life might e'en be too sunshiny:
Nor would I make myself a goose,
   If some big dog should swallow Tiny.

CHARLES STUART CALVERLEY.

## LINES WRITTEN IN AN ALBUM.

[A farmer's daughter, during the rage for albums, handed to the author an old account-book ruled for pounds, shillings, and pence, and requested a contribution.]

| | £. | s. | d. |
|---|---|---|---|
| THIS world 's a scene as dark as Styx, | | | |
| Where hope is scarce worth | | 2 | 6 |
| Our joys are borne so fleeting hence | | | |
| That they are dear at | | | 18 |
| And yet to stay here most are willing, | | | |
| Although they may not have | | 1 | |

WILLIS GAYLORD.

## ON THE BRINK.

I WATCHED her as she stooped to pluck
   A wild flower in her hair to twine;
And wished that it had been my luck
     To call her mine;

Anon I heard her rate with mad,
   Mad words her babe within its cot,
And felt particularly glad
     That it had not.

I knew (such subtle brains have men!)
    That she was uttering what she shouldn't;
And thought that I would chide, and then
    I thought I wouldn't.

Few could have gazed upon that face,
    Those pouting coral lips, and chided:
A Rhadamanthus, in my place,
    Had done as I did.

For wrath with which our bosoms glow
    Is chained there oft by Beauty's spell;
And, more than that, I did not know
    The widow well.

So the harsh phrase passed unreproved:
    Still mute—(O brothers, was it sin?)—
I drank unutterably moved,
    Her beauty in.

And to myself I murmured low,
    As on her upturned face and dress
The moonlight fell, " Would she say No,—
    By chance, or Yes? "

She stood so calm, so like a ghost,
    Betwixt me and that magic moon,
That I already was almost
    A finished coon.

But when she caught adroitly up
    And soothed with smiles her little daughter;
And gave it, if I 'm right, a sup
    Of barley-water;

And, crooning still the strange, sweet lore
   Which only mothers' tongues can utter,
Snowed with deft hand the sugar o'er
    Its bread-and-butter;

And kissed it clingingly (ah, why
   Don't women do these things in private?) —
I felt that if I lost her, I
    Should not survive it.

And from my mouth the words nigh flew, —
   The past, the future, I forgat 'em, —
" Oh, if you 'd kiss me as you do
    That thankless atom! "

But this thought came ere yet I spake,
   And froze the sentence on my lips:
" They err who marry wives that make
    Those little slips."

It came like some familiar rhyme,
   Some copy to my boyhood set;
And that 's perhaps the reason I 'm
    Unmarried yet.

Would she have owned how pleased she was,
   And told her love with widow's pride?
I never found out that, because
    I never tried.

Be kind to babes and beasts and birds,
   Hearts may be hard though lips are coral;
And angry words are angry words:
    And that 's the moral.

CHARLES STUART CALVERLEY.

## THE V–A–S–E.

FROM the maddening crowd they stand apart,
The maidens four and the Work of Art;

And none might tell from sight alone
In which had culture ripest grown,—

The Gotham Millions fair to see,
The Philadelphia Pedigree,

The Boston Mind of azure hue,
Or the soulful Soul from Kalamazoo,—

For all loved Art in a seemly way,
With an earnest soul and a capital A.

.    .    .    .    .    .

Long they worshipped; but no one broke
The sacred stillness, until up spoke

The Western one from the nameless place,
Who blushingly said: " What a lovely vace! "

Over three faces a sad smile flew,
And they edged away from Kalamazoo.

But Gotham's haughty soul was stirred
To crush the stranger with one small word

Deftly hiding reproof in praise,
She cries: " 'T is, indeed, a lovely vaze! "

But brief her unworthy triumph when
The lofty one from the home of Penn,

With the consciousness of two grand papas,
Exclaims: " It is quite a lovely vahs! "

And glances round with an anxious thrill,
Awaiting the word of Beacon Hill.

But the Boston maid smiles courteouslee,
And gently murmurs: " Oh pardon me!

" I did not catch your remark, because
I was so entranced with that charming vaws! "

> *Dies erit prægelida*
> *Sinistra quum Bostonia.*
>
> JAMES JEFFREY ROCHE.

---

## LARKS AND NIGHTINGALES.

ALONE I sit at eventide:
  The twilight glory pales,
And o'er the meadows far and wide
  Chant pensive bobolinks.
    (One might say nightingales!)

Song-sparrows warble on the tree,
  I hear the purling brook,
And from the old " manse o'er the lea "
  Flies slow the cawing crow.
    (In England 'twere a rook!)

The last faint golden beams of day
 Still glow on cottage panes,
And on their lingering homeward way
 Walk weary laboring men.
  (Oh, would that we had swains!)

From farm-yards, down fair rural glades
 Come sounds of tinkling bells,
And songs of merry brown milkmaids,
 Sweeter than oriole's.
  (Yes, thank you—Philomel's!)

I could sit here till morning came,
 All through the night hours dark,
Until I saw the sun's bright flame
 And heard the chickadee.
  (Alas we have no lark!)

We have no leas, no larks, no rooks,
 No swains, no nightingales,
No singing milkmaids (save in books) :
 The poet does his best—
 It is the rhyme that fails!

     NATHAN HASKELL DOLE.

---

## OF BLUE CHINA.

THERE 's a joy without canker or cark,
 There 's a pleasure eternally new,
'T is to gloat on the glaze and the mark
 Of china that 's ancient and blue;

Unchipped, all the centuries through
It has passed, since the chime of it rang,
And they fashioned it, figure and hue,
In the reign of the Emperor Hwang.

These dragons (their tails, you remark,
Into bunches of gillyflowers grew),—
When Noah came out of the ark,
Did these lie in wait for his crew?
They snorted, they snapped, and they slew,
They were mighty of fin and of fang,
And their portraits Celestials drew
In the reign of the Emperor Hwang.

Here 's a pot with a cot in a park,
In a park where the peach-blossoms blew,
Where the lovers eloped in the dark,
Lived, died, and were changed into two
Bright birds that eternally flew
Through the boughs of the may, as they sang;
'T is a tale was undoubtedly true
In the reign of the Emperor Hwang.

ENVOY

Come, snarl at my ecstasies, do,
Kind critic; your " tongue has a tang,"
But—a sage never heeded a shrew
In the reign of the Emperor Hwang.

ANDREW LANG.

29

## A RIDDLE.*

### THE LETTER " H."

'T was in heaven pronounced, and 't was muttered
    in hell,
And echo caught faintly the sound as it fell;
On the confines of earth 't was permitted to rest,
And the depths of the ocean its presence con-
    fessed;
'T will be found in the sphere when 't is riven
    asunder,
Be seen in the lightning and heard in the thunder.
'T was allotted to man with his earliest breath,
Attends him at birth, and awaits him in death,
Presides o'er his happiness, honor and health,
Is the prop of his house, and the end of his wealth.
In the heaps of the miser 't is hoarded with care,
But is sure to be lost on his prodigal heir.
It begins every hope, every wish it must bound,
With the husbandman toils, and with monarchs
    is crowned.
Without it the soldier, the seaman may roam,
But woe to the wretch who expels it from home!
In the whispers of conscience its voice will be
    found,
Nor e'en in the whirlwind of passion be drowned.
'T will not soften the heart; but though deaf be
    the ear,
It will make it acutely and instantly hear.
Yet in shade let it rest, like a delicate flower,
Ah, breathe on it softly,—it dies in an hour.

CATHARINE FANSHAWE.

* Sometimes attributed to Byron.

## A THRENODY.

" The Ahkoond of Swat is dead."—*London Papers.*

WHAT, what, what,
What 's the news from Swat?
    Sad news,
    Bad news,
Comes by the cable led
Through the Indian Ocean's bed,
Through the Persian Gulf, the Red
Sea and the Med-
Iterranean—he 's dead;
The Ahkoond is dead!

For the Ahkoond I mourn,
    Who wouldn't?
He strove to disregard the message stern,
    But he Ahkoodn't.
Dead, dead, dead;
    (Sorrow Swats!)
  Swats wha hae wi' Ahkoond bled,
Swats whom he had often led
  Onward to a gory bed,
    Or to victory,
    As the case might be,
      Sorrow Swats!
Tears shed,
    Shed tears like water,
Your great Ahkoond is dead!
    That Swats the matter!

Mourn, city of Swat!
Your great Ahkoond is not,
But lain 'mid worms to rot.
His mortal part alone, his soul was caught
　(Because he was a good Ahkoond)
Up to the bosom of Mahound.
Though earthy walls his frame surround
(Forever hallowed be the ground!)
And sceptics mock the lowly mound
And say " He 's now of no Ahkoond! "
　His soul is in the skies,—
The azure skies that bend above his loved
　Metropolis of Swat.
He sees with larger, other eyes,
Athwart all earthly mysteries—
He knows what 's Swat.

Let Swat bury the great Ahkoond
With a noise of mourning and
　of lamentation!
Let Swat bury the great Ahkoond
　With the noise of the mourning
　of the Swattish nation!

　Fallen is at length
　Its tower of strength,
Its sun is dimmed ere it had nooned;
Dead lies the great Ahkoond,
　The great Ahkoond of Swat
　Is not!
GEORGE THOMAS LANIGAN.

## LINES TO MISS FLORENCE HUNTINGTON.

Sweet maiden of Passamaquoddy,
  Shall we seek for communion of souls
Where the deep Mississippi meanders,
  Or the distant Saskatchewan rolls?

Ah no,—for in Maine I will find thee
  A sweetly sequestrated nook,
Where the far winding Skoodoowabskooksis
  Conjoiins with the Skoodoowabskook.

There wander two beautiful rivers,
  With many a winding and crook;
The one is the Skoodoowabskooksis,
  The other—the Skoodoowabskook.

Ah, sweetest of haunts! though unmentioned
  In geography, atlas, or book,
How fair is the Skoodoowabskooksis,
  When joining the Skoodoowabskook!

Our cot shall be close by the waters
  Within that sequestrated nook—
Reflected in Skoodoowabskooksis
  And mirrored in Skoodoowabskook.

You shall sleep to the music of leaflets,
  By zephyrs in wantonness shook,

And dream of the Skoodoowabskooksis,
    And, perhaps, of the Skoodoowabskook.

When awaked by the hens and the roosters,
    Each morn, you shall joyously look
On the junction of Skoodoowabskooksis
    With the soft gliding Skoodoowabskook.

Your food shall be fish from the waters,
    Drawn forth on the point of a hook,
From murmuring Skoodoowabskookis,
    Or wandering Skoodoowabskook!

You shall quaff the most sparkling of water,
    Drawn forth from a silvery brook
Which flows to the Skoodoowabskooksis,
    And then to the Skoodoowabskook!

And you shall preside at the banquet,
    And I will wait on thee as cook;
And we 'll talk of the Skoodoowabskooksis,
    And sing of the Skoodoowabskook!

Let others sing loudly of Saco,
    Of Quoddy, and Tattamagouche,
Of Kennebeccasis, and Quaco,
    Of Merigonishe, and Buctouche,

Of Nashwaak, and Magaguadavique,
    Or Memmerimammericook,—
There 's none like the Skoodoowabskooksis,
    Excepting the Skoodoowabskook!
                                        ANONYMOUS.

# V.

## NONSENSE.

---

### NONSENSE.

Good reader, if you e'er have seen,
　When Phœbus hastens to his pillow,
　The mermaids with their tresses green
Dancing upon the western billow;
If you have seen at twilight dim,
　When the lone spirit's vesper hymn
　Floats wild along the winding shore,
The fairy train their ringlets weave
Glancing along the spangled green;
　I you have seen all this, and more—
God bless me! what a deal you 've seen!

THOMAS MOORE.

---

### THE PURPLE COW.

I never saw a Purple Cow,
　I never hope to see one;
But I can tell you, anyhow,
　I rather see than be one.

GELETT BURGESS.

## PSYCHOLOPHON.

[Supposed to be translated from the Old Parsee.]

Twine then the rays
    Round her soft Theban tissues!
All will be as She says,
    When that dead past reissues.
Matters not what nor where,
    Hark, to the moon's dim cluster!
How was her heavy hair
    Lithe as a feather duster!
Matters not when nor whence;
    Flittertigibbet!
Sound makes the song, not sense,
    Thus I inhibit!

GELETT BURGESS.

## THE BAKER'S TALE.

FROM "THE HUNTING OF THE SNARK."

They roused him with muffins—they roused him
        with ice—
    They roused him with mustard and cress—
They roused him with jam and judicious advice—
    They set him conundrums to guess.

When at length he sat up and was able to speak,
    His sad story he offered to tell;
And the Bellman cried "Silence!  Not even a
        shriek!"
    And excitedly tingled his bell.

There was silence supreme! Not a shriek, not a
    scream,
  Scarcely even a howl or a groan,
As the man they called " Ho!" told his story of
    woe
In an antediluvian tone.

My father and mother were honest though
    poor—"
  " Skip all that!" cried the Bellman in haste.
" If it once become dark, there 's no chance of a
    Snark—
  We have hardly a minute to waste!"

" I skip forty years," said the Baker, in tears,
  " And proceed without further remark
To the day when you took me aboard of your
    ship
  To help you in hunting the Snark.

" A dear uncle of mine (after whom I was named)
  Remarked, when I bade him farewell—"
" Oh, skip your dear uncle!" the Bellman ex-
    claimed,
  As he angrily tingled his bell.

" He remarked to me then," said that mildest of
    men,
  " ' If your Snark be a Snark, that is right:
Fetch it home by all means—you may serve it
    with greens,
  And it 's handy for striking a light.

" ' You may seek it with thimbles—and seek it
    with care;
You may hunt it with forks and hope;
You may threaten its life with a railway-share;
    You may charm it with smiles and soap—' "

(" That 's exactly the method," the Bellman bold
    In a hasty parenthesis cried,
" That 's exactly the way I have always been
    told
That the capture of Snarks should be tried! ")

" ' But oh, beamish nephew, beware of the day,
    If your Snark be a Boojum! For then
You will softly and suddenly vanish away,
    And never be met with again! '

" It is this, it is this that oppresses my soul,
    When I think of my uncle's last words:
And my heart is like nothing so much as a bowl
    Brimming over with quivering curds!

" It is this, it is this—"    " We have had that be-
    fore! "
The Bellman indignantly said.
And the Baker replied, " Let me say it once more.
    It is this, it is this that I dread!

" I engage with the Snark—every night after
    dark—
In a dreamy, delirious fight:
I serve it with greens in those shadowy scenes,
    And I use it for striking a light:

" But if ever I meet with a Boojum, that day,
   In a moment (of this I am sure),
I shall softly and suddenly vanish away—
   And the notion I cannot endure!"

CHARLES LUTWIDGE DODGSON (*Lewis Carroll*).

## JABBERWOCKY.

'T WAS brillig, and the slithy toves
   Did gyre and gimble in the wabe;
All mimsy were the borogoves,
   And the mome raths outgrabe.

" Beware the Jabberwock, my son!
   The jaws that bite, the claws that catch!
Beware the Jubjub bird, and shun
   The frumious Bandersnatch!"

He took his vorpal sword in hand:
   Long time the manxome foe he sought—
So rested he by the Tumtum tree,
   And stood awhile in thought.

And as in uffish thought he stood,
   The Jabberwock, with eyes of flame,
Came whiffling through the tulgey wood,
   And burbled as it came!

One, two! One, two! And through and
     through
   The vorpal blade went snicker-snack!
He left it dead, and with its head
   He went galumphing back.

" And hast thou slain the Jabberwock?
   Come to my arms, my beamish boy!
O frabjous day! Callooh! Callay!"
   He chortled in his joy.

'T was brillig, and the slithy toves
   Did gyre and gimble in the wabe;
All mimsy were the borogoves,
   And the mome raths outgrabe.

CHARLES LUTWIDGE DODGSON (*Lewis Carroll*).

---

## FOR A NOVEL OF HALL CAINE'S.

### AFTER KIPLING.

He sits in a sea-green grotto with a bucket of lurid
   paint,
And draws the Thing as it isn't for the God of
   things as they ain't.

ROBERT BRIDGES (*Droch*).

# INDEX: AUTHORS AND TITLES.

# INDEX OF AUTHORS AND TITLES.

*For occupation, nativity, etc., of authors, and the American publishers of American poetical works, see General Index of Authors, Volume X.*

463